Studies in the Anthropology
of North American Indians

POWHATAN'S WORLD AND COLONIAL VIRGINIA

A Conflict of Cultures

Frederic W. Gleach

Published by THE UNIVERSITY OF NEBRASKA PRESS

Lincoln and London ✦ In cooperation with the American Indian

Studies Research Institute, Indiana University, Bloomington

© 1997 by the University of Nebraska Press

∞

First Bison Books printing: 2000
Most recent printing indicated by the last digit below:
10   9   8   7   6   5   4   3   2   1
Library of Congress Cataloging-in-Publication Data
Gleach, Frederic W. (Wright), 1960–
Powhatan's world and colonial Virginia: a conflict of cultures /
Frederic W. Gleach.
p.   cm.—(Studies in the anthropology of North American Indians)
Includes bibliographical references and index.
ISBN 0-8032-2166-5 (cloth: alk. paper)
ISBN 0-8032-7091-7 (pa: alk. paper)
1. Powhatan Indians – History.   2. Powhatan Indians – Government
relations.   3. Powhatan Indians – Social life and customs.   4. Virginia –
Politics and government.   5. Virginia – Race relations.
I. Title.   II. Series.   E99.P85G54   1997   975.5'01 – dc20   96-32723

✦ Contents

✦ Figures

T HE READER MIGHT well wonder, after decades of research and numerous recent publications on the Powhatans and colonial Virginia, what more could be said on the subject. I have repeatedly asked that question myself in the course of researching, writing, and revising this book, but the answer was always there. After years of archaeological and ethnohistorical research in Virginia and elsewhere, followed by extensive studies of the histories of Algonquian and other Native American peoples, and discussions with individual Native people, scholars, and others, much of what I thought I knew about the Powhatans no longer seemed correct. Through these experiences I have learned a great deal. I have tried here to use categories of meaning that would have been relevant to the contemporary Powhatans and colonists, rather than to import categories of meaning arbitrarily from the present. My emphasis is on the role of world-view in the construction of history, not primarily on facts or points of history but on ideas and understandings. These are necessarily fuzzier and harder to document, even within one's own cultural context, and doubly so when attempting to understand another culture, as both the native and the colonial cultures must be considered. Chapters discussing the colonial history are thus preceded by and interwoven with discussions of cultural understandings and institutions for both the Powhatans and the colonists.

One goal of this work is to better explicate some of the meanings of certain events in seventeenth-century Virginia (and, as I shall develop, I don't believe one can speak of *the* meaning of anything, but only of selected meanings), but this goal is embedded in a larger project of understanding the colonial and postcolonial experiences of eastern North America. My frameworks for interpreting the English are thus drawn from a background that encompasses more than those Englishmen who came to Virginia, and my Powhatan frameworks are based on more general understandings of Algonquian peoples. Just as we must use our knowledge of the history and development of European ideas to interpret English activities in Virginia, so we must use the accumulated knowledge of eastern North American Indians to try to reconstruct the pieces of Powhatan culture we see reflected in the written documents of the colonists.

The opportunity to talk through difficult ideas with others — even the process of trying to put them into words — was critical in the development of this work. These others include university faculty, students, and non-academics, Native and Euro-Americans alike. I would like to thank all those with whom I have discussed the ideas that shaped my thinking, but some individuals must be singled out for particular recognition. I could not have produced this work without these interactions.

This book grew out of my doctoral dissertation for the University of Chicago Department of Anthropology (Gleach 1992a), so my first debt of gratitude must be to my committee and other members of the department: committee chair Raymond Fogelson, Leslie Freeman, and Bernard Cohn; and Terence Turner, Marshall Sahlins, Manning Nash, Sol Tax, and Fred Eggan.

My student colleagues were also instrumental to the development of some of these ideas and have my heartfelt thanks: in particular, Ira Bashkow, Catherine Howard, Matthew Lawson, and Larry Nesper; also, William Autry, Margaret Bender, Raymond Bucko, Roger B. Coon, David Dinwoodie, Regina Harrison, John Kelly, Alaina Lemon, Matthew Nadelhaft, Daniel Rosenblatt, and Elizabeth Vann.

A good deal of my research was carried out at the Newberry Library in Chicago, thanks largely to the kindness of Jay Miller, formerly of the D'Arcy McNickle Center for the History of the American Indian. Two other scholars I met at the Newberry, and from whose ideas this work has also benefited, are Rebecca Kugel and Georges Sioui. I would also like to acknowledge the contributions of the staffs of the various facilities where I did my research: the British Library, the British Public Record Office at Kew Gardens, the Bodleian Library at Oxford, the New York Public Library, the National Anthropology Archives in the Smithsonian Institution, the American Philosophical Society Library, the Newberry Library, and the University of Chicago Library. I owe a further debt to the American Philosophical Society, for not only were the staff of their library friendly and helpful, but a Philips Fund grant from that institution helped to finance my research travels. Quotations of manuscripts in the collections of the British Library, the British Public Record Office, and the Bodleian Library are used with the kind permission of those institutions.

Much of the material in this book has seen use in various of my classes (at DePaul University in the fall of 1992 and at Cornell University in the 1993–94 academic year), and I thus have benefited from having to answer the questions of many students. Joshua Piker, a Cornell graduate student, must be singled out for special thanks for many discussions of ideas and for pointing out a few interesting sources I had missed along the way. Several of my colleagues at Cornell have also provided stimulating ideas as I worked to transform my dissertation into the present book. I would like to mention Jane Fajans, Bernd Lambert, and Stephen Sangren specifically, but the entire department has my gratitude.

The contributions of several other individuals must be recognized. My research has benefited from discussions with the participants in the past several Algonquian Conferences and meetings of the American Society for Ethnohistory, and portions of earlier versions of this work have been incorporated into those papers (Gleach 1990b, 1992b, 1993, 1994); parts of an earlier version of chapter 4 were also adapted for use in a recent paper examining methodological issues (Gleach 1996a). In addition to the participants in those meetings already named, I would like to acknowledge Kathleen Bragdon, William Cowan, Regna Darnell, Raymond DeMallie, Clara Sue Kidwell, Lisa Philips Valentine, and Roy Wright. Virginia intellectual influences include Keith Egloff, Jeffrey Hantman, Douglas Mac-Learen, Mel Mednick, L. Daniel Mouer, Stephen Potter, Helen Rountree, and E. Randolph Turner III. This book has also benefited from comments on the manuscript by Raymond DeMallie, Helen Rountree, and two anonymous reviewers. Andie Diane Palmer has also offered reflections on many ideas during the course of my revisions.

Some of these contributions have been specific, and others more general. Although I have not incorporated all of the suggestions of all of these people, they have given me a great many stimulating ideas and interactions over the years, for which I am truly grateful.

Finally, I would like to acknowledge the family and friends who have been so supportive through this work: my mother, Judith Gleach, and sister, Jennifer Gleach, close friends Lawrence and Rhonda Lindberg, and their children, Ilse and Lars. When I began this project I had not yet met Vilma Santiago-Irizarry, now my wife, but she has been with me through the revision process, giving support and assistance.

Whatever good there may be in this work is due to the influences of these mentors, colleagues, friends, and family; any deficiencies are, of course, solely my responsibility.

Powhatan's World and Colonial Virginia

✦ Introduction

There is an etiquette of respect and homage that, if followed, serves to unite and empower people. Such deference does not mean that one must forsake one's own cultural roots. We can all learn from each other. It is important that people be knowledgeable of their own tribal information, but they should be equally knowledgeable in the information of an adopted homebase. And they should respect their hosts — just as we all believe non-Indians should demonstrate respect of American Indians in general.

We don't want English, Germans or Italians to become Indians, and neither should Lakota become Mohegan. But, in Mohegan land, or Paugussett land, others should demonstrate respect. After all the years of destruction it is important now that surviving indigenous nations survive, and we all must assist each other.

— Karen Cooper, "When in Rome, or in the Woodlands"

THE SELF-CONSCIOUS STUDY of European perceptions and constructions of non-Europeans has been a dominant theme in anthropology in recent years (e.g., Said 1978; Bucher 1981; Todorov 1984; Clifford 1988; Hulme 1992). Perhaps partly in response to the implicit Eurocentrism of studies that define the non-European as *Other* (Gleach 1990b), there have also been occasional studies of Native American perceptions of Europeans and Euro-Americans (e.g., Brotherston 1979:28–60; Gleach 1990b; Kugel 1990, 1994; O'Mack 1990). The application of such studies to colonial Virginia is problematic; there has long been a feeling that relatively little could be known of the early Powhatans because of the paucity of early colonial records, particularly of any recording from Powhatan perspectives. In the past, models of Powhatan understandings have been based primarily on generalized psychological models that are ultimately rooted in western culture. I have developed here an approach to reconstructing aspects of a Powhatan world-view, based on Algonquian cultural patterns and on careful attention to details in the historical records, with the goal a more objective treatment of these two sides of the history of early colonial Virginia.

Popular conceptions of Native Americans in the dominant American culture have ranged from "base savage" to "noble savage," with many of these still represented in commonly held stereotypes. All tend to ignore the native cultures as viable entities in their own right, however; they are Euro-American interpretations of distinctly different sets of cultural traditions that must be seen in their own terms for a proper understanding of their histories. Anglo-American policies of enmity and dominance have been so overwhelming that many people are not aware of the dynamic strength of native cultures, or of the ways in which Native Americans have come to be seen as subjugated. This is true not only within our popular culture, but also for many historians of early America, as recently described by Merrell (1989a). There have been anthropological and ethnohistorical studies of Indians and historical studies of the colonial efforts, but the interrelation-ships of the English colonists and the Indians have seldom been the focus of research, despite the acknowledgment over a decade ago of that partic-ular gap (Tate 1979:30–32). This is nowhere more true than in the study of seventeenth-century Virginia (Merrell 1989a; Rutman 1987), where this interaction began, although Rountree's recent work (1990, 1993a) makes a great contribution in this area. The paucity of studies integrating both native and colonial perspectives, and the biases that have continued to haunt ethnohistorical studies of the Powhatans, especially the lack of stud-ies based in a Powhatan world-view, have resulted, however, in continued misunderstanding of the history and misinterpretation of the events of colonial Virginia. *Powhatan's World and Colonial Virginia* intends to begin to change that.

The English who landed in Virginia in 1607, settling at Jamestown, were a small group of poorly supplied men dependent on the native population for their survival. The local natives, a confederation of Algonquian-speaking tribes known as the Powhatans and led by the paramount chief Powhatan, had prior experience with Europeans. In the 1560s one of their chiefs had been taken to Spain; he returned in 1570 as part of a Jesuit attempt to found a mission. That mission was destroyed by the Indians in 1571, and a Spanish military force returned in 1572 to avenge their deaths and rescue any survivors. The English likewise had prior experience with Algonquian Indians, through their attempted colony at Roanoke Island (the "Lost Colony"), and with other native peoples in prior colonial ven-tures, such as in Ireland (see Canny 1973). The colonial policies brought to

America were largely shaped by these experiences, and many of the colonists who came to Virginia had been in Ireland before. For both the Powhatans and the English, the other was understood through already extant cultural categories. The colonists' descriptions of the Indians and their culture — the only record from the time — were thus distorted into Europeanized caricatures from which the native culture in its own terms must be reconstructed.

During the early years of the colony the Powhatans and the English made mutual attempts to civilize each other. Through actions which were largely misunderstood by the other group, each group initially sought to demonstrate to the other its superiority in the relationship and to persuade the other to adopt "appropriate" ways of living. Each group also had certain material goods the other wanted, and the trade in these goods was a significant aspect of their relationship. The Powhatans sought luxury goods that might better be understood as objects of sacred power — particularly copper and glass beads, but also swords and guns — from the English, whereas the English primarily sought food from the Powhatans, particularly in the early years of their interactions. Both groups employed trade, negotiation, and military strength in the pursuit and demonstration of advantage, each group in its own terms. All can be seen as attempts to bring the other to civility, rewarding or punishing actions that were seen as good or bad.

English negotiations were conducted at the beginning by Captain John Smith, a widely traveled military leader who apparently gained a certain amount of respect from the Indians and a rapport with Powhatan himself. In the winter of 1607–8 he was a captive of the Powhatans, during which time a complex series of rituals was performed that brought the English colony into the Powhatan world. Smith departed in 1609, and, as the English began to expand into the heartland of Powhatan territory, violence between the two groups became more frequent. In 1614, relative peace between the two peoples was again obtained, through the marriage of Pocahontas (a daughter of Powhatan) and the colonist John Rolfe. The English saw this as a defeat of the Powhatans, although the resulting social relationships between the two groups were essentially those offered on several occasions by Powhatan as early as 1608. In 1617 Pocahontas died while visiting England, and Powhatan turned over leadership of the Indians to his brother Itoyatan[1] and his cousin Opechancanough.

By 1620–21 the English had expanded far into Powhatan territory, killing a number of Powhatans in the process of occupying essentially the entire

James River drainage in the coastal plain. They were also beginning to proselytize actively among the Indians. The Powhatans were willing to accept the English God into their pantheon, but few, if any, were willing to forsake their religion entirely. These twin assaults on the Powhatans were the primary causes of the Great Massacre of 1622, an attack that has long been seen as a turning point in English-Powhatan relations.

In early 1622, a powerful war-chief, Nemattanew, who the Powhatans considered invulnerable to bullets, was shot and killed by the English. Less than two weeks later, on 22 March 1622, the Indians throughout much of the Powhatan region collected whatever implements were convenient and killed the colonists in a perfectly coordinated attack. The settlements further inland, farthest dispersed into Powhatan territory, bore the brunt of the attack, whereas most of the more easterly settlements emerged unscathed. Of the English population, numbering 1,240, at least 320 were killed that single day. Scalping and other acts of humiliation were practiced on the corpses. This event was perceived by the English as an attempt to exterminate them, an interpretation that has held until very recently. Arguing from the perspective of native cultural institutions, *Powhatan's World and Colonial Virginia* argues that extermination was not, in fact, the intention of this act.

I use the term *coup* for this attack, rather than *massacre*—the contemporary term — or *uprising*—as Fausz (1977) prefers. The word *massacre* has too many pejorative connotations and is not accurate: it properly refers to "unnecessary indiscriminate killing of human beings" (*Oxford English Dictionary* 1971, s.v. "massacre"), which these actions were only in the minds of the English colonists. The term *uprising* is equally problematic. As I show in this book, the Powhatans saw themselves not as inferiors, a requisite for an *uprising*, but rather as morally and politically superior to the English. The Powhatans applied the large-scale attack as a corrective measure to the unruly colonists. While intended to correct a Eurocentric view from which this could only be considered a *massacre*, with all the pejorative connotations, the use of the term *uprising* for this incident is itself an (unintended) case of Eurocentrism, with its implication that the Powhatans must have been, or at least must have perceived themselves as being, under the domination of the English colonists (Gleach 1990b). Finally, by *coup* I do not mean *coup d'etat*—a stroke of state policy — but simply a blow, a successful stroke; most closely, a *coup de main*, "[*lit.* stroke of hand] 'a sudden and vigorous attack' " (*OED* 1971, s.v. "coup de main").

Another term used recently in discussions of these events is *Anglo-*

Powhatan Wars (e.g., Rountree 1990, 1993b; Potter 1993), a phrase first used by Fausz (1977:267); there are supposed to be three wars, one in the early 1610s, and one each following the 1622 and 1644 attacks. Like *uprising*, this term valorizes the violence of these periods, in this case by according it the same status as European military campaigns. This terminology, however, assumes our traditional dichotomy of peace and war, where war is the marked state when one is not at peace. This dichotomy is nearly irrelevant in Native American cultures, where war and peace were often ongoing, simultaneous processes, engaged by different portions of the population; young males were expected to engage in warfare, whereas male elders and females generally did not, although there were certainly exceptions. The colony may have declared war on the Powhatans following the 1622 and 1644 coups, but, although acts of warfare in a general sense, the coups themselves and the violence of the 1610s were not of the sort generally connoted by the term *war*. There were cultural and political factors in these attacks (by both sides) that remove most of them from legally proscribed domains such as assault or murder, but they were not wars as the term is commonly used, much less named, capitalized, *Wars*. I examine the different constructions of the meanings of war and violence in chapters 1 and 2.

Following the 1622 coup the English pursued a war of retribution against the Indians. For several years proclamations and legal decisions reiterated that a state of "perpetual enmity" existed between the English and the Powhatans; at one point, a peace treaty was even annulled because of this enmity (Craven 1970:172–73). In this period, rather than earlier, the Indians must have begun to be aware of the differing constructions of the relationship between the two peoples, as the English reaction was not what the Powhatans' conception of war and dominance allowed them to expect.

This state of aggression on the part of the English was countered by the profits that were to be obtained by trade with the Indians, and for a time in the 1630s it seemed that an uneasy peace had been reached. This was shattered in 1644, however, when Opechancanough, then reckoned to be near one hundred years old, led a second attack against the English. This resulted in an even larger number of English casualties than the first, although it represented a smaller proportion of the colonial population at that time. Opechancanough was captured and ultimately murdered in jail; war was again pursued against the Indians; and the Powhatans' mobility and choice of places to settle were increasingly restricted by law and by the unceasing influx of English settlers.

In 1676 Nathaniel Bacon, a newly arrived settler, led a popular uprising against the governor of Virginia known as Bacon's Rebellion. This began with a series of attacks against nearby Indian groups, culminating in Governor William Berkeley's flight to the Eastern Shore. Bacon was proclaimed governor. He died of dysentery, however, and the movement soon collapsed; Berkeley returned as governor. One result of Bacon's Rebellion, however, was the legal establishment of a number of reservations for the remnants of the Powhatan tribes, of which only two were to survive, those at Pamunkey and Mattaponi. These were the first reservations established in what was to become the United States. Today surviving Powhatans can be found on these reservations as well as in several nonreservation communities in Virginia and elsewhere.

These events of seventeenth-century Virginia established the pattern of Indian-white relations over the next three centuries. Each group sought to further its own aims. At times the behavior of each group fit the way it was perceived by the other; at other times there was a conflict between expected and perceived action. When this conflict became too great, and particularly when there was a perceived threat to the cultural order, the categories of meaning and understanding had to be redefined, and this violent rending of the cultural order was often accompanied by increased physical violence. These events mark changes in cultural perceptions and, thus, in forms of interaction.

THEORETICAL PERSPECTIVES

In eastern North America, colonial history has been the subject of historians and historical archaeologists and has focused primarily on the English colonial population, although recent works have attempted to add the African slave populations to the understanding of colonial America (Deetz 1988; Ferguson 1992). The Indians of the region have been studied by ethnohistorians, anthropologists, and prehistorical archaeologists. The research of Thomas et al. (1978) treats both native and European colonial cultures but generally deals with them separately. Studies integrating both histories and focusing on the relationships between native and colonial groups have been rare (see Merrell 1989a) but include Kupperman's study (1980) of early colonial Virginia and New England, Dickason's monumental study (1992) of the "founding peoples" of Canada, and Merrell's own work (1989b) on the Catawba Nation and colonial South Carolina.

In a more general context, a rapprochement between history and anthropology has long been developing and takes a variety of forms (Cohn

1987a, 1987b; Carmack 1972; Krech 1991). The various elements introduced from the two disciplines can include an interest in chronology, in the playing out of events, in the Other, and in the relevant cultural understandings of events and structures. Examples of such work may be found labeled as historical anthropology, anthropological history, or ethnohistory. Historical anthropology involves much more than the written history of an Other, however; it involves "the delineation of cultures, the location of these in historical time through the study of events which affect and transform structures, and the explanation of the consequences of these transformations" (Cohn 1987b:73). No participant in a colonial situation can be given primacy over others as agents responsible for historical developments. The goal of historical anthropology is to understand the interactions of historical process and conscious action with the unconscious structures of culture.

Historical anthropology is only one of the many approaches that have been called *ethnohistory*; it is rooted in a widely held perception that "people without history" (Wolf 1982) is, itself, a mythic category. As Fogelson and others have noted, history, "a sense of the past," is found among all cultures, although the forms of those histories can take radically different forms from our own (Fogelson 1989:134). A proper understanding of other histories thus demands that we make "a determined effort to try to comprehend alien forms of historical consciousness and discourse" (Fogelson 1989:134) — just as the ideas of western history have been studied (e.g., Collingwood 1956; Furet 1984).

Sturtevant presented the possibility of defining ethnohistory as "the conceptions of the past shared by the bearers of a particular culture, rather than (the more usual sense) the history (in our terms) of 'ethnic groups'" (1964:100), a concept for which Hudson (1966) then suggested the term *folk history*. This is much more than just the "history of primitive or traditional cultures" or the "anthropology of past primitive or traditional cultures" (usages criticized by Dening [1991:356]), but many people used — and continue to use — the term in just such loose fashion (see Sturtevant 1966; Carmack 1972; Krech 1991). A decade later, Fogelson (1974:106) introduced the term *ethno-ethnohistory* to reemphasize the parallels to other ethnomethodologies, but it was seldom used; another decade later, T. S. Turner (1988) used the same term, placing it more explicitly in a theoretical framework of the relations of structure and events.

It is important to recognize, and remember, that taking native terms and concepts into account does not mean that the product of these efforts is a "native" history. Nor should that necessarily be our goal. As DeMallie has observed,

> when we write academic historical narratives, we are not restricted to the particular cultural constraints of the actors, although they form one basis for interpretation. Our work is not usually focused on telling about the past exclusively in its own terms, but rather includes perspectives from the present as well, for just as we are outsiders to other cultures, we are also outsiders to the past. To restrict our narratives to the participants' points of view would be to negate the value of historical study as a moral enterprise, the purpose of which is to learn from the past and, in Ricouer's phrase, "to enlarge our sphere of communication" ([1981]:295). By the very act of composing a narrative, we necessarily impose cultural perspectives and make moral judgements. But to write a narrative about the past without attempting to understand historical cultures in their own terms would vitiate its significance as history. In short, understanding the past in its own terms is a necessary, but not sufficient condition of the writing of history. (1993:525)

The combination of analytical and narrative tools — essentially, using synchronic studies of the structures of culture to inform historical narratives that in turn involve those structures in diachronic processes and thus reveal still more of their nature — is the strength of this approach. Note, too, the significance accorded here to an "outside" position, the value of considering the perspectives of both "insiders" and "outsiders." Dening has also recently commented on this as both "the advantage and the frustration of historical anthropology," observing that "anthropology's vision is built not on the 'primitiveness' of the native but on the advantage of the dialectic between distance and familiarity" (1991:375). At a time when the politics of identity are producing scholarship and academic programs founded on the essentializing principle that one must "be one to study one," it is important to remember the positive effects that can result from an outsider's perspective. Going beyond DeMallie's observation, I would say that both understanding the past in its own terms and submitting that past to analysis and interpretation are necessary but not sufficient conditions for a historical anthropology.

Although the awkward term is only seldom used, the "ethno-ethnohistorical" approach has been employed in a number of significant works by scholars working in various parts of the world (e.g., Gewertz and Schieffelin 1985; Hill 1988), of whom Sahlins is perhaps most notable. Explicitly grounding "histories" in the details of the cultural contexts in which they originate, these approaches jointly implicate structure and event in culturally specific dynamic historical processes.

Sahlins has developed a concept of historical events and cultural contexts in his studies of Fiji (1991) and the Hawaiian Islands (1981, 1985, 1995) in which people's actions are a product of their cultural understandings of the world around them and thus of the cultural systems within which they act. His Hawaiian research has been harshly criticized by Obeyesekere (1992), in a problematic but surprisingly well-received book; Sahlins has recently answered these criticisms (1995). Obeyesekere's chief criticisms are on questions of Western and non-Western modes of thought and expression, on one level, and on readings of documents and questions of voice, on another. Sahlins's case, based on specifics of the Hawaiian context, is much more persuasive, even if expressed through Western voices, than Obeyesekere's claim to an essentialized "native" understanding and invocation of what Sahlins refers to here as "bourgeois rationality" (1995:8–9) — not an *ad hominem* dismissal, but a construct he had developed in detail as *"la pensée bourgeoise"* (1976:166–204) — and at several points in this book my interpretations similarly rebut a kind of imputed universal economic rationality.

The crux of this theoretical framework concerns the relationships of structure and events and of cultural orders and individual actions. Structure and action (or events) have long been treated as opposing ideas — synchrony versus diachrony — partly due to Saussure's analytical need to separate *la langue* from *la parole* in linguistics, in order to isolate the process of signification (Sahlins 1981:3–8; cf. Lévi-Strauss 1963, Saussure 1966). In anthropology a parallel notion to that of linguistic signification developed in which culture is seen as a symbolic means of ordering and thus of interacting with the universe; the history of this concept — and its opposition to a notion of culture derived from function or behavior ("practical reason") — has been set out by Sahlins (1976), tracing its roots to Boas and drawing connections to Durkheim and Lévi-Strauss. The cultural structures emphasized here were generally divorced from historical processes, although history was still commonly seen as important (Lévi-Strauss 1963:23–24, Sahlins 1981:6). This "too simple dualism of 'event' and 'structure'" can be overcome, however, by defining their articulations (Sahlins 1991:44).

Sahlins has called this process the " 'structure of the conjuncture,' meaning the way cultural categories are actualized in a specific context through the interested action of the historic agents and the pragmatics of their interaction" (1991:80–81; cf. 1981). In other words, the action of individuals may produce an instantiation of the cultural structure, a meaningful action, where meaning is derived from a particular cultural [-historical] structure; the individual action is taken to represent something larger. That unique action, in turn, may produce effects upon the cultural structure, through "the attribution of general meanings to particular incidents" (Sahlins 1991:82). Actions become eventful through these structural consequences, which may range from reproduction to transformation (see Cohn 1987a:46).[2]

Furthermore, these actions may be interpreted within a cultural system that is not necessarily the one in which they originated, and thence have effects, thus having the potential to change not only the cultural system in which they originated, but others that are implicated (Sahlins 1985:143–53, 1991:39–48). An action that is eventful in one context may not be so in another (see Fogelson 1989; Sahlins 1988), a condition particularly prevalent in colonial situations, where very different cultures are likely to interact. An understanding of each system of belief, of each world-view — colonial and native — is thus essential to interpret the actions arising from them.

The key to being able to conduct such a study is the availability of information in sufficient detail to reconstruct both the historical contexts and the cultural systems in action in the particular situation of interest. The historical record of the events of seventeenth-century Virginia is less completely detailed than that of the situations studied by Sahlins, but certain classes of available information permit such study. These can be augmented by the available knowledge from archaeological work in the area and from comparative ethnological and archaeological analyses of other Algonquian groups. Because each of these sources carries its own biases and represents a particular cultural construction of reality, none can be given primacy. They must be woven together and their similarities and differences compared, providing an improved understanding of the cultural systems from which they arise and thus of the history of interaction.

In traditional English terms, two types of interaction dominated the relationship between the English colonists and the Powhatans in the earlier seventeenth century: trade and warfare. The English colonization of the New World was a mercantile venture, with overtones of bringing Christianity and civilization to the natives. The Indians were also interested in trade, though their motives were to obtain objects of spiritual power (see Miller and Hamell 1986) and thus maintain and enhance their political and personal positions. Warfare was a normal means of settling conflicts of interest and maintaining the status quo, although other means, such as holding a captive hostage, were also employed by both sides.

The meanings and forms of warfare, trade, and all other forms of action within the Powhatan culture must be reconstructed, for they were recorded only from the English perspective, for the most part by individuals with no interest in understanding them from the Powhatan perspective. Although the Indians accepted many English goods and ideas, they took them and made them their own rather than simply receiving them in the terms of the English (Miller and Hamell 1986). Everything that happened was interpreted within the cultural scheme — or, in the colonial situation, within two or more distinct cultural schemes — and gained significance in terms of its meanings within those cultural schemes.

A key example of the differences in meaning assigned to a particular event is the captivity of Captain John Smith in the winter of 1607–8, when the infamous rescue of Smith by Pocahontas took place. To Smith this was an unconnected series of events over about a month's time, including his capture (a military defeat), accusations of murder (adjudication), inclusion in rituals (to determine his reason for being there), rescue (which was inexplicable), and his return to Jamestown (victory — returning to his prior state of freedom). As I show in chapter 4, for the Powhatans these events were most likely part of a single protracted ritual, making a place for the English colony in the Powhatan world and recognizing Smith as one of the leaders of the colony. To complicate matters further, beginning in the nineteenth century a new meaning was given to the rescue event: it became a myth, a self-aggrandizing story invented by Smith. In recent decades a new layer of complexity has been added to this latter meaning: rather than simple self-aggrandizement, it became archetypical of a process of European invention of Others based on European conventions and traditions. The validity and biases of a text must always be considered, but my interests here lie in the events and their contemporary meanings and effects, not these latter-day interpretations. These events are crucial to understanding the early developing relationships between the Powhatans and the English.

The 1622 coup is another key event to understanding the relationships between the English and the Powhatans. This was an event motivated by the perception of the interactions within the Powhatan cultural system, with effects based on its interpretation within the English cultural system. In the most extensive study of this event to date, Fausz (1977) argued that it was caused by the murder of Nemattanew, that the Powhatans saw their traditional culture as destroyed by 1617, and that Opechancanough was leading a revitalization movement with the goal of annihilating the English, with Nemattanew as his war leader. This reconstruction, however, is based only on English perceptions of the relationship between the two groups.

The 1622 coup became eventful through its effects, first among the English and then, upon English reprisal, among the Powhatans. It prompted both sides to begin to reassess their relationship. The terms of that relationship had developed in the preceding years, following the arrival of the English at Jamestown, and were in turn based on earlier interactions with the Spanish and others. They were to remain in flux to the middle of the century, at which time they began to be codified by the colonists in legislative acts, to which the Indians eventually acceded. The 1644 coup is to be seen as a later example of the contestation of the terms of the relationship between the two groups.

In order to understand these events, and thus the history of the interactions between the two groups, from the Powhatan perspective, one must reconstruct their systems of belief regarding relationships with non-Powhatan others. These involve trade and warfare, both of which are based on Powhatan institutions of authority and in turn on cosmology. These systems can be reconstructed from the records of the English through careful reading of the ethnographic accounts of the Powhatans, both seventeenth-century and later, supplemented by accounts of other related Algonquian groups. Miller and Hamell (1986) provide an example of the way in which this can be done, describing native perceptions of value as they can be reconstructed from the particulars of trade and from ethnographic knowledge of belief systems and color and material symbolism, in a study that is directly applicable to the Powhatan situation.

The type of reconstruction I have employed is an application of what Eggan (1975 [1954]) called "controlled comparison." The control here is based on long-recognized cultural similarities between Algonquian groups (Speck 1924, 1926:299–311; Flannery 1939), and on an assumption that the Powhatans would not have immediately suffered complete culture loss — that some traces of distinctly Powhatan culture could remain, perhaps even into the nineteenth and twentieth centuries. This latter assumption is supported by the ethnographic work of Speck (1925, 1928, n.d.), Rountree (1975, 1990), and passing mentions by Gatschet (n.d.), all of whom found some evidence of cultural continuity beyond the colonial period. As in all historical research, there is also an assumption that documentary sources reflect real phenomena, although they must be interpreted, taking into account biases in observation and transmission. After these sources have been evaluated, the comparisons one makes are between the cultural phenomena represented by the original sources, not the individual sources themselves; "the type, not the single object" (Thompson 1970:359; cf. Collingwood 1956:275).

In cases where there is relatively little information, it may be possible to employ an extension of this process that I have referred to as "controlled speculation," borrowing a phrase from Mednick (Gleach 1996a). These are inherently subjective processes, like any interpretation — including traditional Western histories[3] (see Collingwood 1956:231–49, Furet 1984:17–19) — depending for their success on an ability to assemble sufficient supporting information. The assumptions on which controlled speculation proceeds are essentially those of controlled comparison: recognized cultural similarities. Although some might want to argue that certain things can never be known, or that more speculative reconstructions have no place in scholarly activities, I agree with Dening "that in academic history and anthropology it is better to do what can be done than to declare what cannot" (1991:376). Interpretations and supporting material simply need to be presented sufficiently clearly for the reader to properly evaluate the conclusions, as is true of all scholarship.

In working with comparative material, this information must be evaluated not only for its reliability — which also generally involves comparison with other sources — but also for its relevance to the context. This depends on a knowledge of the cultural meanings and relationships involved. One cannot assume, for instance, that a cultural institution documented in one society would be the same in a neighboring society, or in every society sharing the same language. There is often information to help determine the likelihood of such parallels or similarities, however, in the form of passing mentions and partial accounts. The historical record is replete with tantalizing passages that suggest the presence or form of various rituals, beliefs, institutions, or social structures. Partial descriptions from one group often seem to match more completely described cultural practices from related or neighboring groups, and similarities in other related phenomena may also be documented. In such situations, in the absence of any contradictory evidence, I believe that an assumption of similarity between the two cases is justified.

Because language is a cultural phenomenon that is highly codified and relatively easily analyzed and compared, it is one of the principal factors in comparing Native American groups. In many situations cultural similarities exist despite linguistic differences, and cultural variability within a linguistic group is common; nevertheless, there are often relationships between the two. Care must always be used in arguing from one to the other, but it can judiciously be done.

North America is subdivided into a series of culture-areas, geographic divisions intended also to reflect cultural relationships, or at least similarities; the Powhatan Indians are typically classified in the northeast (Trigger 1978). This might seem unusual, since Virginia is a southern state, but the Powhatans were among the Algonquian-speaking nations, a diverse group occupying a range from North Carolina into northern Canada, and inland west of the Great Lakes (figure 1). Because the historical relationships within this large group are complex and are compounded by the movements of several groups at different times, subgroupings are commonly used, based on linguistic and cultural affinities. The principal division is between central and eastern Algonquians,[4] with all of the eastern Algonquian groups (from the Micmacs in Maine to the North Carolina Algonquians) fairly closely related (Goddard 1978a); they probably diverged from the other Algonquian groups about 3000 years ago, moving east and then spreading southwards (Goddard 1978b:586–87; Rhodes and Todd 1981:60–61). In contrast, central Algonquian languages (which include Shawnee, despite the early location of those people in the southeast) are all historically distinct independent developments of the ancestral "Proto-Algonquian" language (Rhodes and Todd 1981:52). Since they are linguistically distinct from the eastern group, Cree and Ojibwa are typically placed in the central group, although the distributions of those languages range from the Atlantic coast into Alberta and Saskatchewan.

Within these groupings, there are also marked cultural differences from north to south; some based on environment, others adaptations from various neighboring groups, others simply representing different trajectories of cultural change. For instance, the southern groups were more reliant on horticulture, although still employing fishing, hunting, and gathering; horticulture was not even possible for the most northerly Algonquians. In addition to the Algonquian groups there were others in this region, the best known of whom are probably the Iroquoian nations of the northeast, but there were smaller Iroquoian groups in southern Virginia, and the Cherokees of North Carolina; to the west of the Powhatans were less-well-known groups, probably Siouan-speakers. The Powhatans were among the southernmost groups classified in the northeastern culture-area, and as such they also exhibit cultural similarities to neighboring southeastern groups;

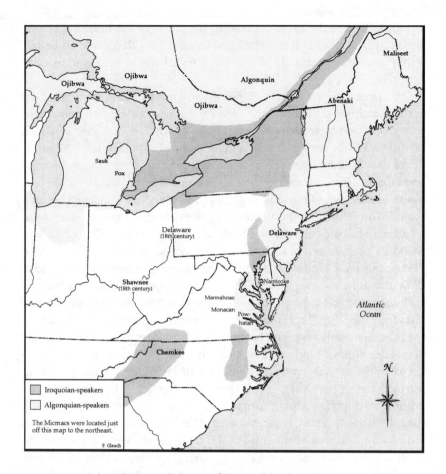

FIGURE I. Selected Native Cultures of Eastern North America

they are sometimes considered southeastern themselves — which certainly makes sense in the political realities of the later colonial and postcolonial period, a realm dominated by the Euro-American culture. Because of the diversity within the region and between Algonquian groups, care must be exercised with comparisons of both sorts. Nonetheless, comparison is possible.

In addition to the written records, the events of seventeenth-century Virginia also left a physical record that can be read in much the same way that historical records must be read, bearing in mind the context within which the record was generated. The physical record forms, to some extent, a complement to the historical record; the biases of the historical record are often race- or class-based (Indians, servants, and slaves tend to be relatively poorly represented), a bias the physical record suffers to a lesser extent.

On a large scale, one aspect of this physical record that is applicable here is the pattern of settlement: the physical locations of English and native settlements and their relationships to each other. The changing locations of settlements for both the native and the colonial populations were a product of the changing interactions of the two groups. It has recently become common in historical archaeology to examine the "landscape" of the colonial Middle Atlantic region (e.g., Upton 1988; Kelso 1989; Rubertone 1989). Most frequently this refers to the study of the changes made in the landscape of a particular site or of a developing urban area. One of the few works to attempt to deal with the cultural landscape as an entity is Isaac's *Transformation of Virginia 1740–1790* (1982). Central to this work is the idea of dramaturgy, referring to the reflection in actions — and thus in the socially constructed landscape (and other physical domains) — of social ideas (Isaac 1982:350–51). This embodiment of the conceptual in the physical is the process that allows going beyond the kinds of regional models of economic development long used by geographers.

On a smaller scale, certain classes of artifacts were important in these interactions: in particular, goods that were exchanged between the two groups. Two such groups of artifacts are Colono-ware pots (Noël Hume 1962; Deetz 1988) and Chesapeake pipes (Emerson 1988), goods that were most likely produced by the Indians and traded to the English colonists or to their servants (Gleach 1990a). The timing of their introductions and popularity, the contexts within which they are found, and the elements of their design all encode aspects of the producing and consuming populations and their relationships, which can be reconstructed through careful study (Deetz 1988; Emerson 1988; Gleach 1990a).

METHODOLOGY AND PREVIOUS RESEARCH

The events on which I focus are the attempted foundation of the Spanish Jesuit mission in 1570, the captivity of Captain John Smith in 1607–8, the coup of 1622, and Opechancanough's second coup of 1644. Bacon's Rebellion of 1676 is also discussed briefly, since a result of this event was the formal establishment of the Pamunkey and Mattaponi reservations, defining in a single act of legislation the restrictions of free movement and territories that had developed over a half-century from practice and a succession of legal rulings.

These events are documented with varying degrees of detail in the historical record — from the English perspective, of course — but they are poorly represented in archaeological work to date. As one way of overcoming the limitations of the historical records, I interpolate from ethnographic accounts, including later descriptions, to reconstruct the native system of beliefs and understanding, in the same way that historians have long reconstructed the English colonial world-view, in order to evaluate the actions that arose from those two very distinct orders. Certain Algonquian-speaking groups are better documented than others and can thus provide more material for comparison. The Delaware Indians, or Lenni-Lenape, inhabited the general area of the Delaware River valley, relatively near the Powhatans, and their language seems also to have been closely related to Powhatan, although there are also some obvious cultural differences. There are extensive missionary accounts of the Delawares from the eighteenth century and further sources from the seventeenth century. The Delawares' proximity and relative cultural closeness makes them a useful comparative case. Some of the New England Algonquians also provide comparative material. The Ojibwas of the Great Lakes area are also well documented; although their environment and thus some of their adaptations are quite different from the Powhatans, many aspects of their culture seem to be closely related. The same is true for other Algonquian-speaking groups. Certain southeastern tribes and Iroquois groups make useful comparative sources for selected aspects of Powhatan culture, but are generally less helpful for the issues of interest here.

In using such comparative material one of course cannot simply assume that, because one tribe employs certain practices or has certain beliefs, other related or neighboring tribes share them. The question of when to accept a comparison as valid is difficult and not one that can be resolved with certainty or subjected to scientific rigor. My decisions here are based not on any set of rules or guidelines but rather on subjective evaluations of interrelated points between the documented seventeeth-century Powhatan case and the various comparative sources. My evaluation of the Powhatan *huskanaw*, for example, is informed by knowledge of vision-quest rituals in other Algonquian-speaking groups. Passing comments and partial descriptions found in the documents of early Virginia fit with more extensive descriptions from other sources. These cannot be used to supply all of the missing details or to reconstruct a ritual completely, but they can be very useful in "seeing through" the cultural biases of the early colonial accounts to get a better understanding of what the meanings of such events might have been in the Powhatan view. Such reconstructions are not likely to capture the exact intent and connotations of Powhatan beliefs and actions, but they provide a much more reliable approximation than either accepting the colonial accounts as given or resorting to generalized psychological models for their interpretation.

A variety of more recent historical studies have informed this research. Smith's captivity and especially his rescue by Pocahontas have attracted copious discussion, including Barbour (1964:158–69, 1970:18–27), Fausz (1977:233–38), Kidwell (1992:99–101), Mossiker (1976:73–88), and Rountree (1990:36–39). Each of these sources has some points I believe to be accurate, but none develops the interrelatedness of all of the events of that captivity, which is key to its proper understanding. Fausz (1977, 1979a, 1979b, 1981, 1985, 1988) has written extensively on Opechancanough and the 1622 coup. I disagree with some of his interpretations, but his works provide a thorough discussion of the conflicts involved in that event, as seen from the English perspective. Craven (1964) provides an excellent study of the causes and history of the dissolution of the Virginia Company in 1624. Bacon's Rebellion has prompted a number of interpretations, ranging from Wertenbaker (1940), who saw Bacon as a patriot and the rebellion as a precursor to the War for Independence, to Washburn (1957), who saw Bacon as a rebel who manipulated popular opinion to advance his own position.

In addition to these histories of specific events, a number of synthetic histories have been written for this period. At the end of the nineteenth century Philip Alexander Bruce compiled both an economic history (1895) and an institutional history (1910) of seventeenth-century Virginia. These works are still considered important compilations in the field. Craven (1970) also provides an historical overview emphasizing economic and political institutions and their roles in the histories of all of the southern colonies. More recently, McCusker and Menard (1985) have written a very detailed analysis of the economic developments of colonial America. Lurie (1959) was the first to consider the Powhatans' reaction to the English arrival. Kupperman (1980) examined the history of interaction in colonial Virginia in light of English perceptions, moving away from the overly simplistic model that English actions were rooted in an inherent imperialist racism that had come to typify writing on the colonial period (see Horsman 1982). Rountree (1990) has provided an excellent history of the Powhatans, particularly noteworthy for its discussion of their history after the seventeenth century, and has edited a volume (1993a) of papers by several scholars on the relations between Powhatans and non-Powhatans.

Ethnographic studies of the Powhatan Indians began at the end of the nineteenth century. The first published was by Mooney (1907), in a study of the history of the Powhatan confederation that included notes on their present condition. Speck (1925, 1928) produced detailed contemporary ethnographies of the Rappahannocks and other Powhatan tribes. Mook and Stern, students of Speck, contributed ethnohistorical and ethnographic overviews (Mook 1943a, 1943b), an ethnography of the Chickahominies (Stern 1952), and a detailed study of Pamunkey pottery making that is essential to the interpretation of locally made pottery in the seventeenth century (Stern 1951). Rountree, who (1972a, 1972b, 1989, 1990) has studied the Powhatans for over two decades, provides an excellent synthesis of information. Ethnographic overviews are provided by the work of Swanton (1979) and Feest (1966a, 1966b, 1967, 1972, 1978, 1990) and can be supplemented by ethnographic accounts of other Algonquian groups, including those of New England and the Great Lakes region (see Trigger 1978) and the Delawares (Heckewelder 1876; Lindeström 1925; Loskiel 1794; Zeisberger 1910). Flannery (1939) provides a summary review of the documentation of many cultural traits for all coastal Algonquian peoples. Siebert (1975) has attempted some reconstruction of Powhatan linguistics, and Barbour (1971, 1972), Harrington (1955), and others have also analyzed the extant vocabularies. This can be augmented by judicious use of the research on Proto-Algonquian (Bloomfield 1946; Aubin 1975) and other Algonquian languages.

Excavations of major archaeological sites dating to this period are very few. Much of the town of Jamestown was excavated in the 1950s (Cotter 1958), but the materials have received little analysis. The site of the Jamestown fort, long thought to have eroded into the James River, has recently been located and is being excavated, a discovery that should greatly increase our knowledge of the period. A small settlement that was destroyed in the 1622 coup, Martin's Hundred, has been excavated, and a popular account published (Noël Hume 1982), and several houses in the Williamsburg area have been excavated and analyzed (Kelso 1984). A number of other, smaller, sites have been excavated but not yet analyzed and reported. Many of these collections are held at the Virginia Division of Historic Landmarks in Richmond, where they are available for study.

Synthetic studies by archaeologists, generally relying on both historical and archaeological materials, are also available. In particular, the recent work of Mouer (1987, 1991; Mouer and Gleach 1984; Mouer, Woolley, and Gleach 1986), has focused on the changing social landscape of seventeenth-century Virginia. Deetz (1988) has also brought together historical and archaeological information, attempting to explain the changing relationships between English colonists and their African slaves in the later seventeenth century. Binford, E. R. Turner, and Potter all brought together ethnohistorical and archaeological information in studies of particular native cultural groups. Binford (1964) focused on cultural diversity in southern Virginia; E. R. Turner (1976) examined the question of social stratification among the Powhatans; and Potter (1982) studied the late prehistoric and early historic settlement patterns of the Chicacoans, an Algonquian-speaking group to the north of the Powhatans. E. R. Turner (1978, 1982, 1985, 1993) has continued his research with the Powhatans, and Potter (1993) has further developed his work on the peoples of the northern fringe of the Powhatans.

All of these sources can be applied to the reconstruction of the historic events of seventeenth-century Virginia both in terms of individual histories and actions and in terms of the contexts within which they took place. These reconstructions, consciously shaped to take into account the perspectives, goals, and methods of the actors, both native and colonial, will provide a more complete understanding of the cultural systems and their effects through interaction. The changes in attitudes and in political "realities" can be seen through the actions of the people living these cultures, once these actions are understood in terms of the cultural systems within which they occurred and had effect.

I begin this work by describing the cultural contexts within which these activities took place and received meaning. Chapter 1 involves considerable reconstruction of the native cultural order, through the use of historical documentation and comparison with other related peoples who have received more extensive ethnographic recording. Chapter 2 presents a similar reconstruction of key points of the contemporary English culture. The reader should not expect these two chapters to be exactly parallel; the critical institutions and their interrelationships differ markedly. Having presented the contexts, in chapters 3 through 8 I discuss the historical events of the colonial situation in early Virginia, in the terms laid out in this introduction and employing the perspectives developed in chapters 1 and 2. This discussion begins with the sporadic contacts of the early sixteenth century and continues through the aftermath of the second coup against the colony, approximately 1646. Chapter 9 provides an overview of the relations between the Powhatans and the Virginia colony in the later seventeenth century, when the relationships worked out over the preceding decades became codified in law. The conclusion presents some of the implications and possible extrapolations of this research for the Powhatans and for the study of other groups.

Throughout this work I use the term *Powhatan* only as an adjective or as a singular noun referring to the specific person Powhatan; *Powhatans* refers to members of the group in plural. Traditionally, historians refer to Native Americans in plural form using an English-language plural, generally ending in *s* (i.e., *one Powhatan*, but *several Powhatans*), and anthropologists use the same form for singular and plural (i.e., one Powhatan, many Powhatan, or even the Powhatan, referring to the whole group). Problems can be noted for both plurals: an *-s* plural has no meaning in the native languages, and many ethnonyms are already plural forms to start with; but using the singular form promotes confusion, and perhaps seems to reify the group into an invariant monolithic entity (i.e., *the Powhatan grew corn*).[5] There is particular capacity for confusion in the Powhatan situation, where *Powhatan* is a specific individual name as well as the group reference, and I have chosen to use the *-s* plural form consistently to minimize possible confusion.

The reader should be forewarned that the text includes extensive quotations from the original documents. This is contrary to the common practice of paraphrasing rather than quoting, but I believe it is essential in a study such as this one, where I am attempting culturally sensitive interpretations of these documents, to allow the voices of the original authors to be heard, to tell their own stories. This is the closest we can get to the actors of colonial Virginia, Powhatan and English alike. In quoting early documents that have been transcribed and published I have regularized spelling, capitalization, punctuation, and italicization where necessary to reflect most accurately the original intent in a more readable form. Since no authoritative source would otherwise be readily available for comparison, unpublished manuscripts have been quoted as written; I have expanded the contractions that would have been typographically difficult to reproduce but have otherwise retained the original spelling and punctuation. In spelling Powhatan words and names I have tried to use spellings that most closely approximate current pronunciations.

1 ✦ The Native Context

It is commonly assumed that Powhatan society was extinct by 1700, and that remnants of their population were wholly assimilated into non-Indian society. This view is based both upon English people's wishful thinking about Indian people and upon the fact that documents about Indians in Virginia after 1700 are few and scattered. In actual fact, Indian society in Virginia was not extinct by 1700; in many ways it was not even much changed. — Helen Rountree, "Change Came Slowly"

W HEN THE ENGLISH arrived in Virginia in 1607, settling at Jamestown, they called the Indians resident in that area the Powhatans, after the common-use and titular name of their paramount chief. The Powhatans were an Algonquian-speaking paramount chiefdom occupying the coastal plain of Virginia from the south side of the James River north to the Rappahannock. Powhatan had inherited the political leadership of six or seven tribes in the late sixteenth century, and then expanded his authority through conquest to over thirty tribes by 1607 (figure 2). It is generally accepted that the time depth of this political organization was not much more than one generation prior to Powhatan himself and that this consolidation was probably at least partly spurred by contact with Europeans in the sixteenth century.

The appropriate terminology to describe the Powhatans' political organization has been a subject of much recent contention. Contemporary accounts referred to Powhatan as "king" (e.g., Smith 1986d:104) or "emperor" (e.g., Smith 1986b:173; Strachey 1953:56), but popular usage has long been to refer to the tribes as the *Powhatan confederacy*; Fiske (1897:94) was one of the first to use that term, followed by Mooney (1907) and others. Fausz (1977:69) states that "Powhatan's empire can be interpreted as a 'centralized monarchy,' a 'traditional state,' or a 'chiefdom,' according to the often ambiguous terminology of political anthropologists." More recently,

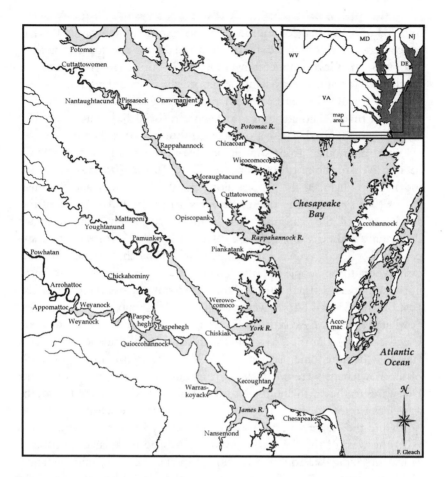

FIGURE 2. Principal Powhatan and Neighboring Districts

he has applied the Powhatan term Tsenacommacah, which properly refers
to the territory (see Strachey 1953:37, 56), to the social and political group-
ing as well (Fausz 1985). Rountree states that "Powhatan's organization was
a paramount chiefdom, not a confederacy" (1989:117), and refers to "Powhatan's 'empire'— which was *not* a 'confederacy'" (1990:10). Barbour (in
Smith 1986d:173n) chides about the same point, noting that "it is interesting to remember that many authorities continue to refer to 'the Powhatan
Confederacy'" despite contemporary descriptions of the Powhatans as a
monarchy. Mooney, however, was quite specific that by confederacy he was
not implying a voluntary alliance: "whereas the Iroquois league was

founded upon mutual accommodation and common interest, the Powhatan confederacy was founded on conquest and despotic personal authority" (1907:136). In a less argumentative tone, E. R. Turner (1985) refers to the Powhatans as a chiefdom, having developed the point at length in his dissertation (1976). The central issue here is not the selection of the "right" term, but that certain attributes of Powhatan social and political organization are recognized. These are discussed shortly in this chapter.

Other Algonquian groups, more loosely or not affiliated with the Powhatans, lived to the north of them (see E. R. Turner 1976:129–32; Potter 1993). These included the peoples along the Rappahannock and Potomac Rivers (both named after one of their resident tribes). The tribes of the south bank of the Rappahannock seem to have been brought under Powhatan's authority, but only at a relatively late date. North of the Rappahannock there is evidence of allegiance to Powhatan, but there are also cases where those people opposed Powhatan; by 1622 the Potomacs were important trade partners for food for the colony. Across the Chesapeake Bay, on the Eastern Shore, were two additional groups that were under Powhatan's rule, the Accomacs and Accohannocks (E. R. Turner 1976:133; Davidson 1993), but they, too, acted with considerable independence, and later they became trade partners with the colony. To the north and south of the Powhatans were unaffiliated groups including the Nanticokes and Delawares to the north and the North Carolina Algonquians to the south, as well as Iroquoian-speaking groups including the Susquehannocks to the north and the Tuscaroras, Nottoways, and Meherrins to the south.

To the west of the Powhatans lived the Monacan Indians, probably a Siouan-speaking (see Tooker 1895:378) group of tribes occupying the James and Rappahannock River drainages in the piedmont of Virginia. Essentially all that is known of them historically is that the Powhatans considered them enemies but nevertheless traded with them to obtain copper.[1] In the first years of the colony Powhatan tried to get the English to fight the Monacans with him, but the English were not anxious to go to war. Since the English did not have extensive contact with the Monacans and since they got most of their information from the Powhatans, there is little documentation of the Monacans. Although what does exist is relatively unreliable, Hantman (1990, 1993) has published two careful studies. The name *Monacan* itself is an Algonquian term by which the Powhatans referred to them (Smith 1986b:145).

This division between the coastal plain and the piedmont seems to have considerable time depth. Pottery types are distinctive by about A.D. 200, which is possibly the approximate time of the arrival of those who later became the Powhatans. It is generally agreed that the eastern Algonquians originated to the north and entered Virginia prior to A.D. 1000. A major change in the most common pottery of the coastal plain between A.D. 200 and 300 (see Gleach 1988) likely represents the arrival of the Algonquian-speaking groups who were to become the Powhatans (see Potter 1993:3–4). The movement of Iroquoian-speaking groups through the area at about A.D. 900 is similarly recognizable by the appearance of new pottery types. E. R. Turner (1993:83–89) has also shown relationships between ceramics and the various groups of Virginia's coastal plain.

The area of the fall line, dividing the coastal plain from the piedmont, appears to have been used by groups from both areas, and likely served as a buffer zone between the two (E. R. Turner 1978; Holland 1979; Mouer 1981) at least as early as the tenth century A.D. (Gleach 1987:225–26). This area was used for fall-winter hunting by both groups; Strachey (1953:83) describes their "hunting in the deserts," in groups "commonly two or three hundred together," employing fire drives to take large numbers of deer. Such burning of large areas has two different effects, both positive, depending on whether it is conducted in old-growth forest or cleared areas. In old-growth forests, burning helps to keep the understory clear, facilitating movement through the forests, and in cleared areas it encourages fresh growth of small leafy vegetation. An environment encompassing both settings can support a greater variety of animal species, and because of the different seasonal availability patterns of nuts and leafy vegetation can support larger animal populations, particularly through lean seasons (see Biswell 1967; Cronon 1983:49–52).

Within the coastal plain, lands were divided into a series of districts, each with a chief's village and other settlements. The territory under Powhatan's control was known as Tsenacommacah, possibly meaning "densely inhabited land."[2] The constituent members of the polity of Tsenacommacah included the groups under Powhatan's control when he inherited the position of paramount chief, and others that he had conquered. The *werowance*[3] of each group governed at Powhatan's sufferance. All villages were required to "pay tribute" to Powhatan; it was recorded that 80 percent of all produce — corn, beans, skins, etc. — was reserved for him (Strachey 1953:87). Barker (1992:61–80) has recently reanalyzed Powhatan productivity and distribution, concluding that Powhatan's desire for surplus led to the expansion through conquest of his control over the central Virginia tribes, but despite the invocation of statistics and demographic and agricultural models it remains uncertain that such a great portion of the production of the Powhatans actually went to Powhatan or even that the English term *tribute* reflects accurately the Powhatan institutions involved.

The core area of Tsenacommacah, that portion inherited by Powhatan, was primarily the inner coastal plain between the James and Mattaponi Rivers, including the districts of Powhatan, Pamunkey, Mattaponi, Youghtanund, Arrohattoc, and Appomattoc. The territory of the Chickahominies was surrounded on three sides by these districts, but they had apparently maintained their independence — presumably by means of their military strength. Hired for that purpose, warriors from the Chickahominies did fight for Powhatan on occasion, and they paid some tribute to Powhatan, but they governed themselves by means of a council of elders, and Powhatan was never able to place a *werowance* over them (Strachey 1953:68–69). The total population of this area in about 1607 has been conservatively estimated at approximately thirteen thousand to fifteen thousand (Feest 1973; E. R. Turner 1982), although Dobyns (1966:399–400) has suggested that it might well have been greater.

Powhatan himself was from the village known by that name, on the James River near the fall line. In 1607, his brothers governed the district of Pamunkey, near the northern edge of the original territory of Tsenacommacah. Feest (1966a:77) and others have suggested that the paramount chiefdom inherited by Powhatan was formed by a marriage alliance between the chiefly families of these two territories, which Powhatan then expanded by conquest.

The districts added by Powhatan were primarily along the James and York Rivers east of the core territory. These groups were not altogether foreign peoples; all spoke the same language as the Powhatans and shared similar cultures. The most eastern of these seem to have been the latest to be conquered. The territories along the south bank of the Rappahannock River were also apparently late additions, with one, Piankatank, at the mouth of that river, having suffered in 1608 a punitive attack similar to that executed against the English in 1622 (Smith 1986d:128; Strachey 1953:44–45).

Although the peoples populating Tsenacommacah shared a common language and culture, this is not to say that there were no differences between the groups. Powhatan culture was not an invariant, monolithic entity. Some of the differences in recorded place names are likely the result of dialectical differences (see Siebert 1975:287–88, 295–96; Gerard 1904), and there were undoubtedly also local differences in ceremonial and other aspects of cultural behavior. This variability can be studied in its own right in detailed microanalyses of particular cultures. Here, however, I apply the available details to the reconstruction of more generalized structures shared by the various Powhatan groups, many of which, in fact, are even more widespread, being found throughout the northeast and in some cases recognizable over much of the continent. The various Algonquian groups shared particularly notable similarities, as the Delawares noted in their histories of tribal relationships:

> All the tribes who had sprung from the Lenape [i.e., the Algonquian tribes] called the mother nation *grandfather*, and received, in return, the appellation of *grandchildren*. They were all united by the strongest ties of friendship and alliance; in their own expressive language, they made but *one house, one fire, and one canoe*, that is to say, that they constituted together, one people, one family. The same thing took place between the Mengwe and the tribes descended from them [the Iroquois]. They and the Lenape had no relationship with each other, though they came over the Mississippi together at the same time. They considered each other as nations entirely distinct. (Heckewelder 1876:96)

Although linguistic classifications that placed Powhatan and Delaware in the central Algonquian group (e.g., Michelson 1933, Bloomfield 1946) have been abandoned (Goddard 1978b:586–87), they are still considered to be closely related to each other and to others of the eastern Algonquian group (Siebert 1975:440–44; Goddard 1978a). Speck (1924) cataloged the effects on their material culture from contact with southeastern Indian groups, later describing them as "less Algonkian in culture than they were in speech. . . . In respect to material and social life the Powhatan tribes had become converted by southern influences to such an extent that their culture status, had we no information concerning language to guide us, would trend more toward classification with the Gulf area than with the Algonkian of the north" (1928:227–28). His descriptions reveal, however, that he was basing this evaluation largely on material factors, such as featherwork, and reliance on corn, bean, and squash agriculture. Politically, although more power was concentrated in the person of Powhatan than was common in most Algonquian groups, it was less than the authority wielded by southeastern chiefs, and it was similar to that held by some southern New England chiefs. In many other aspects, including but certainly not limited to

color symbolism, cosmology and mythology, and burial practices, the Powhatans were very similar to other Algonquian groups.

The Powhatan cultural order may be discussed in terms of three main
themes: authority, warfare, and trade. Each is closely tied to the Powhatans'
cosmology, their understanding of their place in the universe. Although I
have separated these themes here for ease of discussion, they are interrelated
in many ways, particularly through their grounding in the Powhatans' understanding of the universe as a complex and constantly shifting series of
interrelationships between humans and nature, broadly conceived, or between physical and supernatural power — a series of relationships that render such distinctions effectively meaningless. The next section examines the
nature of this mode of perception and some of the cultural institutions
arising from it.

AUTHORITY AND COSMOLOGY

Each village of Tsenacommacah had its *werowance*, who led with the approval of Powhatan; according to Strachey (1953:63) there were approximately thirty-four such villages, although the precise number of districts
has been the subject of some debate (Rountree 1989:9–14, 1993b:3–7).
Powhatan himself, the paramount chief, bore a number of names and titles,
"according to his divers places, qualities, or honors by himself obtained,
either for his valor, his government, or some such like goodness," among
them *Mamanatowick*, or "great king"; his other recorded names were
Ottaniack and *Wahunsenacawh* (Strachey 1953:56), which remain untrans-
lated. Within his domain Powhatan wielded various mechanisms of influence, including alliance through intermarriage (Hamor 1615:41), the replacement of a provincial chief with one more disposed to follow his wishes
(Strachey 1953), or with a brother or son (Strachey 1953:64, 67), and the
purchase of military force to maintain control (Strachey 1953:107). Nevertheless, his authority was not unquestionable. There are numerous examples of individuals not following their chief's wishes and of individual provincial chiefs exercising their autonomy from Powhatan. Throughout the
early histories, there are accounts of Powhatan telling the English that he
could not be held responsible for the actions of all of his subjects, saying
that "even our King James (commanding so many divers men) must have
some irregular and unruly people" (Strachey 1953:58).

Rountree refers to this as " 'incomplete' power," seeing it simply as a
manifestation of "a considerable disjunction between status and role,"

where Powhatan and other Native American chiefs had a high status but relatively limited power. As she notes, however, "much of the disjunction we observe comes from our using European terminology" (Rountree 1993b:8). Calling this power incomplete does not avoid such problems of terminology, which are embedded in different cultural systems of meaning. Rountree (1993b:8) questions "historians and anthropologists who have dealt with the heads of chiefdoms or states, in North America or elsewhere, [who] often have settled for recording the more easily collected data on the leaders' status, rather than carefully reporting on the long-term behavior which indicates the actual roles they played." But status is an anthropological construct dealing with culturally embedded meaning, not simply a question of perceived deference, and is anything but simple. Furthermore, perceptions of status are derived from behavior, raising serious questions about the precise meaning of this opposition. By rejecting the repeated observations and reports of many people that Powhatan was a person of great authority, she is left to assert that "the English probably overestimated Powhatan's ability to make and carry out a determined policy; he was actually less of a power behind the scenes than they believed" (Rountree 1993b:12). This may be literally true in the sense that the English accorded Powhatan more absolute authority than he had, but Rountree's statement in turn leads to an undervaluation of the authority that is well attested for Powhatan. The "power of individual Indian people to make up their own minds about foreigners and then act accordingly" (1993b:18–19) certainly needs to be considered — in the context of cultural notions of morality and individual behavior that I present below — but Powhatan's leadership should not be so lightly dismissed. Rountree (1993b:13–18) attempts to justify her notion of limited chiefly power by a worldwide cross-cultural comparison, an approach that assumes some level of universality and thus only works on a most general level. This is not necessary; the nature of chiefly power can be examined using a more controlled comparison to develop a characterization and set of terms appropriate to the particular cultural situation. The power of Native leaders was limited, but it was not "incomplete"; it was simply of a different, less coercive, form than similar European concepts, based in a different world-view, and needs to be understood as such (see W. B. Miller 1955).

At the time of contact, Powhatan resided at Werowocomoco, near the mouth of the York River; this location was near the recently conquered territories. His three brothers were *werowance*s at Pamunkey, as was his son Parahunt (also known as Tanx-Powhatan [Little Powhatan]) at Powhatan.

This dispersal, and particularly Powhatan's presence in the eastern territories, probably reflects the need for physical proximity to maintain his authority over this large region that had only recently been brought under his control.[4]

The position of *werowance* was normally inherited through the matriline, succeeding first to the brothers of the deceased chief, then to his eldest sister and her sons. This held for both the provincial chiefs (for which a few examples were recorded) and the paramount chief (Strachey 1953:77), but it was apparently possible for an older brother to authorize a younger to rule for him (see Smith 1986d:290–91). Although an individual thus held the position of chief, he or she did so because of his or her position in the family, not simply because of individual ability or achievements (cf. Biard 1897:87). The position of the paramount chief as leader of all of the tribes of the chiefdom, and his consequent role in both political and trade relations with the English, gave him a privileged position in the determination of the actual interaction. This position was further enhanced by the fact that all chiefs and priests were considered lesser gods (*quioccosuks*), with the paramount chief holding the ranking position among these earthly deities.

Powhatan's authority as paramount chief was extensive, but it was as much a personal as an official authority. As was typical for Algonquian groups, he ruled with the support and advice of his people, through the republican structure of a council composed of all the chiefs and priests. William Penn (1855:18) noted this of the Shawnees: "It is admirable to consider how powerful the kings are, and yet how they move by the breath of their people." Although frequently alluded to, this is not explicitly stated in any of the Virginia accounts. Strachey (1953:58) refers to Powhatan receiving word from his sentinels at his "court, or hunting house, wheresoever he, and his *cronoccoes*, [that is], councilors, and priests are; and then he calls to advise, and gives out directions what is to be done." Again, "when they intend any wars, the *werowances* usually advise with their priests or conjurers, their allies and best trusted councilors and friends" (Strachey 1953:104). Indeed, the Chickahominies had no *werowance* but were led by a council alone (Strachey 1953:68–69).

In the more usual form, the paramount chief led the council, and in practice could generally manipulate it to his desired ends (see Zeisberger 1910:96–97; Biard 1897:89–91). Nevertheless, as Zeisberger noted for the Delawares in the eighteenth century, "a chief may not presume to rule over the people, as in that case he would immediately be forsaken by the whole tribe, and his counsellors would refuse to assist him. He must ingratiate himself with the people and stand by his counsellors. Hence, it is that the chiefs are generally friendly, gracious, hospitable, communicative, affable and their house is open to every Indian" (Zeisberger 1910:92–93). Powhatan also had the power of life and death over his people, however, and could act on his own initiative; several cases were recorded where he had individuals summarily killed for various offenses. This would seem out of keeping with the above observations concerning the council's leadership, but what was important was not that the council had made a decision prior to the chief's action, but that it would support his action. Although the office of chief was passed through the matriline, "[t]he principal captain may choose a chief and inaugurate him, and it is also in his power to take him out of office if the chief proves a poor regent, acts contrary to the customs, does according to his own wishes and refuses to accept counsel. The captains, who always have the people on their side may thus forsake a chief, not only refusing to support him but even publicly announcing that they do not agree with him, and thus his power is at an end" (Zeisberger 1910:98, on the Delawares). The great authority of the chief rested upon the respect in which he was held.

Unquestionably, Powhatan had supreme authority — and support — within the council. This would have been true for any paramount chief but is especially notable for him: "It is strange to see with what great fear and adoration all these people do obey this Powhatan, for at his feet they present whatsoever he commands, and at the least frown of his brow, the greatest will tremble; that may be because he is very terrible, and inexorable in punishing such as offend him" (Strachey 1953:59–60). This seemingly absolute authority was probably partly due to Powhatan's holding shamanic, or priestly, power in addition to his inherited position in the political structure. Strachey (1953:60–61) discusses "the impression of the divine nature" of Powhatan in terms of an infusion of godliness; this state of Powhatan was obvious to the English as well as to the Indians. Hallowell (1976b:432–33) described the perception of such an individual among the Ojibwas: "Men who are believed to have acquired much power from other-than-human sources occupy a special position in Ojibwa culture. Since they have both the power to cure, as well as the power to kill, people's attitudes towards them are ambivalent: they may exercise a great deal of personal influence because they are feared, and may outrank other men in power, though not in material wealth or formal social ranking." Spiritual and social position could also be united in one person, of course. Father Biard

(1897:91) noted the combination of these two powers among the Algonquians of New France: "It happens sometimes that the same person is both
Autmoin [priest] and *Sagamore* [chief], and then he is greatly dreaded."
Lescarbot's description of Membertou, the great chief of the Micmacs in
the early seventeenth century, yields more detail:

> He has under him a number of families whom he rules, not with so
> much authority as does our king over his subjects, but with sufficient
> power to harangue, advise, and lead them to war, to render justice to
> one who has a grievance, and like matters. He does not impose taxes
> upon the people, but if there are any profits from the chase he has a
> share of them, without being obliged to take part in it. It is true that
> they sometimes make him presents of beaver skins and other things,
> when he is occupied in curing the sick, or in questioning his demon
> (whom he calls *Aoutem*) to have news of some future event or of the
> absent: for, as each village, or company of savages, has an *Aoutmoin*,
> or prophet, who performs this office, Membertou is the one who,
> from time immemorial, has practiced this art among his followers. He
> has done it so well that his reputation is far above that of all the other
> Sagamores of the country, he having been since his youth a great Cap-
> tain, and also having exercised the offices of soothsayer and medicine-
> man, which are the three things most efficacious to the well-being of
> man, and necessary to this human life. (1896:75–77)

This case is probably closely parallel to that of Powhatan and is simply the
fullest development of normal chiefly characteristics. One does not have to
go back to the seventeenth century to find this pattern; Shkilnyk (1985:101–
2) noted in an Ontario Ojibwa community that "until the year 1962 . . . all
the chiefs were men who epitomized the 'ideal' person, combining religious, economic, and kinship roles in the exercise of leadership."

The name *Powhatan* itself seems to suggest that he held this dual position
of authority. It has traditionally been translated as "falls on a rapid stream"
(Trumbull 1870a:10), following Smith's statement (1986d:138) that this
name was derived from his original village, near the falls of the James River.
It is unclear, however, why this place would have been singled out by this
name in an area where all of the major rivers fall as they cross from the
piedmont to the coastal plain. Furthermore, although it was not unusual
for a place name to be taken from a person's name (Trumbull 1870a:37),
the reverse is not likely, given native naming conventions. Trumbull
(1870a:43) notes that "Indian place-names are not *proper names*, that is un-

meaning marks, but significant *appellatives*, each conveying a *description* of the locality to which it belongs." In the same way, personal names also tend to be descriptive. Finally, Strachey (1953:183) gives, in his Powhatan word-list, the following listing: "The falls at the upper end of the king's river — *Paquachowng*." This word is probably related to the Proto-Algonquian root **pak-*, "strike, beat" (Aubin 1975:#1787) — the action and sound of the rapids at the fall line. The name *Powhatan* was probably related to the term *powwáw*, the Narragansett term for a priest, with both derived from the Proto-Algonquian root **pa:w-*, "dream (stem)" (Aubin 1975:#1781, cf. #1782: **pa:wa:qe:wa*, "he, she dreams of him, her"). Aubin (1975) also lists the Micmac "*pewat* 'he dreams.' " J. M. Cooper (1934) gives the Cree word "*pōwā'gàn* ('guardian spirit')," and Hallowell gives the Ojibwa "*pawáganak*" ("*pawágan*," singular) as "dream visitors" (1976a:379), or "other-than-human persons . . . conventionally referred to, in the anthropological literature, as 'guardian spirits' " (1976b:406). The Ojibwa historian Warren (1984:30) noted that the name *Powhatan* meant "a dream," and "*Powatanep*," which Voegelin translated as "shaman" (1954:121), appears in the Walam Olum.[5]

Barbour (1971:297) began to correct the misunderstanding of this name, giving the meaning of the place-name Powhatan as "Medicine-man's (shaman's) village or hill." He correctly noted that the village of Powhatan was located about a mile below the falls of the river, dismissing the usual derivation. His construction, however, would be "dreamer-village" or "dreamer-hill" (*powwáw-otan* or *powwáw-adené* would be an approximation) and would still leave Powhatan the person named after his location. Note that all such linguistic reconstructions of meaning are speculative; the personal derivation, as approximately "one who dreams," with the place named after the person, seems to provide a better fit here, however. Further support for this interpretation is found in his other recorded title-name, *Mamanatowick*; embedded here, despite the spelling variation, is the word *manito* (*Mà-mánito-wek*), the widespread Algonquian term for a spirit-being.

This posited meaning of his name is particularly significant in that dreaming was the source of shamanic power (cf. Simmons 1986:41–45), as Barbour alluded in his derivation. This belief was still in evidence among the Powhatans as recently as this century, as recorded by Speck (1925:81): "Dreams are held in high esteem. The photograph of James Johnson . . . shows the wearing of a beaded headband to induce dreaming. He is an herb doctor who works his profession through dreams." Cass (1826:99–

100), in a critical discussion of the Shawnee Prophet, describes the acqui-sition of spiritual power through dreaming, and continues: "These proph-ets, as they are improperly termed, frequently make their appearance among the Indians, and acquire a wonderful ascendancy over them." The strength resulting from his dual position of authority, with both inherited political power and achieved religious power, could help explain how Pow-hatan was able to assemble the tribes that made up his chiefdom.

In addition to the *werowance*, there was also a position of leadership recorded by the English only as captain, or war-chief, with no Algonquian equivalent given. Mechling described this division among the Maliseets and Micmacs:

> Besides these peace chiefs there were war chiefs, *ginap*, or what may more accurately be called war leaders or band leaders. They were really not chiefs at all, for they were not political officials. A *ginap* was a man who had, through previous bravery and skill in war, made a reputation for himself, and who, therefore, was able to obtain a following in war time. . . . Even though a *ginap* may not be a [shaman], he is supposed nevertheless to have supernatural power, but only along particular lines. For example, as the shaman is able to perform certain things which other people cannot, such as cure the sick or make his enemies sick, so the *ginap* is able to perform other things, e.g., to run very fast and for a long distance, to swim under water . . . and to perform feats of strength which would be impossible to ordinary individuals. How much supernatural power he is supposed to have is well shown by the fact that a war party, no matter how numerous, is entirely helpless before a much less numerous enemy if it loses its *ginap* or *ginaps*. (1958:141–42)

In Virginia, Strachey (1953:104) recorded that the war-chief could be a *werowance*, but could also be simply "some lusty fellow." The war-chief could be recognized for his abilities with gifts of beads or copper and could gain prestige that lasted beyond the time of war. He could also be given "a name answerable to the attempt," one "which they take for the most eminent and supreme favor" (Strachey 1953:114).

The distinction between peace-chief and war-chief is common among Algonquian groups and in the southeast; the position of war-chief was achieved by a demonstration of bravery and ability to lead, and not inher-ited (see Callender 1978:640–41; Erickson 1978:131–32; Johnston 1990:68; Mechling 1958:141–42; W. B. Miller 1955:283–85; Zeisberger 1910:101). A dream or vision often provided the evidence that one was to be a captain, but this had to be made good through action (Zeisberger 1910:101; cf. Heckewelder 1876:246–47). The division was probably not simply between peace and war but rather between internal and external matters in general (Raymond Fogelson, personal communication). The peace-chief held the higher ranking position but depended on the support of the war-chief in council. The position of war-chief could, of course, take on a greater importance in a context of interaction with powerful outsiders. Powhatan was the paramount chief of his people, ranking over the chiefs of all of the villages of Tsenacommacah. In the same way, Opechancanough was his war-chief; there were other war-chiefs, just as there were other, lesser, *werowances*.

The existence of this division in Virginia has not been properly recognized by historians, primarily because of the particular history of interactions. Captain John Smith, attempting to meet with Powhatan, whom he had been informed was the chief leader of the Indians, was first met by Opechancanough. Only after some time and the performance of certain rituals was he taken to Powhatan. These rituals were probably to cleanse him of dangerous elements that could have been brought in from outside; they also were likely part of a process by which Smith and the English colony were adopted into Powhatan's nation, as is discussed in chapter 4. Smith's insistence on dealing with Powhatan — whom he saw as an "emperor" — was paralleled by Powhatan's desire to meet with Captain Newport, whom Smith had described as his "father," the person in charge of the Englishmen (Smith 1986a:55, 63). This reflected the Powhatan's perception of a dual structure among the English: as they saw it, Smith primarily dealt with the "outside," like a war-chief, whereas Newport, the ship's captain they seldom saw, dealt more with internal (English) affairs and was seen in the superior position of the peace-chief.[6]

The dual nature of chiefdom is reflected in the structure of the Powhatans' cosmology, which was also poorly understood by the English. Strachey's account (1953:88) is typical: "their chief god they worship is no other indeed than the devil, whom they make presentments of and shadow under the form of an idol which they entitle *Okeus* and whom they worship as the Romans did their hurtful god [Jupiter] more for fear of harm then of hope of any good." This is the Powhatans' god generally recognized by the English colonists, a god that needed to be pacified by sacrifices and offerings. But in the same account, Strachey writes of their "great God," who governs all the world, and makes the sun to shine, creating the moon and stars his companions, great powers, and which dwell with him, and by whose virtues and influences, the under earth is tempered, and brings forth her fruits according to her seasons, they calling Ahone, the good and peaceable god, requires no such duties, nor needs be sacrificed unto, for he intendeth all good unto them, and will do no harm, only the displeased Okeus looking into all men's actions and examining the same according to the severe scale of justice, punishes them with sicknesses, beats them, and strikes their ripe corn with blastings, storms, and thunderclaps, stirs up war and makes their women false unto them, such is the misery and thraldom under which Satan hath bound these wretched miscreants. (1953:89)

The same duality, and the same emphasis, is found in accounts of the beliefs of the Algonquians of the Massachusetts area (see Simmons 1986:38–40) and in Jesuit descriptions of the northeastern Algonquians (e.g., Biard 1896a:77). This is quite different from the English view of the world, where order was imposed by man and threatened by a potent evil (Satan) that could only be resisted, not compelled. The colonists dwelt on the god Okee, who required external worship by offerings and sacrifices, just as they emphasized the war-chief, who engaged in action with the outside. This identification of the devil as the god of the Powhatans made the Natives heathens — devil-worshippers — who needed to be converted and made it proper for the English to take the Powhatans' lands into God's dominion.

For the Powhatans, the sacrifices made to Okee were simply an example of right behavior, of actions made to maintain order in the world, to keep potentially dangerous powers in balance. The true God, the active creator, did not judge or require sacrifices made to him but rather was worshipped through the subordinate spirits, the *manitoac* (Loskiel 1794:40), and Okee, who corresponds to the natural world and sits in judgment (Strachey 1953:88–89). The individual was seen as in a particular and personal relationship to the world, one emphasizing proper behavior as part of a living system — of a family. Hallowell has discussed this relationship for the Ojibwas, where *pīmädäzīwin*, "life in the fullest sense, life in the sense of longevity, health and freedom from misfortune" (1976a:383) could only be achieved by maintaining approved standards of conduct with the help of others, both human and other-than-human (the latter generally referred to as "grandfathers"), resulting in a situation in which human and nonhuman beings are involved in reciprocal relations and held to the same values. A moral distinction is drawn between the kind of conduct demanded by the primary necessities of securing a livelihood, or defending oneself against aggression, and unnecessary acts of cruelty. The moral values implied document the consistency of the principle of mutual obligations which is inherent in all interactions with "persons" throughout the Ojibwa world. According to Hallowell (1976a:385), in Ojibwa culture "a balance, a sense of proportion must be maintained in all interpersonal relations and activities. . . . The central importance of this moral value in their world outlook is illustrated by the fact that other-than-human persons share their power with human beings." This emphasis on right behavior reflected poorly on the colonists and highlights one of the difficulties encountered by the English in their efforts to convert the Indians to Christianity. The Reverend Heckewelder gives a typical response from the Delawares:

> these white men would always be telling us of their great Book which God had given to them, they would persuade us that every man was good who believed in what the Book said, and every man was bad who did not believe in it. They told us a great many things, which they said were written in the good Book, and wanted us to believe it all. We would probably have done so, if we had seen them practise what they pretended to believe, and act according to the *good words* which they told us. But no! while they held their big Book in one hand, in the other they had murderous weapons, guns and swords, wherewith to kill us, poor Indians! Ah! and they did so too, they killed those who believed in their Book, as well as those who did not. They made no distinction. (1876:188)

For the Indians, rightness was based in practice, not simply on belief. The practice was based in belief, however — fundamentally, in a belief in the connection between every individual and the supernatural, or the spirit world. Such a connection was culturally defined but was obtained through individual action. It was based in gnosis, in individual knowledge, rather than in the Logos of the English, institutional knowledge recorded in the Bible. Power–the ability to act rightly — was derived from the individual's connections with the various spirits: "And *as there is a spirit in all things,* the united spirit of myself and those that have sent me will have power in this matter. I fear not hunger," wrote the Penobscot Joseph Nicolar (1893:45–46, emphasis added), recording the teachings of the elders. The presence of this power — the capacity for right or just action — in the priests and chiefs is reflected in the fact that they were considered *quioccosuks*; the word possibly meant "the just, the upright ones" (Barbour 1972:42).

This relationship with the powers of the supernatural was closer for some than for others, but was present for all. Zeisberger (1910:132–33) wrote, from the Delawares: "There is scarcely an Indian who does not believe that one or more of these spirits has not been particularly given to him to assist him and make him prosper. This, they claim, has been made known to them in a dream. . . . If an Indian has no *Manitto* to be his friend he considers himself forsaken, has nothing upon which he may lean, has no hope of any assistance and is small in his own eyes. On the other hand those who have been thus favored possess a high and proud spirit." There were greater and lesser spirits, and ordeals were undertaken specifically for the acquisition of powerful spirits (see [Cass] 1826:99–100, on central Algonquians; Simmons 1986:39–41, on the New England tribes). Their influence would be reflected in the abilities and position of the individual. These contacts with the spirit and outside worlds could be dangerous; Purchas notes (1617:955) that the priest Uttamatomakkin could not enter a temple after his return to Virginia from England "till *Okeeus* shall call him," suggesting a time of purification (Rountree 1989:132; cf. Helms 1988) to control the dangerous powers and influences he may have brought back.

The one religious ceremony relatively well described for the Powhatans, the *huskanaw*,[7] was probably a vision-quest rite, by means of which a young man acquired such a tutelary spirit, establishing a personal connection with the supernatural world which would help him to employ the powers available in the world in the right ways (cf. Johnston 1990:119–33). It involved boys generally in their teens, "the choicest and briskest young men of the town, and such only as have acquired some treasure by their travels and hunting," and was essential "before they can be admitted to be of the number of the great men" (Beverley 1947:207). The ceremony began with a morning of singing and dancing, followed by the boys having to pass through a gauntlet three times. They were largely shielded from the blows by older boys at this point. There followed a great feast, ending with the boys again having to run the gauntlet, after which they were as dead (Rountree 1989:80–81). Indeed, many English observers thought they were dead or were soon to be sacrificed; none were allowed to observe what followed: "the principal part of the business is to carry them into the woods, and there keep them under confinement, and destitute of all society, for several months; giving them no other sustenance, but the infusion, or decoction of some poisonous intoxicating roots; by virtue of which physic, and by the severity of the discipline, which they undergo, they become stark staring mad: In which raving condition they are kept eighteen or twenty days" (Beverley 1947:207). According to Smith (1986b:172) their isolation lasted nine months; after this, they were reborn and returned to their village as men, having forgotten all that they knew in their youth (Beverley 1947:208–9). This alternation of socially integrated and isolated components is typical of Native American ceremonies for obtaining a guardian spirit; whereas the spirit is generally received in isolation, the group rites validate the individual experience for the society (Benedict 1923:51–57). From the perspective of the individual, his relationships to both society and to the spiritual elements of the natural-supernatural universe are emphasized.

Smith (1986d:125) notes that from those who completed the *huskanaw* "were made their priests and conjurers," who, with the *werowances*, were all considered *quioccosuks*, or lesser gods. As such, their actions were supposed to define right behavior — not because they were the rulers, but because they had a closer affinity to, or a better understanding of, the spiritually defined quality of "rightness." This was largely due to their having been through the *huskanaw*. Beverley describes the Indians' views on this point:

> [they] pretend that this violent method of taking away the memory, is to release the youth from all their childish impressions, and from that strong partiality to persons and things, which is contracted before reason comes to take place. They hope by this proceeding to root out all the prepossessions and unreasonable prejudices which are fixed in the minds of children, so that, when the young men come to themselves again, their reason may act freely, without being bypassed by the cheats of custom and education. Thus also they become discharged from the remembrance of any ties by blood, and are established in a state of equality and perfect freedom, to order their actions, and dispose of their persons, as they think fit, *without any other control, than that of the Law of Nature*. By this means also they become qualified, when they have any public office, equally and impartially to administer justice, without having respect either to friend or relation. (1947:209, emphasis added)

The English seem to have only partly understood this spiritual basis of rightness; they sought codified rules of conduct among the Indians: "nor have they positive laws, only the law whereby he ruleth is custom; yet when he pleaseth his will is law, and must be obeyed, not only as a king, but as half a god, his people esteem him so. His inferior kings are tied likewise to rule by like customs, and have permitted them power of life and death over their people as their command in that nature" (Strachey 1953:77). The main point of misunderstanding in this interpretation is that Powhatan "custom" was not "a habitual or usual practice" or "an established usage which by long continuance has acquired the force of a law or right" (*OED* 1971, s.v. "custom"), the established English usages at the time. Custom, for the Powhatans, was a directly and individually received moral code of "divine" origin, coming from the "supernatural," or spirit world, a consequent extension of their world-view.

Dividing the world into "natural" and "supernatural" does not reflect a Native American perception, however, since spirits and gods were seen as part of the living world. This belief is widespread but has been well described from the Ojibwa culture: "Yet to call these beings supernatural slightly misinterprets the Indians' conception. They are a part of the natural order of the universe no less than man himself, whom they resemble in the possession of intelligence and emotions" (Jenness 1935:29; cf. Hallowell 1976a, 1976b). These beings were frequently encountered in dreams and visions, which were considered at least as "real" as everyday waking encounters (Heckewelder 1876:246–47; Hallowell 1976a). Like many Algonquian groups, the Powhatans recognized the concept of *manit* (Feest 1978:262); Hariot recorded of the North Carolina coastal Algonquians that "they believe that there are many Gods, which they call *Mantóac*, but of different sorts and degrees" (1588:E2ᵛ). *Manit*, the singular noun form of the word, refers to "spiritual power that could be manifested in any form" (Crosby 1988:192–93). *Manitu* was a frequently used expression recorded by Roger Williams from seventeenth-century Massachusetts Algonquians:

> there is a general custom amongst them: at the apprehension of any excellency in men, women, birds, beasts, fish, etc. they cry out *Man-ittóo*, that is, it is a God; as thus if they see one man excel others in wisdom, valor, strength, activity etc. they cry out *Manittóo* a God; and therefore when they talk amongst themselves of the English ships, and great buildings, of the plowing of their fields, and especially of books and letters, they will end thus: *Manittôwock* they are Gods; *Cumman-ittôo*, you are a God, etc. A strong conviction natural in the soul of man, that God is; filling all things, and places, and that all excellencies dwell in God, and proceed from him. (1973:191)

Williams's translation of *manit* or *manitu* as "God" was common; "great

Manitu" was a common reference for the English God (cf. Heckewelder 1876:101–2), and the root *anit* was used in constructions referring to specific deities within the native pantheon (see Gatschet 1899; R. Williams 1973:190). The Crees in the early twentieth century seem to have recognized three aspects of a single *manitu*: the least powerful, with mastery over food; next an aspect with mastery over life, and curing; and the most powerful, the aspect of death (J. M. Cooper 1934:11–12, 16–17). *Manit* was also used as a more generalized term, however, referring to " 'that which is more than,' 'passes beyond,' or 'exceeds,' the common or the normal" (Trumbull 1870b:340; cf. Jones 1905; Loskiel 1794:39–40). Crosby (1988:193) has described the ways in which *manit* "as spiritual power was observed as a quality or an ability expressed in the appearance, behavior, or strangeness of animals, plants, people, and things, both Indian and European." Note, however, that among northern Algonquian peoples *manitu* "always denotes a supernatural *personal* being," not impersonal supernatural force (J. M. Cooper 1934:38; cf. Hallowell 1976a:382).

These *manitoac* were most likely the tutelary spirits with whom connections were made through the *huskanaw* ceremony. Hallowell (1976a:384–85) discussed the "so-called 'puberty fast' or 'dreaming' experience" of Ojibwa boys as "the means by which it was possible to enter into direct 'social interaction' with 'persons' of the other-than-human class for the first time." Walter Miller (1955:287) notes "an internalized *manitu* guardian" among the Fox that is obtained through a vision quest that is quite similar to the *huskanaw*, although of shorter duration. Brightman (1993:76–102) describes the vision quest as it survives today among the Crees, and Heckewelder (1876:245–48) described the process of initiation for the Delawares in the late eighteenth century. All of these rituals put young men in contact with the tutelary spirits they would work with throughout their lives. As in Virginia, these initiates learn that they are to be, variously, warriors, physicians, sorcerers, "or that their lives are to be devoted to some other civil employment" (Heckewelder 1876:247).

The relationship between an individual and *manit* has also been extensively documented for the Fox Indians of the Great Lakes region:

> Manitu power is actualized or manifested only when it is acquired by some particular being, who then *becomes* manitu. . . . A significant characteristic of manitu power is that it is never possessed permanently by any being or group of beings; it is always held conditionally. It is lost, gained, lost again — its possession being measured by quality of

performance in a particular area of activity. To succeed means that manitu power is possessed; to fail means that it is lost. . . . Fox cosmology presents a picture of scores of powerful manitus jockeying with one another in a constant and unending struggle for temporary superiority.

. . .

The Fox pantheon is extremely elastic, always ready to accommodate any deity, of whatever origin, who can demonstrate the possession of power. (W. B. Miller 1955:279, 281)

This condition of the Algonquian pantheon is reflected in statements made by individual Powhatans, such as the *werowance* of Quioccohannock:[8] "he believed our god as much exceeded theirs as our guns did their bow and arrows" (Strachey 1953:101) — despite the fact that most Powhatans strongly resisted the conversion sought by the English. In the same way, Simmons (1986:40) has noted that two of the first Indians to enter the Pilgrims' settlement at Plymouth, Hobbamock and Squanto, had considerable *manit* and "hoped to add the Christian God to their personal arrays"; nevertheless, "the English counted them, although tentatively, among their first converts."

The shamans and priests also dealt with the supernatural and had gained this ability through dreams and visions obtained through ordeal, but they had less institutionalized authority than the *werowance*s. The principal duties of the shamans, also referred to as conjurers, "included forecasting plans of enemies, revealing thiefs, finding lost objects, and aiding the priests within the temples" (E. R. Turner 1976:117). The priests performed many of the same duties as the shamans, but in addition the priests were in charge of the temples and the interments of the deceased chiefs (Strachey 1953:94–95). Priests provided counsel to the living chiefs and in particular were consulted in questions of war (Strachey 1953). Priests also engaged in travel, like Uttamatomakkin, who visited England with Pocahontas in 1616–17. Among the Chickahominies there was no *werowance*, and all decisions were made "by their priests, with the assistance of their elders" (Strachey 1953:69), structurally formalizing the decision-making process evident for the Powhatans in general.

Political and spiritual power were thus closely related for the Powhatans; at the time of contact, both were probably instantiated in the person of Powhatan. His conquest of neighboring groups was due to the application of both military strength and moral rightness; indeed, his ability to command such military strength rested largely on his personal ties to spiritual power obtained through dreams. This interrelationship, verging on identity, of political and spiritual power — of might and right — becomes even more apparent in considering the native institution of warfare.

THE POWHATANS AND AN ALGONQUIAN AESTHETIC OF WAR

Little actual warfare between native groups was observed by the English in early Virginia, although they were told that the piedmont tribes were considered enemies of the Powhatans and that there had been wars with them in the past. Two raids into the coastal plain by piedmont tribes were recorded in the first years of the colony, both on the fringes of the territory controlled by Powhatan, on the Rappahannock (Smith 1986d:175) and on the Potomac (Spelman 1910:cxiv). When Powhatan staged a mock battle for the English, the two sides represented the Powhatans and the Monacans (Strachey 1953:110). What the English would term *war* had certainly taken place within the coastal plain; much of the territory of Tsenacommacah had been gained by conquest. Indeed, the English were told by the Powhatans of their conquest of Piankatank in 1608 (Strachey 1953:44), and of Kecoughtan (Strachey 1953:68) and Chesapeake (Strachey 1953:104–5) at somewhat earlier dates.

The mock battle witnessed by Captain John Smith took place in an open field with the warriors arrayed in ranks. It was highly formalized and not typical of any actual battle observed or described in Virginia, or indeed for any other Algonquian group:

> Having painted and disguised themselves in the fairest manner they could devise, they divided themselves into two companies, well near 100 in a company. The one company they called Monacans, the other Powhatans; either army had their captain. These (as enemies) took their stands a musket shot one from another, ranking themselves fifteen abreast, and each rank from other four or five yards, not in file, but in the opening betwixt their files, so as the rear could shoot as conveniently as the front. Having thus pitched the field, from either went a messenger with conditions, that whosoever were vanquished, such as escaped, upon their submission or coming in, though two days after, should live, but their wives and children should be prize for the conquerors. The messengers were no sooner returned but they ap-

proached in their orders, on each flank a sergeant and in the rear an officer for lieutenant, all duly keeping their ranks yet leaping and singing after their accustomed tune, which they use only in wars. Upon the first flight of arrows, they gave such horrible shouts and screeches as so many infernal Hellhounds. When they had spent their arrows, they joined together, prettily charging and retiring, every rank seconding other. As they got advantage they caught their enemies by the hair of their head, and down he came that was taken; his enemy with a wooden sword seemed to beat out his brains, and still they crept to the rear to maintain the skirmish. The Monacans decreasing, the Powhatans charged them in the form of a half moon; they unwilling to be enclosed fled all in a troupe to their ambuscados, on which they led them very cunningly. The Monacans dispersed themselves among the fresh men, whereupon the Powhatans retired with all speed to their seconds, which the Monacans seeing took that advantage to retire again to their own battle, and so each returned to their own quarter. All their action, voices and gestures both in charging and retiring were so strained to the height of their quality and nature that the strangeness thereof made it seem very delightful. (Strachey 1953:109–10, following Smith 1986b:166–67)

A pitched battle fought in this way would result in immediate destruction for both groups, given the demonstrated effectiveness of the Indians' archery — if the intent was indeed to inflict the greatest possible damage. This mock battle, however, suggests that a ceremonial or ritual conflict rather than a purely physical one was being demonstrated. Although the Powhatans were victorious, as Rountree (1989:123) notes, "one suspects that the outcome was prearranged."

Their actual style in combat, as was both observed and experienced by the English, was "by stratagems, surprises and treacheries; yet the werowances, women or children they put not to death, but keep them captives" (Strachey 1953:109). The account of Powhatan's attack on Piankatank is typical:

First, he sent divers of his men to lodge amongst them one night (pretending a general hunt), who were to give the alarm unto an ambuscado of a greater company within the woods, who upon the sign given at the hour appointed, environed all the houses, and fell to the execution. Twenty-four men they killed (the rest escaping by fortune, and their swift footmanship), and the long hair of the one side of their heads, with the skin, cased off with shells or reeds, they brought away to Powhatan. They surprised also the women, and children, and the werowance, all of whom they presented to Powhatan. (Strachey 1953:44)

These survivors of the conquered would be incorporated into the conquering group, sometimes on their original lands, along with others, and sometimes moved to a new location, as with the people of Kecoughtan, who were moved to Piankatank (Strachey 1953:68). This incorporation of the conquered has also been noted for other Algonquian groups (Heckewelder 1876:217–18; Warren 1984:94).

This style of warfare by stratagem and deceit is typical for Algonquian groups and for the eastern woodlands in general. Eid (1982) provides several examples from northeastern Iroquois and Algonquian groups. Hariot (1588:E2) described the same approach among the North Carolina Algonquians: "Their manner of wars amongst themselves is either by sudden surprising one another, most commonly about the dawning of the day, or moon light, or else by ambushes, or some subtle devices. Set battles are very rare, except it fall out where there are many trees, where either part may have some hope of defence, after the delivery of every arrow, in leaping behind some or other." And even in relatively set battles, warriors stealthily stalked opponents (Spelman 1910:cxiv) or even camouflaged themselves with branches for cover (Smith 1986d:174). This is counter to Fausz's assertion (1979b:34) that Indian warriors abandoned traditional formal warfare for these "guerilla tactics" because of the frightening power of firearms. I address Fausz's misconceptions about the effectiveness of firearms relative to the bow and arrow in the context of seventeenth-century Virginia in chapter 2; note here simply that the "guerilla tactics" he dismisses were widespread in native North America, were noted quite early on, and were evidenced in a number of battles that took place at later times when both sides were similarly equipped in terms of weapons. Gabriel Archer (1969:91), for example, records for the Powhatans, in 1607, "the manner of their own skirmishes, which we perceive is violent, cruel and full of celerity; they use a tree to defend them in fight, and having shot an enemy that he fall, they maul him with a short wooden sword." Drawing on materials from southern New England, Malone (1991) has described this Algonquian warfare as "the skulking way of war."

Although often disparaged in comparison with firearms, the killing potential of the Powhatans' bows and arrows was ably demonstrated in what was meant to be a demonstration of their inferiority: "One of our gentle-men having a target [shield] which he trusted in, thinking it would bear out a flight shot, he set it up against a tree, willing one of the savages to shoot; who took from his back an arrow of an ell long, drew it strongly in his bow, shoots the target a foot through, or better; which was strange, being that a pistol could not pierce it. We seeing the force of his bow, afterwards set him up a steel target; he shot again, and burst his arrow all to pieces" (Percy 1969:140). Powhatan archers were accurate to 40 yards and could shoot 120 yards "at random" (Smith 1986b:164), quite effective when shooting in a volley. Malone reports a somewhat greater range, based on historical accounts from New England and on an experimental replica of a Massachusetts bow (1991:15, 17–18). It was estimated in 1590 that an archer could fire four to five arrows in the time it would take a soldier to load and fire a single shot from a musket (Smythe 1973:F4ᵛ). The matching of Powhatan warrior against English soldier was thus not so straight-forward.

Another notable example of this Algonquian style of warfare by strata-gem is the taking of Fort Michilimackinac by the Ojibwas, in 1763 (Warren 1984:200–209). On the birthday of the English king, the British were told that in honor of the day the Ojibwas and the Sauks would play a game of lacrosse, for a high stake, "for the amusement of the whites." The game began and "became exciting"; while the commandant watched from his opened gates,

> His soldiers stood carelessly unarmed, here and there, intermingling with the Indian women, who gradually huddled near the gateway, carrying under their blankets the weapons which were to be used in the approaching work of death.
>
> In the struggle for its possession, the ball at last was gradually carried towards the open gates, and all at once, after having reached a proper distance, an athletic arm caught it up in his bat, and as if by accident threw it within the precincts of the fort. With one deafening yell and impulse, the players rushed forward in a body, as if to regain it, but as they reached their women and entered the gateway, they threw down their wooden bats and grasping the shortened guns, toma-hawks, and knives, the massacre commenced, and the bodies of the unsuspecting British soldiers soon lay strewn about, lifeless, horribly mangled, and scalpless. The careless commander was taken captive without a struggle, as he stood outside the fort, viewing the game,

which the Ojibwa chieftain had got up for his amusement. (Warren 1984:203–4)

Note here that ball games and war were closely related for many Indian groups (Blanchard 1981:128; Fogelson 1962); indeed, one Cherokee term for the ball game is "little war" (Fogelson 1971:330).

This battle exemplifies the nature of Algonquian warfare in several ways and can thus help in understanding the Powhatans' warfare. I have argued that there was an *aesthetic* of warfare among the Algonquians, one which was not understood by the English colonists (Gleach 1993). I use this term not only in the sense of "having or showing an appreciation of the beautiful or pleasing" or "in accordance with the principles of good taste" (*OED* 1971 s.v. "aesthetic"), but also in the more specific sense described by Kupfer (1983) in his work on aesthetics and everyday life. Here, an experience or action is aesthetic if it expands one's understanding, if it tends towards an inclusionary rather than an exclusionary self-definition and relationship to the universe. Truth and beauty are brought together. The aesthetic experience is a nonrational, emotional understanding of the inclusive, encompassing nature of reality; the beautiful or pleasing quality derives from a recognition of truth in the experience. This concept of the aesthetic reflects the emphasis on beauty and morally right action described in the previous section.

This aesthetic takes the form of a spirit of play in Algonquian warfare, an element of playful irony or wit that should be brought to bear. Such wit is evident in employing a ball game as a ruse in the preceding example; it is also evident in the killing of the English with their own tools rather than with weapons, when possible, in the 1622 Virginia coup. Walter B. Miller (1955:279–80) notes, in speaking of mythic battles between the Fox *manitus*, that "conquest depends, not on possessing an intrinsically superior amount of power, but rather on how carefully, or shrewdly, or skillfully each antagonist utilizes the resources he possesses in any particular encounter." Similarly, Brinton described the Algonquin culture hero: "Michabo does not conquer his enemies by brute force, nor by superior strength, but by craft and ruses, by transforming himself into unsuspected shapes, by cunning and strategy. He thus comes to be represented as the Arch-Deceiver" (1885:139). Finally, Heckewelder (1876:177) describes the Delawares' attitude in war: "Courage, art, and circumspection are the essential and indispensable qualifications for an Indian warrior. When war is once begun, each one strives to excel in displaying them, by stealing upon his enemy unawares, and deceiving and surprising him in various ways."

In all these examples the importance of strength or power is downplayed in favor of cunning — an attitude expressing one's superior knowledge of and ability to employ the resources and situations in a particular exchange. The emphasis is on individual expression, but an individual expression of knowledge of and integration with natural and supernatural forces and resources is most important. Deception of the enemy reveals both his inferior understanding and control of the situation and his need (or inability) to improve.

The Ojibwa battle described by Warren is also typically Algonquian in the practice of scalping and torture, which were also part of their aesthetic of warfare. Scalping transferred the victim's humanity, or at least his sign of being a man, to the victor, and rewarded the victor with tangible evidence of his greatness and strength. At the same time, it demonstrated a certain respect for the slain, an acknowledgment that he had been a worthy opponent. Henry Spelman, who had then lived among the Powhatans for a year, described the prelude to the execution of four murderers and a thief: "Then came the officer to those that should die, and with a shell cut off their long lock, which they wear on the left side of their head, and hung that on a bough before the king's house" (Spelman 1910:cxi). These criminals were symbolically deprived of their manhood *before* their executions, which was symbolically very different from scalping a slain enemy. In contrast to removing the scalp — and thus an aspect of the man's soul — from a worthy defeated opponent, this act forced the criminals to confront their existence without that soul. Certainly, no honor was intended by this gesture, and we can assume that such a scalp would not receive the same treatment as one taken in battle.

A man's hair was carefully maintained in a style dictated by the Powhatan god as proper for all human males; the Powhatan priest Uttamatomakkin objected to the English god on the grounds that he had not taught the English to wear their hair properly (Purchas 1617:954). Heckewelder (1876:215) gives the Delawares' reasoning for wearing one lock of hair long: " 'When we go to fight an enemy,' say they, 'we meet on equal ground; and we take off each other's scalps, if we can. The conqueror, whoever he may be, is entitled to have something to shew to prove his bravery and his triumph, and it would be *ungenerous* in a warrior to deprive an enemy of the means of acquiring that glory of which he himself is in pursuit. A warrior's conduct ought to be *manly*, else he is *no man.*' " Although Williamson (1979) has elaborated an argument that Powhatan men's hair marked them symbolically as both male and female, it is clear here that the wearing of that lock of hair was part of proper manly conduct and that its removal marked an end through conquest of that state (see Axtell and Sturtevant 1980:466–67). The complexities of scalping include not only the symbolic meanings mentioned here, which could range from insult to honor depending on whether the victim was alive or dead and the context in which the scalping took place, but also social meanings, as represented in the adoption of war-trophy scalps and the dance by which such scalps were ritually welcomed into the villages of their takers (Friederici 1985).

The embodied spiritual value of strength and rightness is also illustrated in a story told by the central Algonquian Sauk Indians (Jones 1905:185), in which a Comanche hunter sacrificed his life to enable his comrades to escape from a larger Sauk hunting party they encountered. The Sauk party so admired the bravery of this man that they did not count coup or take his scalp, but instead shared in eating his heart. The Comanche was allowed to keep his outward evidence of manliness — his hair; he was a great warrior, and his spirit was allowed to remain whole. The excision and ingestion of his heart was an even greater honorific act; the Sauks did not take a physical trophy representing that they had been able to overcome even this great warrior, but they hoped to acquire his greatness for themselves by eating his heart, the locus of the *manitu* essence responsible for that greatness.

The same spirit of playfulness or irony noted for warfare in general can be seen in torture. Warren quotes a traditional story of the nineteenth-century Ojibwas:

> A noted warrior of the Ojibwas was once taken prisoner by his own nephew, who was a young warrior of the Foxes, son of his own sister, who had been captured when young, adopted and married in this tribe. This young man, to show to the Foxes his utter contempt of any ties of blood existing between him and his Ojibwa uncle, planted two stakes strongly in the ground, and taking his uncle by the arm, he remarked to him that he "wished to warm him before a good fire." He then deliberately tied his arms and legs to the two stakes, as wide apart as they could be stretched, and the unnatural nephew built a huge fire in front of his uncle. When he had burnt his naked body to a blister on this side, he turned him with his back toward the fire, and when this had also been cruelly burned, he untied him, and turning him loose, he bade him to "return home and tell the Ojibwas how the Foxes treated their uncles."

The uncle recovered from his fire wounds, and in a subsequent war excursion, he succeeded in capturing his cruel nephew. He took him to the village of the Ojibwas, where he tied him to a stake, and taking a fresh elk skin, on which a layer of fat had purposely been left, he placed it over a fire till it became ablaze; then throwing it over the naked shoulders of his nephew, he remarked. "Nephew, when you took me to visit the village of your people, you warmed me before a good fire. I now in return give you a warm mantle for your back." (1984:106–7)

Such tortures were seen by the colonists as barbaric, but for the Powhatans, like other Algonquians, they were part of the right way to live, just as war was (Knowles 1985). The shrewdness, skill, and wit employed in these actions were the important performative elements in their aesthetics for the victors; the victim was expected to display strength and composure in the face of such torture. William Byrd, writing in the early eighteenth century, described the practices in war of the Virginia Indians:

The prisoners they happen to take alive in these expeditions generally pass their time very scurvily. They put them to all the tortures that ingenious malice and cruelty can invent. And (what shows the baseness of the Indian temper in perfection) they never fail to treat those with the greatest inhumanity that have distinguished themselves most by their bravery; and, if he be a war-captain, they do him to honor to roast him alive, and distribute a collop to all that had a share in stealing the victory.

. . .

In the mean time, while these poor wretches are under the anguish of all this inhuman treatment, they disdain so much as to groan, sigh, or show the least sign of dismay or concern, so much as in their looks; on the contrary, they make it a point of honor all the time to soften their features, and look as pleased as if they were in the actual enjoyment of some delight; and if they never sang before in their lives, they will be sure to be melodious on this sad and dismal occasion. (1967:220, 222)

Jouvency (1896a:273), writing at about the same time, described the same attitude among the Montagnais: "The prisoner who has beheld and endured stake, knives and wounds with an unchanging countenance, who has not groaned, who with laughter and song has ridiculed his tormentors, is praised; for they think that to sing amid so many deaths is great and noble." Few examples of torture or mutilation were recorded in detail for the Powhatans in the seventeenth century, but one provides evidence for the point here. During the Starving Time, the winter of 1609–10, hunger moved several parties of Englishmen to try to join the Indians or to steal food from them. One such party was later found "slain, with their mouths stopped full of bread, being done, as it seems, in contempt and scorn, that others might expect the like when they should come to seek for bread and relief amongst them" (Percy 1922:265). The contempt and scorn assumed by Percy was precisely what was meant to be communicated by this act. A similar incident was recorded in the late eighteenth century in the Great Lakes area, where "the warriors slaughtered many of their prisoners, torturing some. They stuffed the mouths of the dead with soil — satisfying in death their lust for Indian land" (White 1991:454). White (1991:440) has suggested that it was only after the American Revolution, after decades of contact in this area, that "torture less often took place in its original ritualized form than as a random and unpredictable exercise in individual cruelty. Sacrifice — that is, ritualized public murder — had become simply murder." This distinction was not recognized by the English settlers of seventeenth-century Virginia, however, who viewed such actions as irrational and barbaric rather than as motivated by a logic other than their own.

This attitude, the deprecation expressed by such acts, is to be expected given the generalized motivations of war among the Indians. War was undertaken to right a wrong, to correct improper actions; it was a means of restoring justice and teaching proper behavior. Biard (1896a:73), writing in the early seventeenth century, noted of the northern Algonquians that "they wage war as a tribe on account of wrongs done to a private individual. The whole race is very revengeful and, after the fashion of savages, insolent in victory, carrying about the heads of their captives as trophies and spoils of victory." Such revenge did not necessarily involve a group beyond the family: "The great offenses, as when some one has killed another, or stolen away his wife, etc., are to be avenged by the offended person with his own hand; or if he is dead, it is the duty of the nearest relatives" (Biard 1897:94–95). Presumably, revenge would be pursued by the larger corporate group when the offense had been so received, as in the case of repeated incidents committed against many members of the group over time. Trowbridge noted for the Shawnees that "the cause of general war between nations has almost always been found in individual murders, which have been so often repeated on both sides as to embroil the whole of the tribe and at length the nation en masse" (Kinietz and Voegelin 1939:23). Closer to Virginia, Heckewelder describes the causes of war for the Delawares:

> It is a fixed principle with the Indians, that evil cannot come out of good, that no friend will injure a friend, and, therefore, that whoever wrongs or does harm to another, is his ENEMY. As it is with individuals, so it is with nations, tribes, and other independent associations of men. If they commit murder on another people, encroach on their lands, by making it a practice to come within their bounds and take the game from them, if they rob or steal from their hunting camps, or, in short, are guilty of any act of unjust aggression, they cannot be considered otherwise than as ENEMIES; they are declared to be such, and the aggrieved nation think themselves justifiable in punishing them. (1876:175)

Heckewelder (1876:176) continues to describe the form of this war of vengeance: "they generally endeavour to make at once a bold stroke, so as to strike their enemies with terror." War would thus right a wrong on two levels: the act of revenge would reestablish the balance of power, and the form of revenge (punishment) would impress upon the original offender both the wrongness of the act and the strength of the avenger. This concept of the corrective, moral nature of war is crucial to an understanding of the events of colonial Virginia, as I discuss later.

The moral nature of Algonquian warfare is illustrated by the Algonquians' attitudes towards defense and defeat. Trowbridge (Kinietz and Voegelin 1939:21–22) described this attitude for the Shawnees in the nineteenth century, noting that they relied on the aid of their tutelar spirits and "war medicines" for defense, rather than armor, and that "if any who were reputed brave, met death in battle the Indians acknowledged themselves mistaken and such persons were set down as cowards, because it would have been impossible to kill them had they possessed true courage." This moral propriety in war is reiterated from the northeast; as already cited, "a war party, no matter how numerous, is entirely helpless before a much less numerous enemy if it loses its *ginap* or *ginaps*" (Mechling 1958:142). One further example was recorded in early colonial Virginia; in this case it was the loss of a representation of *Okee* rather than of the war-chief that brought the conflict to an end:

> Sixty or seventy of them, some black, some red, some white, some

parti-colored, came in a square order, singing and dancing out of the woods, with their *Okee* (which was an idol made of skins, stuffed with moss, all painted and hung with chains and copper) borne before them. And in this manner, being well armed with clubs, targets, bows and arrows, they charged the English, that so kindly received them with their muskets loaded with pistol shot, that down fell their God, and divers lay sprawling on the ground. The rest fled again to the woods, and ere long sent one of their *quioccosuks* to offer peace, and redeem their *Okee*. (Smith 1986d:144)

If the cause and its leader were just, the force would be undefeatable. The rightness of the cause and the concomitant power of the leader must prevail. Upon the revelation of falseness through the loss of the leader, the warriors were defeated; there would be no point in fighting, since the supernatural powers were obviously against them on that occasion.

The notion of an appropriate balance of power between groups, maintained through a sequence of acts of vengeance, suggests another important element in the understanding of Powhatan warfare: the results were neither permanent nor static but rather subject to change with the next encounter. A defeated group could gather greater powers to bring against the victors at a later date, thus the importance of strongly impressing the defeated with their impropriety. This dynamic nature of relationships can be seen in a variety of forms and modes of interaction, on an individual as well as on a group level. On the individual level, relationships between the Powhatans and the English were constantly being "tested" (Rountree 1989:86–87); such testing was common throughout native North America (Lowie 1908). Strachey (1953:74, 75) notes that "they are inconstant in everything, but what fear constrains them to keep," that "they dare come unto our forts, truck and trade with us and look us in the face, crying all friends, when they have but new done us a mischief, and when they intend presently again, if it lies in their power, to do the like." This reflects the state of flux that was seen as the natural state of relationships in the native culture. Note the similarity here to Miller's description (1955:280) of the struggle for superiority among Fox deities, where a temporary advantage in prestige was the best that could ever be obtained; although the loser would feel shame, because of his direct access to *manitu* power there was always the potential to defeat his adversary later.

Techniques could be employed to help prevent future conflicts from occurring and thus to avoid the likelihood of any reversal. Such were Powhatan's attacks at Piankatank and Kecoughtan, for example, where he up-rooted the populations and forced them to live with his people. Although this might not remove the threat completely, it was intended to impress upon the conquered the superiority of the victor, sufficient to remove any will to contest the relationship further.

This lack of finality is evident not only in war but also in diplomatic exchanges. Captain John Smith, who seems to have been able to engage in this process of negotiating "one-upmanship," would trade speeches with Powhatan, each carefully presenting himself as having been wronged (see Smith 1986d:194–98), and Smith would elaborate the English colonists' military prowess, and the strength of their "mines, great guns, and other engines" (Smith 1986d:148). This word-play was constant, as were other forms of "testing" the relationship between these two peoples, including testing through trade.

THE NATIVE CONSTRUCTION OF ENGLISH-POWHATAN TRADE

That the Powhatans' understanding of exchange was different from that of the English is apparent from the historical record. Trade for the Indians demanded that open generosity be maintained, a generosity rooted in the perception of the world as a place of sufficient riches for all. Heckewelder describes this attitude among the Delawares:

> They think that [the Creator] made the earth and all that it contains for the common good of mankind; when he stocked the country that he gave them with plenty of game, it was not for the benefit of a few, but of all. Every thing was given in common to the sons of men. Whatever liveth on the land, whatsoever groweth out of the earth, and all that is in the rivers and waters flowing through the same, was given jointly to all, and every one is entitled to his share. From this principle, hospitality flows as from its source. With them it is not a virtue but a strict duty. (1876:101)

This attitude not only demanded generosity; it also led to expectations of generosity in return (cf. Hallowell 1976a:384–86). The Indians expected the English to give freely not because the English had received much from them, but because the English had much to give. Smith (1986d:156) records Powhatan as "scorning to trade;" following several days of Powhatan's having feasted the English, he said to them, "Captain Newport, it is not agreeable to my greatness, in this peddling manner to trade for trifles;

and I esteem you also a great werowance. Therefore lay me down all your commodities together; what I like I will take, and in recompense give you what I think fitting their value." It was important to the Indians to receive "fair value," a subjective quality, but it was not important to accumulate as much as possible.

This contrasted markedly to English notions of trade, where one tried to obtain the greatest benefit in exchange for the least cost. Captain John Smith was, again, more astute in his manipulations of these exchanges than were most of the English: in 1608 he demonstrated this ability in trade, getting much more corn for far fewer trade goods than Captain Newport had been able to get (Smith 1986d:156), while still maintaining the respect of the Powhatans. He was able to do this by emphasizing the value of the trade goods he offered in terms that had meaning to the Indians: the color of the beads he offered, "not to be worn but by the greatest kings in the world" (Smith 1986d:156). This is probably very like the negotiation of position through trade that existed in the Powhatans' exchanges with the piedmont Monacans prior to the arrival of the English, the trade through which they obtained copper. When the English arrived, they took the place of the Monacans in that trade relationship.

The English saw the accumulation of the finest goods by the chiefs as evidence of their power to seize goods, rather than as evidence of their high moral position. This perception distorted their understanding of Powhatan institutions, producing a number of false parallels in English descriptions, including their consideration of Powhatan as an emperor. Strachey's statement (1953:87) that Powhatan collected as tribute 80 percent of everything produced is likely another such misunderstanding. The generosity of Powhatan chiefs is evident in accounts of their giving of gifts in exchange for services, including planting fields (Spelman 1910:cxii) and fighting in battle (Strachey 1953:107). Honored by being given gifts when he visited (Spelman 1910:cxiii), Powhatan kept a storehouse at Orapaks, "in which he keeps his kind of treasure, as skins, copper, pearls, and beads, which he stores up against the time of his death and burial. Here also is his store of red paint for ointment, and bows and arrows" (Smith 1986b:173).

The Indians universally saw themselves as superior to the Europeans at the time of contact and for long afterward. In New France in the early seventeenth century, Biard (1897:75; cf. 1896b:173) wrote, "you will see these poor barbarians, notwithstanding their great lack of government, power, letters, art and riches, yet holding their heads so high that they greatly underrate us, regarding themselves as our superiors." The Delawares recognized the ingenuity of the Europeans but considered the European life-style "wearisome and slavish," considered themselves much superior as hunters and woodsmen, and saw no reason they should abandon their own way of life (Zeisberger 1910:121–22; Loskiel 1794:17–18). Hallowell (1946:201–2) describes this as a general attitude among the Indians of the Northeast, and he quotes Peter Grant on the Saulteaux in much the same terms as both Loskiel and Zeisberger. There are three main points in these criticisms: a disdain for the European way of life — and their refusal to adopt or at least tolerate the Indians' way of life — acknowledgment of their technological abilities, and a fear of their greed for land.

These feelings partially account for the English colony's lack of success in trying to convert and "civilize" the Powhatans, and they are echoed in the willingness of the Indians to accept the English God without giving up their own, as already noted. As William Byrd (1967:118) noted in the early eighteenth century, "many children of our neighboring Indians have been brought up in the College of William and Mary. They have been taught to read and write, and have been carefully instructed in the principles of the Christian religion, till they came to be men. Yet after they returned home, instead of civilizing and converting the rest, they have immediately relapsed into infidelity and barbarism themselves." Even at that late date, the Indians were selective in their acceptance of the Euro-American culture. The material goods and technological innovations were desired, but these were drawn into the Powhatans' culture; the English religion and world-view were consciously rejected or taken only as they fit with the native Powhatan culture.

This was not a special treatment accorded the English but was rather the continued application of the Powhatans' traditional view of the world. Power, and powerful objects, originated "outside" and had to be admitted to the immediate Powhatan world from the outside. This distinction must not be overdrawn; even the physically distant and spiritual "outside" realms were only relatively outside, given the encompassing nature of the Pow-hatan world. This movement of power is evident in the form of the guard-ian spirits, powers that were seen as omnipresent, but that had to be man-ifested in a person through the mechanism of a dream, or socialized through the *huskanaw*, in order to be controlled. That the *huskanaw* took place outside of the village is significant here. This movement from outside to inside is also evident in the trade for copper, which had to be obtained from other Indian groups or from the English. All copper went to the chiefs and priests, who were best able to control its power. Powerful objects were stored in a "treasure house," which, like the temples, was located outside the village. Some could be given by the chiefs to the common people, in recognition of service, but only after the objects had been socialized through the chiefs.

It is significant that the most eagerly sought trade good from the English was copper. Miller and Hamell (1986) have pointed out that copper was widely valued among native American peoples because of its reddish color and its reflecting qualities, both of which had ritual significance. Warren (1984:98–99), writing of the Ojibwas in the nineteenth century, notes: "Copper, though abounding on the lake shore, they never use for common purposes; considering it sacred, they used it only for medicinal rites, and for ornament on the occasion of a grand Me-da-we." The reflecting quality of metal objects in general identified copper objects with the spirit world. Reflecting materials were widely used in divination and were seen as reflecting a spirit (Miller and Hamell 1986:316); Jay Miller (1991:26) notes the use by Moravian missionaries to the Delawares of the Delaware word for mirror to refer to the Christian soul, a usage appropriating this relationship, "which traditional Delawares recognize but find confusing." The color of blood, red was probably seen as "charged with powerful destructive energy," as described by Fogelson (1990:173–76) for the Cherokees (cf. Loskiel 1794:27; R. Williams 1973:132, 240). In Virginia, when Sir Thomas Dale negotiated a treaty with the councilors of the Chickahominies (who had at that time no single chief), their payment consisted of "a red coat, or livery, from our king yearly, and [to] each of them the picture of His Majesty, engraven in copper, with a chain of copper to hang it about his neck" (Hamor 1615:14).

Other items in great demand were beads, especially blue beads. The parallel between glass beads and the native-produced shell beads is obvious and may be one reason they were so readily accepted. The preference for blue trade beads parallels the greater value placed on "blue" wampum beads. Following the lead of Miller and Hamell, however, it is important to note that what we call blue or purple shell in wampum was referred to by the natives as black. Jay Miller (personal communication) notes that the Delaware term for black refers to any dark tone (cf. Loskiel 1794:27). This term is not among the few recorded for the Powhatans, but the same was likely true here, given the cultural and linguistic similarities between the two groups.

Like red, black had spiritual significance; Callender (1978:643) notes that, for the Fox, "blackening one's face with charcoal invoked the spirit of fire, a messenger to the manitous." For the New England Algonquians, black was associated with Hobbamock, the principal deity who appeared to humans in dreams and who was also associated with the dead (Simmons 1986:39). In the Powhatan context, black and red were commonly used as body paint for warriors and in ritual contexts, certain participants in the *huskanaw* were painted black, copper was restricted to chiefs and priests, a black bird was worn by shamans, and the body was frequently painted with red dyes.

As Miller and Hamell (1986:318) have noted, metals and other materials having these qualities of reflection and color were, in fact, seen as "otherworldly" in origin throughout the eastern Woodlands, obtained by humans through exchange with other-than-human persons. As such, they were both powerful and dangerous, and these materials were thus incorporated into sacred objects and embedded in ritual traditions. These beliefs were shared by the Powhatans, and they were also noted among the neighboring Algonquians of North Carolina, who believed that items of English technology were considered "rather the works of gods than of men, or at the leastwise they had been given and taught us of the gods" (Hariot 1588:E4). When the English arrived with their trade goods, the Powhatans thus already had in place a system of meaning into which these goods fit. Trade with the English was understood in the same way as pre-contact trade with the Monacans (see Hantman 1990), as a means for obtaining and controlling power from the outside.

Even the shell beads produced by the coastal Indians themselves were seen as having a mythic origin, as coming from "outside." Speck (1919:8–15) gives a series of origin myths for wampum and describes this situation as it existed among the New England coastal tribes, "where a fictitious origin is almost always ascribed to the material despite the fact that the Indians really knew that it was a hand manufactured product" (1919:9). The most frequently cited origins were from a bird, but one origin, recorded from the Wabanaki, is instructive here. The informant indicated that wampum came from a sorcerer's (or shaman's) mouth, after lighting his pipe, in council (Speck 1919:9). Tobacco smoke was seen as opening a channel to the supernatural; this shaman produced wampum — a physical manifestation of power — in the same way that oral manifestations of power were produced: via the mouth, in council, after opening a connection to the spirits. The source of the power was from beyond the shaman, but it entered him and became socialized through his person before being brought forth into the group. This socialization, or control, is an important step, since power uncontrolled can be very dangerous.

The myths of origin from a wampum bird also demonstrate the movement from outside to inside. The tales generally involve the bird, whose body or feathers produce wampum, being killed by a young man and thus providing the source of wampum. In those recorded from both the Iroquois and the Wyandot, two groups somewhat removed from the coast, the young man is "from a neighboring tribe" or "of a strange people" (Speck 1919:13, 14), who is then adopted into the tribe. In the text recorded from the Penobscot, themselves a coastal people, the hero is a boy of the people, but "lost to his parents," who lives with a cannibal before returning to gain control over the source of wampum (Speck 1919:14). All thus have a character embodying youth, wildness, and "outsideness" who gains the power of creating wampum and is then brought into the tribe. This freedom to bring something in from the outside was a reflection of the fact that even the "outside" world was only relatively so; ties could readily be made through trade, just as ties with the spirit world were made through dreaming. This potential connection was a major shaping factor in Powhatan relations with the English.

One "outside" item desired from the English was firearms. Immediately upon the arrival of the English, the Indians sought to obtain guns for their own use. The only traditional story surviving among the Powhatans from this period, recorded in the nineteenth century by a free black who was half-Powhatan, relates an account of just such an attempt, where Manotee, a chief and a grandson of Powhatan, executed a plan to take a cannon from the English through cunning artifice (Archer 1844:22–24). This story, although clearly mythic in some aspects, seems to reflect real attitudes among the Powhatans (see Gleach 1992b). The deception involved echoes the importance of the application of wit in warfare already discussed. Note, too, that the stolen cannon was not used — nor apparently intended for use — in military action against the English. In the story, several colonists who later observed the Indians firing the cannon were neither killed nor imprisoned to keep the theft secret; rather, they were returned to the colony with gifts. Indeed, what they observed was not a demonstration of *killing* power of any sort, but rather the "novelty and curiosity of gunpowder," suggesting a much more abstract form of power, involving perhaps the noise and smoke of the firing, or perhaps simply Manotee's mastery of the gun. This mastery of a powerful object obtained from the "outside," a proper chiefly action in the Powhatan world, would not be affected by the fact that the "outside" here was the English colony.

The English were not seen as alien or incomprehensible. Miller and Hamell noted that for Native Americans in general the English represented "creatures different from themselves in appearance, yet related to them in a metaphorical and ceremonial sense" (1986:325), and this attitude was almost certainly shared by the Powhatans. Their offering of copper and beads was an echo of the trade that had existed between the Powhatans and the Monacans, and it immediately placed the English within the Powhatans' universe, although they would have needed to be domesticated, coming from the "outside"; for the English, on the other hand, the Powhatans were fundamentally external, savages who had to be civilized, or converted, even to be brought into the English universe as outsiders, and certainly to have a chance of being perceived as fully human.

The statesmen of the day were not indifferent to the enterprise [the Virginia colony], for since the war with Spain had ceased, the streets of London had been filled with men, who had been soldiers in Ireland and in the Netherlands, averse to return to the quiet peasant life from which they had been pressed into military service, and yet unfitted to obtain a living by honest industry. Too indolent to handle the spade, they were forced to beg or to steal, and became a terror to the peaceable citizen on the side-walk, or the traveller on the highway.

  Military officers also favored the scheme, in the hope that the development of a new commonwealth would furnish an occasion for them to draw once more the swords that hung upon the wainscoted walls of their houses, and beginning to rust in the scabbards.
— Edward D. Neill, *Early Settlement of Virginia and Virginiola*

Sea Gull: — Come boys, Virginia longs till we share the rest of her Maiden-head.
— Chapman, Jonson, and Marston, *Eastward Hoe*

B Y 1607, THE ENGLISH had been seeking a permanent settlement in the New World for over twenty years. Spanish maritime dominance had been broken with the defeat of the Armada, encouraging the English to build upon the explorations begun under the Cabots before 1510 (Hulton 1984:3). Their attempts at establishing a colony in the 1580s, initiated by Sir Walter Raleigh under charter from Queen Elizabeth, had failed primarily because of delays in and the lack of resupply. While delayed in England awaiting the availability of ships for the much-needed resupplying voyage, held up by the war with Spain, the expeditions' scientist, Thomas Hariot, produced a printed volume (1588) that provides considerable insight into the goals of colonization in Elizabethan England.

   Given the context of publication — the Spanish Armada had already delayed the supply expedition by a year and Raleigh had had to sell stock in his company in order to raise money to fit out the expedition (Livingston

1903:xi) — it seems evident that Hariot's volume was intended to persuade prospective settlers and backers. Indeed, the introduction addresses itself "to the Adventurers, Favorers, and Well-willers of the enterprise for the inhabiting and planting in Virginia"[1] (Hariot 1588:A3). The interests of the intended audience are evident from the volume's organization. In his brief introduction, Hariot informs his readers that the negative rumors they may have heard were being circulated by people who could not be trusted. The remainder of Hariot's volume is broken into four sections: marketable commodities, food resources native to the area, resources for building, and, finally, the natives themselves. This sequence appears to represent the relative importance in the audience of different factions; the investors come first, with marketable commodities to yield a return on their investments, followed by the settlers, who are necessary for the extraction of those marketable commodities.

Hariot describes native inhabitants last, although the tenor of his descriptions makes it clear that he was favorably impressed by their abilities:

> In respect of us they are a people poor, and for want of skill and judgement in the knowledge and use of our things, do esteem our trifles before things of greater value. Notwithstanding, in their proper manner considering the want of such means as we have, they seem very ingenious. For although they have no such tools, nor any such crafts, sciences and arts as we, yet in those things they do, they show excellency of wit. And by how much they upon due consideration shall find our manner of knowledges and crafts to exceed theirs in perfection, and speed for doing or execution, by so much the more is it probable that they should desire our friendship and love, and have the greater respect for pleasing and obeying us. Whereby may be hoped if means of good government be used, that they may in short time be brought to civility, and the embracing of true religion. (Hariot 1588:E2ᵛ)

His description of the natives is given, however, "that you may know, how that they in respect of troubling our inhabiting and planting, are not to be feared; but that they shall have cause both to fear and love us, that shall inhabit with them" (Hariot 1588:Eᵛ).

Hariot's description of the natives begins with their clothing, weaponry, towns and houses, government, and manner of war. These strategic issues are laid out so that it may be apparent that "the turning up of their heels against us in running away was their best defence" (Hariot 1588:E2). It is only after thus making clear the fact that settlers need have little fear of the natives that he indicates that they "seem very ingenious" and "may in short time be brought to civility, and the embracing of true religion" (Hariot 1588:E2ᵛ).

This balance between religious and economic interests was to be worked out both verbally and in action over the next half-century, with the emphases varying both between individuals and between the colony in Virginia and the Company in England. Although historians have argued the relative importance of these interests, ranging from studies of purely religious factors (Porter 1979) to studies of purely economic factors (Vance 1970) to those discounting religion as a cover for economic interests (Jennings 1975, esp. 53–56; Sale 1990, esp. 258–66), the two were very closely linked in the context of seventeenth-century England (see Wright 1943). A group of merchants and religious leaders through the Virginia Company of London acted upon these interests, seeking to establish a colony to "civilize" the Indians and bring them to the true religion — while extracting a due profit for themselves. This effort also involved employing military force to bring about and to enforce order and discipline in the colony. Military force, economic interests, and proselytism were related, by the specifically English perception of the universe.

As is always the case, there was variability within the English culture — by class, individual, etc. — but for the purposes at hand we examine the general form of the culture, just as we did for the Powhatans. The "Great Chain of Being" that dominated European thought for centuries was endemic in late sixteenth-century England (Notestein 1954:27). This fixed hierarchical model of the universe placed humans beneath the heavenly beings but above the animals, plants, and inanimate objects, with all of creation intended for the benefit of humanity. Herein lies the fundamental difference between the English and the Powhatan cultures of the time. Whereas the Powhatans saw the universe as an entity in which they were merely participants, living alongside other animal and spirit beings as equals at best, the English saw the universe as created specifically for human benefit, with man having "dominion over the fish of the sea, and over the fowl of the air, and over the cattle, and over all the earth, and over every creeping thing that creepeth upon the earth" (Genesis 2.26). The relationship between God and profit, between religious belief and economic action, is rooted in this view. This Western world-view also assumed a fundamental division between mind and matter, where "thought alone has no impact on the structure and operation of reality, and spoken words have no power

to control matter or energy" (Witherspoon 1977:9). This, again, is in opposition to the world-view of the Indians, which did not construe a division
between mental and physical phenomena. Finally, the English believed that
humanity was fundamentally flawed, having constantly to struggle to overcome natural sinfulness. In a sermon delivered to those with concerns in
Virginia, Patrick Copland[2] (1622:23) stated: "I showed you before the danger of your people sent to Virginia, the danger of your colony planted
there, and the danger of your own selves here at home. And now if you
look to the primitive and original cause of all these your great dangers, and
many disasters that have heretofore befallen to your plantation, I suppose
you shall soon find the cause to be sin." He enumerated some of the sins
of the colonists: "they neglected God's worship, lived in idleness, plotted
conspiracies, resisted the government of superiors, and carried themselves
dissolutely amongst the heathens. If any of these they have offended, was
not God's rod of Mortality justly upon them for their sins?" (Copland
1622:24). William Crashaw[3] had earlier preached on this need for salvation:

> Particularly, as the body, so the soul stands in need of three sorts of
> physic. First, it is necessary that it be purged from the corruption of
> sin, which else will kill the soul; then, being purged, it is to be restored
> to life and strength; lastly, being so restored, it is requisite that it be
> preserved in that state unto the end. Answerable unto these there is a
> threefold kind of physic we receive from Christ: viz. purgative, re-
> storative, and preservative. (1610:A1^v–A2)
>
> To keep us from deadly relapses (into which without Christ we were
> sure to fall) we do finally receive from Christ preservative physic, by
> the virtue whereof we are preserved in the state of grace, and favor of
> God. (1610:A2^v)

This definition of humanity as fallen, as doomed by sin and needing the
salvation of Christ, significantly affected the English approach to colonization.

Unlike other English colonies, the Virginia colony consisted primarily
of non-Puritan Anglicans. Although the Church of England had recently
rejected the Puritan movement, a wide range of beliefs were manifested
within the church (see Notestein 1954:156–71). This extended to the colony;
a contemporary letter included the news: "there is an unhappy dissension
fallen out amongst them, by reason of their minister, who being, as they
say, somewhat a puritan, the most part refused to go to his service, or to

hear his sermons, though by the other part he was supported and favored" (Beaulieu 1969:287). There were relatively few clerics of any sort in Virginia, roughly one-eighth the per-capita proportion in Massachusetts (Porter 1979:380). A contemporary minister in England, addressing Parliament, attributed the lack of success in conversion to a "want of able and conscionable ministers, as in *Virginia*; they themselves are become exceeding rude, more likely to turn heathen, than to turn others to the Christian faith" (Castle 1747:773). There was thus in Virginia little of the piety for which the Puritans were noted and less insistence "that men ought not to strive for great riches" (Notestein 1954:167). The relationship between godliness and wealth was free to flourish.

MERCANTILISM AND THE CHURCH OF ENGLAND

Unlike the Spanish, who used military force to conquer the natives in order to extract immediate wealth, or the French, who traded with the natives for their goods and raw materials, the English established the Virginia colony as a mercantile venture. The English sought both a source of the raw materials they needed — and the wealth they desired — and a market for the goods they produced, ones over which they could exercise control — that is, supplies and markets not already under foreign dominion. England was deforested, overpopulated, and underemployed. As Richard Eburne urged his readers in his 1624 treatise propounding colonization:

> Look upon the misery and want wherein you do and, abiding in England, you cannot but live. Look upon the plenty and felicity wherein, going hence, you may live.
>
> . . .
>
> Be not too much in love with that country wherein you were born, that country which, bearing you, yet cannot breed you, but seems and is indeed weary of you. She accounts you a burden to her and encumbrance of her. You keep her down, you hurt her and make her poor and bare; and, together with your own, you work and cause, by tarrying within her, her misery and decay, her ruin and undoing. Take and reckon that for your country where you may best live and thrive. (1962:10, 11)

By directing people to overseas colonies, he hoped to improve conditions both in England and in the colonized lands, to better provide for the people in both places. He further noted that timber "so fast decays with us that very want of it only within few years is like to prove exceeding hurtful to our land" (Eburne 1962:48). The Virginia colony was expected to produce the food and raw materials it needed, as well as a surplus of commodities that could be sent to England in exchange for goods that could not be produced in the colony, notably the textiles and ceramics that were coming to dominate English production. The ease with which food and other goods could be obtained by trade with the Indians, however, would prove a constant temptation to the colonists in Virginia and a source of irritation to the company officials.

Hariot's (1588) discussion of commodities makes plain England's — and the colony's — needs. It is notable for this period, when the Spanish were removing vast quantities of gold and silver from the New World, that gold is not even mentioned among the marketable commodities, and silver is mentioned only briefly. This proved realistic, since these metals are not found in abundance in Virginia. It ran counter to the popular aspirations, however. Fueled by the riches obtained by the Spanish, the common perception was probably closer to that voiced by a character in *Eastward Hoe*, in a paraphrase from Sir Thomas More's *Utopia*:

> I tell thee, gold is more plentiful there than copper is with us; and for as much red copper as I can bring, I'll have thrice the weight in gold. Why, man, all their dripping pans, and their chamber pots are pure gold; and all the chains, with which they chain up their streets, are massy gold; all the prisoners they take, are fettered in gold; and for rubies and diamonds, they go forth on holidays and gather them by the sea-shore, to hang on their children's coats, and stick in their caps, as commonly as our children wear saffron gilt brooches, and groats with holes in them. (Chapman et al. 1926:50–51)

Hariot (1588:A4ᵛ) notes that one reason for the spread of negative rumors about Virginia was that gold was not found immediately; the Jamestown colonists persisted in the search for several years after their arrival (see Yeardley 1933:30) despite the opinions of others among them that this search was a waste of time (Smith 1986d:157–59). After initial excitement over finding a gold ore in 1607 — which ore proved to be false (Quinn 1974:487) — the company in London returned its focus to other commodities. Quinn (1974:485) observed that the English needed a colony that could produce the goods that England could not: "sugar, wines, raisins, citrus fruit, rice, dyes (woad especially), and possibly leather and iron. . . . Perhaps a colony just outside the Spanish zone in North America would produce some of the minor riches of the Indies, such as tobacco, dyes, and cotton." Having been effectively excluded from the Mediterranean trade by the Spanish and by North African pirates, the English merchants hoped an American colony would prove a source for those goods to which they had lost access.

Hariot identified the marketable commodities abundant in Virginia: silk, flax, and hemp; other organically derived substances such as pitch, turpentine, oil, and wine; skins, furs, and woods; and iron and copper. He describes pearls as common, but this information is buried in the midst of the more mundane resources. Silver is only mentioned as having been seen and found in "the same place or near, where I after understood the copper was made" (Hariot 1588:B3ᵛ). His second part describes the various food crops of the natives and the richness of the soil, along with the indigenous wild fruits, nuts, and animals. He also describes the native use of tobacco and mentions that members of his company had also taken the habit, claiming that it was partly responsible for the great health of the natives, of which "the use of it by so many of late, men and women of great calling as else, and some learned physicians also, is sufficient witness" (Hariot 1588:C3ᵛ). It is tempting to view this passage as prophetic; Hariot devotes more space to the description of tobacco than to any other resource, and it became, of course, the principal crop in both Virginia and North Carolina.

These commodities were not those of instant wealth, but rather those that would require an investment of time and effort, with a more sustained profit in return. Vance (1970:68–72) has discussed the importance of mercantilism in the early American colonies, observing that they were born as mercantile efforts even before political and social situations produced movements of national emigration. These early American colonies were dependent upon economic success to attract settlers and only gained some measure of success when a reliable commodity was found — tobacco in Virginia and beaver furs in the St. Lawrence valley. Given the long-term commitment that was required to turn a profit through farming, the economic importance of good relations with the natives is apparent. Trade with the Indians was also the easiest way to obtain furs, also an early staple in Virginia.

Furthermore, trade was also seen as an important part of "civilizing" the Indians. William Crashaw (1610:D3ᵛ–D4) spoke to this in defending the colony's actions, stating that no wrong had been or would be made to the natives of Virginia, as Christian doctrine and the instructions and resolutions of the colony required. Instead, that which the colony needed would be obtained by fair trade, with the Powhatans having land and natural resources to spare. The English would provide them in return with "such things as they greatly desire," but more importantly, "out of our humanity and conscience, we will give them more, namely such things as they want and need, and are infinitely more excellent then all we take from them: and that is 1. Civility for their bodies, 2. Christianity for their souls; the first to make them men, the second happy men; the first to cover their bodies from the shame of the world; the second, to cover their souls from the wrath of God" (1610:D4). It was this notion of civilizing through exchange that differentiated this colonial enterprise from an invasion for many Englishmen. Richard Eburne had written in his dialogue: "I neither am nor can be persuaded that it may be lawful for one nation to fight against and destroy another in that sort, and upon no better title than the desire of their lands and goods to bereave each other of their rights and lives," and his interlocutor replies:

> Indeed, the Scripture saith, "All the whole heavens are the Lord's, the earth hath He given to the children of men" (Ps. 115:16), by which words I gather that whatsoever country any people do possess and inhabit it is God's gift unto them; God has allotted and bestowed that on them for their portion. Which being so, it seems to me to stand with reason and religion both that every people whatsoever they be should be permitted quietly and peaceably to hold and enjoy their own country, and that it ought not of any by violence to be taken from them. (Eburne 1962:127)

Peaceful coexistence was essential if the English colonists were to remain in Virginia long enough to produce a surplus in crops and other goods to be sent to England and to provide a market for English goods. But this pursuit of wealth was not merely sanctioned by the church and was not separate from the Englishmen's desire to "civilize" and convert the Indians.

In a letter of instruction dating to early 1611, the members of the Virginia Company in London wrote of "the eyes of all Europe looking upon our endeavors to spread the Gospel among the heathen people of Virginia, to plant our English nation there, and to settle in those parts which may be peculiar to our nation, so that we may thereby be secured from being eaten out of all profits of trade, by our more industrious neighbors" (Virginia Co. 1878:41). In closing, the letter refers to the colonization as "this action, that tends so directly to advance the glory of God, the honor of our English nation and the profit and security in our judgement, of this kingdom" (Virginia Co. 1878:43). This was not an idiosyncratic view; other examples elaborate on the point, but this quote clearly equates the glory of God, English honor, and profits. An individual could emphasize any of these points in his or her life without necessarily going against the Church. This view made it easy for the rhetoric of colonists and their supporters to emphasize bringing Christianity to the natives, while their actions were devoted to extracting a profit. Both missionization and the advancement of profit were acceptable ways to increase the glory of God and English honor, but only one had the added incentive of immediate personal material enrichment. The choice, for most of the colonists, was clear.

The close relationship of godliness, wealth, and power in the Anglican Church was fundamental and thus tenacious; indeed, the text of the ultimate chorus of Handel's *Messiah*, composed during the following century, conveys a similar idea: "Worthy is the Lamb that was slain, and hath redeemed us to God by his blood, to receive power, and riches, and wisdom, and strength, and honor, and glory, and blessing. Blessing, and honor, glory and power, be unto him that sitteth upon the throne, and unto the Lamb, for ever and ever" (following Revelations 5.12–13). Riches (and power, etc.) are due the faithful because of their redemption — and thus "blessed is the Lord!" This is far from the Puritan notions regarding the pursuit of wealth that dominated the Massachusetts colony, but it is at the core of the beliefs behind the Virginia colony.

The natives were also to be brought to the English god. This was written into the original charter of the company by King James (James I 1969a:25) and was repeated in several instances. The instructions prepared for Sir Thomas Gates when he was sent to Virginia as governor stated that the conversion of the Indians to Christianity was "the most pious and noble" goal of the colony and that the colony should attempt to "procure from them some convenient number of their children to be brought up in your language, and manners." It was also recommended that the colony take all the Powhatan religious leaders as prisoners to make this task easier. Gates was even authorized to kill these leaders — "murtherers of soules and sacrificers of gods Images to the Divell" — for the sake of advancing the Christian cause (Virginia Council 1609:ff 179–79ᵛ).[4] In addition to the desire for religious conversions, there was a pragmatic side to these instructions. By that time (two years after the founding of the colony) there was some concern that the Powhatans might distrust the English; for their part, the English certainly did not trust the Powhatans. Gates was further instructed to watch for a chance to seize their werowances and all known successors, so that the future leaders could be educated and instructed "in your Manners and Religion" in order to then lead their people to "become in tyme Civill and Christian" (Virginia Council 1609:f 181).

Variations on these instructions continued to be given out for some time. They were discussed by the Virginia General Assembly ten years later, when a college was being planned for the education of the Indians. Individual settlements were authorized to take in "five or six" of the "better disposed" Indians, with the consent of the governor, "to do service in killing of deer, fishing, beating of corn, and other works," as long as a good guard was kept on them at night; preferably, a separate house would be built for them. A certain number of children were also to be taken in, "of which children the most towardly boys in wit and graces of nature [were] to be brought up by them in the first elements of literature, so to be fitted for the college intended for them; that from thence they may be sent to that work of conversion" (Virginia General Assembly 1933:165–66). The service that could be supplied by Powhatan workers — servants — was a strong incentive, but even so this endeavor enjoyed only limited success.

Not only were the Powhatans uninterested in trading their faith for the English church, but most colonists also gave a low priority to proselytism. Some even questioned the propriety of attempting conversion: how could it be known that the time for the Indians' conversion had come, that this was God's will? Richard Eburne answered that "the inclination and readiness alone of those people . . . [who] even of their own accord offer themselves to be taught, suffer their children to be baptized and instructed by us, and, as weary of and half seeing the grossness of their own abominations and the goodness of our observations, do make no great difficulty to prefer our religion before theirs and to confess that it is God that we and the devil that they do worship" (1962:27). Thus was the Indians' willingness to incorporate foreign ideas into their own belief system turned against them and used to justify their forced conversion.

The English preconception of the proper relationship between God, themselves, and the Indians is further exhibited in an arrangement of biblical verses published with Crashaw's sermon (1610:L3), a passage that concisely illustrates the period use of religion to justify the English colonial enterprise:

GOD TO EUROPE.
> *THE kingdom of God shall be taken from you, and given to a Nation that shall bring forth the fruits thereof.*

GOD TO ENGLAND.
> *But I have prayed for thee that thy faith fail not: therefore when thou art converted strengthen thy brethren.* Luk.22.32.

ENGLAND TO GOD.
> *Lord here I am: Send me.* Esay 6.7.

GOD TO VIRGINIA.
> *He that walketh in darkness, and hath no light, let him trust in the name of the Lord, and stay upon his God.* Esay 50.10.

VIRGINIA TO GOD.
> *God be merciful to us, and bless us and cause the light of thy countenance shine upon us: let thy ways be known upon earth, and thy saving health among all Nations.* Psal.67.1.2.

ENGLAND TO VIRGINIA.
> *Behold, I bring you glad tidings: Unto you is borne a Savior, even Christ the Lord.* Luk.1.

VIRGINIA TO ENGLAND.
> *How beautiful are the feet of them that bring glad tidings, and publish salvation!* Es.52.7.

ENGLAND TO VIRGINIA.
> *Come children, hearken unto me: I will teach you the fear of the Lord.* Psal.34.11.

VIRGINIA TO ENGLAND.
> *Blessed be he that cometh to us in the name of the Lord.* Psal.118.

Other European nations had forfeited their rights by not bringing the natives to the true faith. The conversion and civilization of the Virginia Indians by the English was not only ordered by God but was requested and welcomed by the Indians. The Indians were compared with children, who needed proper education and time to mature in order to enter the kingdom. This conceit, an essential part of their justification for colonization, would shape all interactions between the two groups.

Religious conversion and bringing the Indians to "civility" was seen as a great work for humanity, demonstrating and improving the position of the English before God. As Crashaw (1610:C4ᵛ) noted in his sermon, the English had also been savage until civilization and Christianity were brought to them by the Romans and later Christian disciples, and it was thus incumbent upon them to "labor to procure the same good to others." This would be accompanied by the accumulation of wealth, following the ideals of that great promoter of colonialism, the Reverend Richard Hakluyt, who wrote that "Godliness is great riches, and that if we first seek the kingdom of God, all other things will be given unto us" (Hakluyt 1935:178). Crashaw had preached the same message: "if we first and principally seek the propagation of the Gospel and conversion of souls, God will undoubtedly make the voyage very profitable to all the adventurers and their posterities even for matters of this life. . . . Now the high way to obtain that, is to forget our own affections, and to neglect our own private profit in respect of God's glory; and he that is zealous of God's glory, God will be mindful of his profit" (1610:G3). For these followers of the Anglican Church, religion and mercantilism were thus one and the same (cf. Fausz 1977:145–54). This permitted different individuals to join the enterprise for their own reasons. Although some of the writings of the religious, with their lofty ideals and aspirations, have been preserved, the thoughts of the individual colonist or merchant are less well represented. Captain John Smith's late reflections on the members of the Virginia Company may be indicative, or they may represent the cynical thoughts of a great egotist who had been forced from his position in the colony; he described them as "making religion their color, when all their aim was nothing but present profit" (Smith 1986e:272) — a charge repeated by Jennings (1975:53–56).

I suspect that this was true for many who actually went to Virginia, although certainly not for all. Many writers, Smith included, have noted the tendency among the colonists to pursue any avenue that seemed to offer immediate profits; Crashaw spoke of the many deterred from joining by lack of immediate profits, "because the greater part of men are unconverted and unsanctified men, and seek merely the world and themselves, and no further." Richard Eburne (1962:12) summed it up in his address to his countrymen: "Englishmen above many others are worst able to live with a little."

Even the Puritans who went to Virginia were to have little effect on this tendency. After the earliest days of the colony, despite the presence of a series of active clerics, the church played less of a role in the everyday lives of the colonists; Wertenbaker (1927:116) even suggested that the colony's incipient "democratic tendencies," along with the dispersed nature of the settlements, interfered with their "development of a truly religious life." Nevertheless, the relationship within the church between godliness and wealth and power encouraged the pursuit of worldly goods as part of a religious life. Even the more religious of those who were involved with the colony, both in England and in Virginia, supported the pursuit of riches. These expectations of advancement in the material and spiritual worlds together determined the Virginia Company efforts of the early seventeenth century.

THE VIRGINIA COMPANY AND COLONIZATION

English attempts to colonize the New World did not begin with the Virginia Company, of course. Following early explorations that were never pursued toward colonization (see Quinn 1974:91–194), three attempts were made in the 1580s to establish a colony at Roanoke Island, in what is now North Carolina but was then Virginia. The last of these attempts failed because ships needed for the colony's resupply were instead diverted to the Anglo-Spanish war in 1588, which was fought largely at sea. That war ended in 1602; by 1603 there had been at least two English visits to Virginia, and there were Virginia Indians with their canoe on the Thames, apparently having been brought back from one of those expeditions (Quinn 1974:419–31). Nothing more is known of these Indians, but the public interest in Virginia is evident in the popularity and in the text of the play *Eastward Hoe*, published in several editions in 1605 (see Neill 1878:4; Tyler 1904:36; Harris 1926:lii–lviii).

The next English colonial efforts were undertaken by the crown-chartered Virginia Company, founded in 1606 (see Quinn 1974:482–88; Craven 1970:60–65), with one center in Plymouth to focus on the northern part of "Virginia" (what was to become New England) and one in London to exploit "the Old Virginia of the Roanoke colonies" (Quinn 1974:483). Both were supervised by a royal council but acted independently. Quinn (1974:484–87) has described the differences between these two groups of investors. The East India Company had demonstrated the potential for profit in such speculative investments, and merchants were eager to participate in other offerings. Merchants in the west of England were already invested in fish and oil and sought an area that could be exploited year-round to extend their season; the fishing banks of the northern Atlantic coast provided such an opportunity. The resources that interested the London merchants required the sustained presence of a colony, as "the whole basis of their economic program rested on agriculture, industry, and possibly mining, even though there was subsidiary Indian trade to be obtained" (Quinn 1974:487). Emboldened by the successful return of the first fleet of the East India Company in 1603, the English established the Virginia Company to provide sufficient funding for this effort. The major problem with Raleigh's privately funded attempts in the 1580s had been difficulties with resupplying the colony; although some of those difficulties were related to wartime demands, there had also been a shortage of funds, which broad support through the sale of stock would improve.

As already described, the situation in Virginia demanded long-term settlement in numbers and was seen as an effort with economic, nationalistic, and religious ends. The Virginia Company was to provide a financial and leadership base to ensure the longevity of this effort. The structure of the company (see James I 1969a:27–28) was analogous to the "great chain of being" (Lovejoy 1936) seen as the structure of the universe: at the top was the king, under whose authority the colonization was begun. The company was governed by a thirteen-member Royal Council in England, which supervised both the Virginia Company of London and that in Plymouth. Each of the two colonies was also to be governed by a council within the colony, answerable to the corresponding company. The king, the Royal Council, and the London and Plymouth Companies may be seen as analogous to the heavenly host: God and the ranks of angels; the colonies as analogous to earthly beings with their governing bodies. Whereas England was governed by a Parliament and headed by the king, the colonies were governed by a council with a president elected from their number (James I 1969b:36). This council, its role to interpret and implement the acts of the company in London, was to become a ground for great personal disputes and factionalism.

This structure was altered several times during the colonial period, and the company was finally dissolved in 1624. Throughout the lifetime of the company several features remained intact, including the involvement of the Crown and the ties of the Virginia colony to London merchants. These merchants, in order to protect their interests and to see the colony develop as quickly as possible, sought strong leaders in the colony, leaders without outside interests of their own to pursue in the colony. Gentlemen proved to be less than ideal in this capacity. The first president appointed in Virginia, Edward Wingfield, a gentleman "of a distinguished family, and [a] middle-aged veteran of wars in Ireland and the Netherlands" (Craven 1970:71), was removed after only a few months and sent back to England following squabbles over food supplies and individual status (cf. Smith 1986a:33–35, 1986c:143; Wingfield 1910). The next president was the "vile commander" (Smith 1986c:218) Captain John Ratcliffe; when Smith returned from his exploration of the Chesapeake Bay, he "found the last supply all sick; the rest, some lame, some bruised; all unable to do any thing but complain of the pride and unreasonable needless cruelty of their silly President [Ratcliffe] that had riotously consumed the store; and to fulfill his follies, about building him an unnecessary palace in the woods" (Smith 1986c:229). Captain John Smith himself was then elected president. Smith left the weakened company to recuperate and went on another trip of discovery that summer (Smith 1986c:229). Upon his return in September, he set the colonists to repairing and rebuilding, and he instituted field exercises (1986c:233–34).

Ultimately, the company came to rely on such military commanders and on their experience in leadership and maintaining discipline, their willingness to gain glory directing the actions of their men, and their ability to follow orders. Time and again the colony was to falter, only to be saved by these military leaders. Although harsh discipline was sometimes applied, at other times effective leadership seems to have consisted simply of inspiring the proper community spirit.

Smith was exasperated by these early colonists, but the situation was only to worsen. The first two years saw relatively small numbers of colonists traveling to Virginia. The original expedition included approximately one hundred men; the first supply, one hundred twenty; the second supply, seventy (Craven 1970:65n). The lists are dominated by craftsmen and gentlemen, with only about one quarter listed as "laborers" (Smith 1986c:207–9, 222–23, 241–42). Not until the third supply in 1609, after Smith's departure, did larger numbers of colonists begin to arrive (Earle 1979:108ff; Smith 1986d:241). The typical person leaving England for Virginia was probably similar to those entering the English army at the time: "out-of-work and rather ne'er-do-well," "when not engaged in warfare he was taking to parasitic or other questionable modes of existence" (Watteville 1954:27). The new colonists came from all parts of the country, rural as well as urban, but they were not the cream of English society, as noted by Josiah Child (1733:34) in 1692. Patrick Copland (1622:24) described these early colonists in a sermon delivered to Virginia Company members: "most of them at the first, being the very scum of the land, and great pity it was that no better at that time could be had"; William Crashaw (1610:F4) referred in more general terms to "the pusillanimity, the baseness, the tenderness and effeminateness of our English people: into which our nation is now *degenerate* from a strong, valiant, hardy, patient and enduring people."[5]

Morgan (1975:61–68) suggested a series of economic factors to account for this condition, including overpopulation and underdevelopment, with a consequent overspecialization to make jobs for everyone. But the attitudes deriving from this excess of free time, and their negative attribution as "laziness," is cultural, not inherent. Gentlemen of the time did less work than laborers, and they were not defined as "lazy" (although they generally are in modern constructions). Sale (1990:273, 272) has tried to explain the laziness noted repeatedly in early colonial Virginia as "a psychological impotence, a withdrawal, a kind of mental fetal-positioning" resulting from the confrontation between "the psyche of Europe" and "the wilderness of America." Although it is conceivable that this was a contributing factor, such a reaction was by no means universal among the colonists, and the condition was noted among soldiers, gentlemen, and laborers without regard to their prior experiences with other cultures. Indeed, from Smith's account, it seems the gentlemen were apt to be the more productive members of the society.

It seems more likely that this endemic laziness — "that evil disease of this land [England], which, if it be not looked unto and cured the sooner, will be the destruction of this land" (Eburne 1962:34) — was related to the self-interest inherent in the English culture of the time. Certainly there was no end of creative energy expended in the private trade and search for gold decried by Smith, as already noted. Most of the English colonists traveled to Virginia as indentured servants; they were to work for a time for the colony, to cover the cost of their transport and maintenance, during which time the company would keep them alive. Personal industry would not yield personal reward, except for those colonists who had come to Virginia at their own expense and particularly for those who were also investors in the company; these (relatively few) individuals had the greatest incentive for hard work. The colony was on the verge of collapse or abandonment repeatedly in its early years, a condition known even to the Spanish; John Digby (1613:f 170ᵛ) wrote from Madrid[6] that "they understood that our Plantation of Verginea is likely to sinke of itselfe." The importance of the "preaching of God's word" (Crashaw 1610:E4ᵛ) was argued by many, but there continued to be relatively few ministers in Virginia. The Virginia Company itself seems to have recognized eventually that some incentive was needed to maintain interest in the colony; in 1614, for the first time, private distributions of land were authorized, with settlers to receive fifty acres of land "for their personal adventure," and nonsettlers could obtain fifty acres of land in the colony for an investment of £12 10s (Craven 1970:117). The size of land grants was increased in 1619, and they were even extended to indentured servants on completion of their indenture. The private ownership of land seems to have begun to spark the interest of some of the planters.

Prior to the provision of this "carrot," the application of the "stick" was frequently needed to keep the colony from literally falling apart; military discipline never had to be imposed after this catering to the self-interest of the colonists with the provision for privately owned land. This discipline is most closely associated with Sir Thomas Dale, who served the colony from 1611 to 1616, first as High Marshall and then as governor. The punishments inflicted under Dale should be seen as differing only in degree and frequency, however, not in kind, from the disciplinary measures employed by others in the colonies, or in England, for that matter. Compiled by William Strachey (1969:9–39), the laws Dale enforced were prepared by the company and were very similar to those enforced in the armies in the Low Countries (cf. Styward 1581:48–64), where Dale and many other early colonial leaders had served. Punishments authorized included death, for acts ranging from murder to bearing false witness; consignment to the galleys, for slander against the colony, the company, or its officers; whipping, for stealing or losing tools, or for doing laundry or excreting in or near the fort; cutting off or burning various body parts; and "such punishment, as shall be thought fit by a court martial" (Strachey 1969:17).

Sale mistakenly describes these as laws "with a severity of punishments that not only strike the modern temperament as harsh but were seen at the time, by such as the Virginia secretary, Ralph Hamor, at least, as 'cruell, unusuall and barbarous' " (1990:276). This was not Hamor's opinion; the quotation is taken out of context, and Sale actually inverts Hamor's meaning. The passage refers to Dale's command:

> It was no mean trouble to him, to reduce his people so timely to good order, being of so ill a condition; as may well witness his severe and strict imprinted book of articles, then needful with all severity and extremity to be executed, now much mitigated, for more deserved death in those days, then do now the least punishment, so as if the law should not have restrained by execution, I see not how the utter subversion and ruin of the colony should have been prevented. . . . So as Sir Thomas Dale has not been tyrannous, nor severe at all; indeed the offences have been capital, and the offenders dangerous, incurable members, for no use so fit as to make examples to others. But the manner of their death, may some object, has been cruel, unusual and barbarous — which in deed they have not been: witness France, and other countries for less offences; what if they have been more severe then usual in England, there was just cause for it; we were rather to

> have regard to those whom we would have terrified, and made fearful
> to commit the like offences, than to the offenders justly condemned.
> (Hamor 1615:27)

Clearly, Hamor, who was in Virginia at the time, believed the punishments
were necessary and just; as Sale (1990:277) notes disparagingly, Smith
agreed, and many historians have credited the enaction and enforcement
of these laws with having saved the colony. This assessment would seem
to be accurate; as already discussed, the typical colonist acted in self-interest, narrowly defined, and seems to have responded only to threats to his
person or to opportunities to enrich himself.

Nor should these laws and punishments be seen as out of line with what
was being enforced in England at the time. Wertenbaker compared punishments inflicted in England and in the colonies, finding examples of death
and mutilations in sixteenth- and seventeenth-century England having "no
parallel in the history of the American colonies" (1927:210). Indeed, with
the exception of the heights of Dale's administration, "punishments [in the
colony] were far milder than in the mother country" (Wertenbaker
1927:210). After that time, he notes that criminals who would have received
death sentences in England would be punished for the same crime in the
colonies by "fines, imprisonment or at most whippings," explaining this
disparity "by the fact that crime was more common in the mother country
and human life cheaper" (Wertenbaker 1927:211–12). Although this may
run counter to romantic perceptions of Shakespeare's England, documents
of the times attest to it repeatedly. The sociological factors cited by Wertenbaker to explain seventeenth-century English ethics have also been invoked by others (e.g., Morgan 1975:58–91), but it is equally important to
consider the effects of the English perception of the place of man in the
universe, and the relationship between godliness, power, and wealth, as
laid out in this chapter, in evaluating this social condition.

ENGLISH MILITARY FORCE IN THE SEVENTEENTH CENTURY

If the discipline imposed by the English on their own people could be
harsh, so too was the military force exerted against the Powhatans. George
Percy describes several instances of fighting, including the following from
August 1610:

> we marched towards the town having an Indian guide with me named
> Kempes, whom the provost marshall led in a hand lock. This subtle

savage was leading us out of the way, which I misdoubting bastinaded him with my truncheon and threatened to cut off his head, whereupon the slave altered his course and brought us the right way near unto the town. So then I commanded every leader to draw away his file before me to beset the savages' houses that none might escape, with a charge not to give the alarm until I were come up unto them with the colors. At my coming I appointed Captain William West to give the alarm, which he performed by shooting off a pistol. And then we fell in upon them, put some fifteen or sixteen to the sword, and almost all the rest to flight. Whereupon I caused my drum to beat and drew all my soldiers to the colors, my Lieutenant bringing with him the queen and her children and one Indian as prisoners, for the which I taxed him because he had spared them. His answer was that having them now in my custody I might do with them what I pleased. Upon the same I caused the Indian's head to be cut off, and then dispersed my files, appointing my soldiers to burn their houses and to cut down their corn growing about the town, and after we marched with the queen and her children to our boats again, where being no sooner well shipped my soldiers did begin to murmur because the queen and her children were spared. So upon the same a council being called it was agreed upon to put the children to death, which was effected by throwing them overboard and shooting out their brains in the water. Yet for all this cruelty the soldiers were not well pleased, and I had much to do to save the queen's life for that time. (1922:271–72)

This woman was killed later in the same expedition (Percy 1922:272–73). Although taking prisoners who would later be killed was unusual, the brutality evident here was typical of the English attacks on the Powhatans, particularly in the first half of the seventeenth century. At times the English attacked the Powhatans by destroying their crops, but English attacks against Powhatan people were at least as brutal as Powhatan attacks against English people, and they were marked by an undercurrent of uncertainty about the humanity of the Indians.

The seventeenth century saw the English military forces in the midst of a technological revolution that casts further light on the relationship in that culture between power and right (righteousness) and between individuals and power. Fortunately for scholars, the period from the mid–sixteenth into the seventeenth century is also marked by a great increase in published works on military theory and practice, publications that were often rapidly translated and published throughout western Europe; and, judging from the wear and marginal annotations on the surviving copies, these publications were used extensively. The firearm had finally gained ascendancy over the bow and arrow by the end of the sixteenth century, after decades of debate over their relative merits within the English army (see Smythe 1973; Barwick 1973). The English archer, responsible for English victories from the thirteenth through the sixteenth century in such notable battles as Agincourt, Crécy, and Falkirk, and raised to a position of great respect and honor, had been an almost supernatural force in Europe (Heath 1973:v–vi). Nevertheless, the firearm did replace the bow as the mainstay of the English army in the mid–sixteenth century. As Rogers (1960:35) notes, "this was due more to the shortage of trained archers than to superiority in the firearms of the day. It took practice from youth up to train an archer, and in the hey-day of archery it was practised on every village green. But the spread of firearms and their use for sport inevitably resulted in a growing dearth of young men who could draw the long bow." The armies of many other nations had already relinquished the longbow, for the crossbow or early firearms, but the skill of the English archer was remarkable. An Italian observed in 1557 that "they draw the bow with such force and dexterity at the same time, that some are said to pierce corslets and body-armor; and there are few among them, even those that are moderately practised, who will not undertake at a convenient distance, either aiming point-blank, or in the air (as they generally do, that the arrow may fly further), to hit within an inch and a half of the mark" (quoted in Rogers 1960:39). Although the cross-bow was not widely used by the English, the firearms that ultimately replaced the long-bow there had similar strengths and weaknesses. They were relatively inaccurate and slow to fire and reload, but they did not need the years of physical training and mental discipline that archery required (see Ascham 1571). They did, however, involve a complicated series of steps in loading and firing, a mistake in any one of which could result in a misfire — "a series of movements by comparison with which the most complicated kinds of drill in more modern times appear simplicity itself" (Falls 1950:45).

This difference in the need for training reflects another distinction between the archer and the soldier with a gun. Whereas the power of an archer comes from his own mind and body, developed through years of training, the power of the soldier armed with a firearm lies essentially in the gun itself. The advantage of a firearm is that it supplies more force than the human body could produce, whereas a bow simply stores the energy produced by the archer. This change in technology meant that military improvement no longer need come from better soldiers (people), but rather should be pursued through the perfection of weapons (objects), it transformed the human soldier into a simple manipulator of power, rather than a receptacle of power. The almost symbiotic relationship between an archer and his weapon was replaced by a relationship of control over an external power. The development of strength and discipline thus became superfluous and dwindled, to be replaced by training in the technicalities involved in the operation of the firearm. The low quality of the soldiers, noted previously, can thus be traced directly to this change in emphasis from person to object as the locus of power.

The forms of European warfare of this time, involving vast numbers of men organized into large formations directed as a unit by their commanders, further decreased the importance of individual ability or action for the common soldiers. Henry Hexham thus described the duties of a soldier:

> In marching or standing, he must have a singular care to keep his rank and file, and not to stir out of it (without command), yea, if he were sure to kill an enemy. He ought also in fight, and in the day of battle, to hearken well to his officer's command. . . .
> The first duty then required in a gentleman or private soldier is obedience. . . . For without this a whole army is worth nothing. (1642:1)

Robert Ward gave a slightly different ordering of priorities: "In the first place, let a soldier's resolution be truly and sincerely to serve God; keeping a quiet conscience within their breast, which otherwise will gnaw at the roots of valor, and undermine all resolutions, wherefore a just and righteous conversation ought to be a soldier's companion, for his life is daily in danger" (1639:150). He then listed obedience, silence, secrecy, sobriety, hardiness, truth and loyalty as the next important qualities (Ward 1639:150–52). The keeping of these duties would produce a valorous soldier:

> True valor in subjects and soldiers is the summoning of the faculties of the irascible parts to a mature consultation with reason, judgement being the principal engine, and resolution the model that turns all the wheels, both of invention and execution, which makes a man truly valiant, to undertake without rashness, and to perform without fear, bearing down dangers with a lofty courage, trampling on them with success; it makes a soldier look death in the face, and pass by it with

> a smile; it makes him afraid of nothing, but to be betrayed by fear,
> desiring rather to have his blood seen, than his back; it makes a soldier
> disdain life upon all base conditions, making him prodigal of his
> blood, when God, his King and country shall command it. His bold-
> ness proceeds neither from ignorance nor senselessness. But first he
> values the danger, and then disdains it, having his fears least, when
> perils are greatest. (Ward 1639:172)

These dispassionate soldiers were, of course, the ideal, and the reality was
often far removed, as the accounts of period battles demonstrate. Nevertheless, this distancing from events (the "lofty courage," disdaining danger
and "base" life) is yet another instance of the externalizing of the world,
making it an object to control and dominate in a final and one-sided sense.
It is also the antithesis of the emotional, aesthetic approach to war of the
Native Americans described in chapter 1.

Several levels in the hierarchy of authority directed the actions of these
soldiers, in yet another parallel to the "great chain of being." As employed
in Virginia, the hierarchy was even more rigid than in Europe (Shea
1983:15). In his classic comparative analysis of authority, Miller (1955:277)
describes a generalized European model in which authority is reified as a
substance with the qualities of a liquid: "We speak of the 'flow' of authority,
of 'going through channels,' of the 'fountainhead' of authority. As a substance, authority can be quantified, and thus we speak of a great deal of
authority, little authority, no authority." This "substance" of authority was
held — and doled out — by individuals in "positions of authority." One of
the more important offices in the English military chain of command, especially as taken to America, was that of captain, a less formal office than
exists today with that title. Whereas officers of the time were gentlemen,
the captains were soldiers, chosen from the ranks to lead after demonstrating that they could "be circumspect, skillful, and expert in the noble art of
martial affairs; also hardy, and valiant of courage, painful and ingenious;
liberal in rewarding; just in service to their powers, above all things on the
earth, ever mindful to render a just account of that charge" (Styward
1581:34; cf. Hexham 1642:4). Their duties included training, disciplining,
and leading their soldiers, and seeing that all needs were supplied, as they
carried out the commands of their officers.

In training their men, these captains had prescribed drills to teach the
use of arms, a set of rules for individual soldiers' handling of arms that was
codified beginning in the early seventeenth century (Barriff 1635; Ward

1639; Hexham 1642, 1643; Markham 1643; Elton 1668), following the cod-ification of forms for large-scale troop movements that began in England in the mid–sixteenth century (Whitehorne 1573; Cataneo 1574; Styward 1581; Gutierrez de la Vega 1582; Fourquevaux 1589) and continued to be elaborated in later works. As the use of firearms compelled the individual to manipulate an external force rather than develop his own strength and ability, these drills applied external forces to the control of the individual soldier rather than encouraging his development. The soldier was to be-come an interchangeable unit, a tool for the use of his commanders.

In the only relatively detailed analysis of firearms in seventeenth-century Virginia to date, Fausz (1979b:44) has argued that the English guns were technically and symbolically superior weapons to the Powhatans' bows, that the early matchlocks were rapidly replaced by more advanced early flintlocks, and that these arms were "the only proper weapon for use in New World warfare," "for either side." Although this is a common as-sumption — compare Sheehan (1980:162): "Firearms, more than any other item in the material culture of European civility, gave Englishmen a tech-nical edge in the New World" — Fausz's assertion is best taken as an example of the continued Western reliance on external sources of power, but it does not accurately reflect the conditions of seventeenth-century Virginia. Fire-arms did come to dominate the colonists' military strategy earlier in Vir-ginia than in Europe, as Fausz noted (1979b:44) — but it is important to bear in mind that the force they replaced was pikemen, not archers, who were never tested in Virginia. A further importance of this shift was that, whereas pikemen generally wore back- and breastplates, musketeers did not (Falls 1950:40) because of the weight of the weapons they had to carry. This left them much more vulnerable to arrows, which could have been stopped by steel armor.

The kind of war fought in Virginia called for projectile weapons, with accuracy and rate of fire the most important criteria. There were no massed battles on an open field, or sieges of fortified settlements; the engagements were more akin to guerilla warfare. As developed in the previous chapter, and contrary to Fausz's assertion, this was a native style of war for the Powhatans, one where skill and the ability to strike fast and to retire were essential. Pikemen and halberdiers — soldiers with pole-arms — were essen-tially useless in this kind of combat. As already noted, by this time the English no longer had highly trained archers and so had no alternative but to rely on the gun.

Several types of guns were brought to Virginia. There were a variety of cannons, but these were of use primarily in defending a fortified site, such as Jamestown. These would have been important in defending against a Spanish naval attack, but although this was feared and planned for, it never happened. As field weapons, cannons were as useless in roadless Virginia as they were in roadless Ireland (Falls 1950:37). Handguns included muskets, large guns requiring an additional support in the form of a forked rest that had to be carried; calivers, lighter than muskets, and not requiring a rest; and pistols (see Peterson 1956:12–15; Cotter and Hudson 1957:71; Rogers 1960:51–53). In the early years of the colony handguns were almost entirely matchlocks, particularly the calivers and muskets; even by 1618, the outfitting for thirty-five men included only twenty muskets, of which only half had the vastly superior early flintlocks (Sandys et al. 1933:95–96). These flintlocks were considerably more expensive than the matchlocks and were often carried by officers: Strachey's laws of 1611 specify a flintlock arm only in reference to officers (Strachey 1969:46), and all his other references to arming the soldiers refer to powder, ball, and *match*—clearly indicating matchlocks. It was only in the early 1620s — after the first coup — that matchlocks were essentially retired (Brown 1980:84; Cotter and Hudson 1957:71; Peterson 1956:43).

The type of guns commonly carried in Virginia is important because even the early flintlocks were significantly more reliable than matchlocks. No longer was it necessary for a soldier to attend constantly to his match to keep it lit. There was almost no difference in either rate of fire or accuracy with the new locks, however, leaving the English with a weapon that was neither faster than matchlocks nor more accurate than the bow. The only advantages of firearms were the severity of wounds produced when the bullets hit their target, and the possible psychological advantage of its noise and smoke (Peterson 1956:19). The Frenchman Raimond de Fourquevaux[7] (1589:25–26) compared firearms and bows in the late sixteenth century, observing that despite the desire of most soldiers to be harquebusiers — either to fight from a greater distance or to have less weight to carry — they were not very effective: "in a skirmish wherein ten thousand harquebussados are shot, there dies not so much as one man, for the harquebusiers content themselves with making a noise, and so shoot at all adventures. . . . And although the harquebusier may shoot further, notwithstanding, the archer and crossbow man will kill 100 or 200 paces off as well as the best harquebusier."

Reliable estimates of the capabilities of seventeenth-century handguns are difficult to obtain. The flintlock musket of the early nineteenth century, with a number of refinements over its earlier counterparts to improve its reliability, accuracy, and rate of fire, is better known: "To load and fire the single-shot weapon required at least twelve separate movements in a standing position. Well-drilled troops could at best deliver three or four rounds per minute. Under battlefield conditions the musket misfired every six pulls of the trigger, for the flint might wear, the powder dampen, or the touch-hole clog" (Kimball 1967:169). The firearms available to the colonists in Virginia would have been considerably less effective even than this. Indeed, following the 1622 coup there was concern that English bows and arrows, which were given to the Virginia Company by the king, not fall into the Powhatans' hands, "in respect the use and scattering of them amongst the Indians might prove a thing dangerous to our own people" (Virginia Co. 1906a:100); they were sent to the Summer Islands, instead.

Fausz's acceptance of the (probably exaggerated) English account of their toll in the Powhatans' early attacks on Jamestown belies this state of affairs: "the Indians' 'custom' of falling down 'and after run[ning] away' whenever a musket was fired in their direction" (Fausz 1979b:36; quotes from G. Archer 1969) was a moderately effective defense, especially at distance, from the inaccurate musket-fire (see Shineberg 1971:65–66, 72, 76–77). When a musket shot found its target, however, the large, tumbling bullet inflicted a serious wound. Strachey stated that "a compound wound, as the surgeons call it, where besides the opening and cutting of the flesh any rupture is, or bone broken, such as our small shot make amongst them, they know not easily how to cure, and therefore languish in the misery of the pain therof" (1953:110).

For the kind of war being fought in Virginia, however, the bow and arrow would be at least as effective a weapon as the firearms of the time. Land-war in Europe at this time was essentially of two sorts: open-field and siege. Open-field war was fought between massed armies acting as units, with pikemen playing a major role. This was soon found to be an ineffective tactic against the Indians, so the use of pikes rapidly declined (Peterson 1956:99). Du Praissac (1639:26–30; cf. Rohan 1640:123–26) described the goals and methods of this European form of warfare in general terms. One should seize the most advantageous ground and attempt to divide the enemy's forces, while allowing one's own soldiers no opportunity to flee battle, and artillery should be used to disorder the enemy's ranks, even before battle is engaged. The battle would be engaged by forces consisting largely of pikemen; the flanks should be sharply attacked along with the front, and reserves should be brought up both to the weakest and strongest of the enemy's positions, but one's advance should not be so hasty as to become disordered. Psychological tactics were also advised: "If you attempt to conquer the enemy's country, you are to publish the victory, for that will cause his confederates to shrink from their alliance, it will affright your enemy, and will make the neutrals to declare themselves for the victor; it will keep your confederates faithful and constant, your subjects obedient, and will procure favor from all men" (Du Praissac 1639:29). If defeated, "If you be pursued with extremity, you must retreat in the best order you shall be able, making it appear you are not vanquished in your courage, though you be so in your fortunes" (Du Praissac 1639:30).

Often involving armies of thousands of soldiers, this was the kind of warfare learned by the English soldiers in their experiences in the wars in the Netherlands. Sir Roger Williams described one such battle from 1572:

> The enemies . . . kept themselves close in the village until York and we entered the ambush. Then they delivered a hot volley of shot upon us and withal charged with some hundred pikes. . . . True it is, the enemy stood in the village round about . . . where we marched and received us at the entry of some hundred of ours into the village out of the narrow way, where we passed and could not march above five in a rank, wherefore they found us good cheap. Our retreat was so fast that the enemy followed us upon the heels into the troops which Captain Morgan led, who charged them resolutely with his armed men in such sort that the enemies ran back. But wisely he had placed half his men in the village for his retreat, who delivered their volley on Captain Morgan.
>
> . . .
>
> The next morning we dislodged towards Goes. Our vanguard being arrived within half a mile of the town, we made a stand until the rest arrived. In the meantime the enemies sallied and gave furiously into our guards, forced our first guards to run amongst our battles of pikes, . . .
>
> Notwithstanding, Captain Morgan with his brave shot entered an orchard and flanked the enemy, which stood on the high ditch beating on our pikes with volleys of shot. Withal, Sir Humphrey and his armed men passed the bridge and charged the enemy with great resolution, in such sort that the enemy fell to running. (1964:70–72)

Even in Ireland, battles were fought in much the same way, with only slightly smaller forces (see Falls 1950). The campaigns in Virginia involved far fewer men than most of these European battles, but the tactics remained the same: the effort was to maintain one's massed unit, for the greatest concentration of power, and to entice the enemy into a position where parts of their unit could be cut off and subjected to the full force of one's army (Styward 1581:72–76; Markham 1643:130–53). The ability — and desire — to deliver massive assaults and to endure all responses without retreat, in order to achieve the absolute destruction of the enemy's forces, has always been the trademark of the "Western Way of War," a tradition that can be traced to classical Greece (Hanson 1989:9).

Sieges laid against fortified sites demanded large guns of the sorts carried by ships and emplaced at Jamestown. None was ever engaged in Virginia, however; few Powhatan villages were even palisaded. The relatively immobile massed force of the English colonists was of little use against an enemy who would readily flee in the face of impending defeat, only to consolidate forces and attack again later.

There were also rules in war for the proper treatment of the defeated and particularly of prisoners. Styward discussed these, citing examples from the history of Western warfare to illustrate his points. His Christian morality demanded mercy to prisoners, but he also noted repeatedly that humane treatment was not only proper Christian behavior, but also a pragmatically sound policy: since "fortune is uncertain," the tide of battle could reverse, leaving the earlier victor in defeat, and subject to the mercy of his enemy (1581:143). The fact that the Powhatans were not accorded humane treatment in the early years of the colony suggests that the English considered them no serious potential threat, and perhaps somewhat less than human. This again echoes the relationship between religion and political and economic pragmatic concerns in the English colonial culture. Each individual chose his own concerns — the more pragmatic ones, particularly economic, seem to have been preeminent for most — but trade, "civilizing," conversion, and warfare were simply different faces of a single policy brought by the English to Virginia, a policy rooted in their conception of the universe as falling under their domination and control. By the time Jamestown was founded, this policy had also been shaped by previous colonial experiences, particularly those in Ireland and the "Lost Colony" of Sir Walter Raleigh.

3 ✦ Prolegomena

The Colonization of Virginia
Sir Walter Ralegh was responsible for the first attempts to plant Englishmen in "Virginia" (modern North Carolina and Virginia). Ralegh saw these efforts as both an act of patriotism and a stepping stone for his own ambition. A combination of great ambition, misplaced idealism and greed meant that the colony established in 1584 struggled for a few brief years and died. Further attempts involved a similar tragic waste of energy and lives.
— seen in the "Bloody Tower" of HM Tower of London, where Raleigh was imprisoned 1603–16 (Dec. 1990)

ENGLISHMEN HAD VISITED the New World at least as early as 1497, when John Cabot explored parts of the East Coast, including Newfoundland (Quinn 1974:6), and it is possible that sailors from Bristol may have discovered what was then referred to as the "Isle of Brasil" prior to Columbus's famed voyage, perhaps as early as 1480 (Quinn 1961, 1974:5–23). Cabot's grant to explore issued from King Henry VII, and from 1497 into the early sixteenth century a series of voyages were undertaken by a cooperative association of Bristol and Portuguese merchants and sailors. These seem to have been unprofitable, and for more than seventy years after 1505 the English did not challenge the efforts of other nations to seek fortune in North America. English fishermen continued to make annual trips to the Labrador and Newfoundland fishing grounds throughout the sixteenth century, but they engaged in little trade or exploration during that time.

The French, Portuguese, and Spanish continued to explore the New World through the sixteenth century, with the French more involved in the north and the Spanish and Portuguese most active from Florida south. The Spanish and Portuguese in particular were wide-ranging in their explorations, exploring large parts of the coast of North and South America. In fact, a Portuguese pilot in the employ of the English, Simão Fernandes, guided them when they again began to explore in 1578 and 1580. These were the expeditions of Sir Humphrey Gilbert and Walter Raleigh, who searched for a site to found a colony (Quinn 1974:246–63).

This culminated in attempts by the English in the 1580s to colonize what is now North Carolina, with what has become known as the Lost Colony. Although the English had some experience with colonies in Ireland, wartime pressures and supply difficulties prevented the colony from succeeding as "the first attempts to plant Englishmen in 'Virginia.' " The jingoistic qualification of this statement is necessary because of the Spanish. They had established a settlement in Florida at San Augustín in 1565, and Spanish Jesuits had established missions in present-day Georgia and South Carolina by 1568 (Gradie 1988:139). They then attempted a mission among the Virginia Indians in the early 1570s. Although short-lived, this was the first European effort to establish a colony in Virginia.

This pre- and protocolonial period is relatively poorly documented and until recently has been little known. It has been intensively studied in recent decades, however, and there is general acceptance of the widespread and repeated visits of Europeans to the New World through the late fifteenth and sixteenth centuries. Although the Spanish, Portuguese, French, and English were involved in the exploration and exploitation of America, by the mid–sixteenth century the Spanish and the English were the main rivals in Virginia.

FISHERMEN AND MISSIONARIES
IN THE NEW WORLD

Throughout the sixteenth century, the Spanish were the most visible Europeans in the New World. The papal bulls of 1481 and 1493, further redefined in the Treaty of Tordesillas of 1494, had divided the New World between Spain and Portugal (Quinn 1974:70, 111–12). The English, of course, having separated from the Roman Catholic Church, were not recognized by the Pope. The French were largely content to raid Spanish ships and to exploit the fishing banks off the American coast, although they twice attempted colonies in the early 1560s (Parry 1982:94–95). Most of the inland exploration of North America was thus conducted by the Spanish working from colonies established along the Gulf coast and in Florida. The interior was thereby little exposed to Europeans, but fishermen, raiders, and smugglers annually visited the coasts — the "great quantities of cod" off the Newfoundland coast were noted by English sailors as early as 1497 (Quinn 1974:95) — and some land contacts are indicated by the parrots, wildcats, and other kinds of goods mentioned in contemporary documents as being brought back to England (Quinn 1974:123–26). A series of six-teenth-century maps of the North American coast also attest to the coastal navigations conducted at this time (Lewis and Loomie 1953:250–62).

The fishing fleets off the North American coast seem to have been largely English and French, although most of the maps were made by the Portu-guese and Spanish (see Quinn 1974). Portuguese pilots, in particular, seem to have been frequently employed in these expeditions. The frequency of these voyages has been demonstrated by Quinn through scrupulous ex-amination of letters, logs, and accounts books, particularly those of the Bristol seafarers. Although these voyages were not colonial in nature, they are clearly related to the later colonial ventures: not only did they provide needed information to the Europeans, but they also likely produced the first interactions of Europeans and the native peoples along the North American coast. We know of three Indians being taken to England in 1502 (Quinn 1974:118), Micmacs in Portugal in 1501, seven Indians in France in 1508 (Foreman 1943:8–9), and of Baffin Island Eskimos brought back by Frobisher in 1577 (Hulton 1984:8); this practice had begun with Colum-bus's first voyage. There were many other contacts, including the taking of slaves from North America by the Spanish (Foreman 1943:1–21); the in-troduction of European diseases seems to date to this period, also. Virginia provides a case in point. On one of the early visits to Virginia, in the first half of the 1560s, a group of Spanish sailors returned with a Virginia Indian, a young chief, to whom they gave the name Don Luis de Valasco, after his sponsor. This man lived in Mexico, in Spain for at least two years, where he was educated at the court of King Philip II, and in Havana. When he was returned to Virginia in 1570 with the Jesuit mission attempted in his home territory, he was astounded at the hardships his people had suffered in his absence: "We find the land of Don Luis in quite another condition than expected, not because he was at fault in his description of it, but because Our Lord has chastised it with six years famine and death, which has brought it about that there is much less population than usual. Since many have died and many also have moved to other regions to ease their hunger, there remain but few of the tribe" (Quirós and Segura 1953:89). We see in later chapters that the Indians in Virginia possessed sufficient stores of food in the early seventeenth century to survive considerable deprivation, and there is no reason to assume that this represented any change from their sixteenth-century way of living. Furthermore, six years of famine caused by climate would likely have been noted elsewhere in the world; such severe conditions could hardly be so localized. The conditions seen by Don Luis and the Spanish seem much more likely to be attributable to the long-term actions of disease, which could weaken even those who were not killed, making them less effective as farmers, hunters, and gatherers and more susceptible to the effects of climatic and dietary stress.

This mission of 1570 — the first attempt to establish a permanent European settlement in Virginia that actually resulted in settlement being made — would not last long. The mission consisted of ten men, including Don Luis (Philip II 1953:96), and they made landfall on 10 September 1570 (Lewis and Loomie 1953:36), with extremely small food supplies. Don Luis did not stay long with the Jesuits; as recounted by the sole Spanish survivor of the mission, a young boy named Alonso:

> After they arrived there, Don Luis abandoned them, since he did not sleep in their hut more than two nights nor stay in the village where the Fathers made their settlement for more than five days. Finally he was living with his brothers a journey of a day and a half away. Father Master Baptista sent a message by a novice Brother on two occasions to the renegade. Don Luis would never come, and Ours stayed there in great distress, for they had no one by whom they could make themselves understood to the Indians. They were without means of support, and no one could buy grain from them. They got along as best they could, going to other villages to barter for maize with copper and tin, until the beginning of February. (Rogel 1953a:109)

During this time Don Luis had taken several wives, an action that the Jesuits saw as evidence that he had fallen "into evil ways" and "was now completely corrupted" (Rogel 1953b:119). Although the Jesuits did not recognize it as such at the time, this was another instance of a Virginia Indian's willingness to accept European religion into his own system of beliefs without rejecting his earlier beliefs, as previously discussed. Don Luis's acceptance of the Catholic faith, in his own way, is as evident in his actions as his bond with his own people.

At this time, in early February 1571, Father Baptista sent Father Quirós with two brothers to bring back Don Luis, who sent them back saying he would follow, apparently in good faith. Then,

On the Sunday after the feast of the Purification, Don Luis came to the three Jesuits who were returning with other Indians. He sent an arrow through the heart of Father Quirós and then murdered the rest who had come to speak with him. Immediately Don Luis went on to the village where the Fathers were, and with great quiet and dissimulation, at the head of a large group of Indians, he killed the five who waited there. Don Luis himself was the first to draw blood with one of those hatchets which were brought along for trading with the Indians; then he finished the killing of Father Master Baptista with his axe, and his companions finished off the others. . . . This boy [Alonso] then told Don Luis to bury them since he had killed them, and at least in their burial, he was kind to them. (Rogel 1953a:110)

Alonso's account changes slightly in each version, but several features remain constant. In Rogel's later version,

He said that when Don Luis arrived with his tribe armed with clubs and lances, he greeted Father Baptista who was as we described ["in bed, sick and praying . . . on the eve of Our Lady's Purification"]. Raising his club and giving his greeting were really one gesture, and so in wishing him well, he killed him. All the rest were murdered also. Then going out to search for Brother Sancho de Zaballos, who at that time had gone to the forest to get firewood, they slew him there. . . . After the Indians were sated, Don Luis summoned Alonso and told him to show the Indians how to bury the bodies of the Fathers as was the custom of the Christians. (1953b:119–20)

Later accounts became increasingly exaggerated, perhaps by Alonso himself, and certainly by his recorders; the Rogel letters — written shortly after the event by someone who had known Don Luis and who, as part of the expedition that rescued Alonso, had the opportunity to speak at length with him — are considered the most reliable source (Lewis and Loomie 1953:48; Gradie 1988:142n).

Since Alonso possibly did not actually witness the slayings (Lewis and Loomie 1953:46–47) but only heard the details from the Indians with whom he lived for the next year and a half, some variability should be expected. Consistent are the points that it was not a purely surprise attack, that there was some greeting or verbal exchange between Father Baptista and Don Luis; that all of the adults — all of whom were religious persons — were killed, sparing only the boy Alonso; that the bodies of the slain were buried; and that the religious goods of the Jesuits were then distributed:

Finally Don Luis distributed the clothes of the Fathers among himself and his two brothers who shared in the murders. The boy [Alonso] took nothing but the relics and beads of Father Baptista which he kept till now and handed over to us.

. . .

When this boy was with Don Luis, following the death of the others, Don Luis left the vestments and books and everything else locked up in chests. On returning, they took up their share of spoils. He said that a brother of Don Luis is going around clothed in the Mass vestments and altar cloths. The captured chief told me that Don Luis gave the silver chalice to an important chief in the interior. The paten was given to one of those Indians we captured, while the other images were thrown away. (Rogel 1953a:110, 111)

Every account also describes an incident whereby three Indians were killed by the power of a large crucifix in one of the Jesuits' chests, although the details differ. Several accounts place the killing of Father Baptista in the context of religious activity, the priest either praying or at Mass. The account recorded by Carrera, embellished with a number of imaginative details of the killings themselves, offers an additional possible insight: "As the boy recalls, the wicked Indian who fostered this crime, though evil and hardened in his errors and sins, was so touched at seeing them dead that he wept copiously and called them martyrs" (1953:136). Several of the later accounts allege that Don Luis was desperate to kill Alonso and that the boy was only saved by the successive actions of two other chiefs. One should bear in mind, however, the apparent closeness of Don Luis and Alonso evident in the accounts cited here, where they consulted on burial practices and where Alonso was given some of the relics of Father Baptista.

Don Luis's desperation has been generally accepted by recent scholars as part of an attempted psychological understanding first invoked by Lewis and Loomie (1953:47), who invoked A. I. Hallowell's cultural psychology studies to suggest that "we may expect Don Luis to manifest extreme sensitivity to overtones of anger or public criticism, in his case a sensitivity perhaps heightened by a disturbed conscience if his conversion had been genuine." More recently a variation on this has been elaborated by Rountree (1990:16–17), who suggests that "his eagerness to help the Jesuits faded" when Don Luis left the physical presence of the mission to live with his people; he was then caught in the middle, and took the easy way out: "whatever he did, he would be publicly criticized and shamed by somebody, a terrible fate for one brought up in the Powhatan world. But the Jesuits were more ready than his own people to blame him for disloyalty just then, and the missionaries were few in number. Therefore, the solution Don Luis chose was to eliminate the Jesuits" (Rountree 1990:17). Although Gradie's earlier study (1988) attempted to explain these killings as an instantiation of the Indians' ethnocentrism (following Fausz's interpretation of the 1622 coup) — an argument also involving the native culture at a merely superficial level, as a somewhat variant form of the ethnocentrism of the Europeans — more recently she has adopted Rountree's argument (Gradie 1993).

This kind of rational cost/benefits analysis, even if reflection through "the Powhatan world" is admitted, may be imposing too much of a Western notion of causes and causality on this situation, trivializing the culturally constructed meanings of the Powhatan world and its capacity for accepting and integrating difference. Implicit in all of these interpretations is a notion of ethnic boundaries as rigid "either/or" lines where an individual can exhibit only the traits of the category in which he or she "belongs." From this perspective, Don Luis was thus "converted" when he lived among the Spanish, but presumably "unconverted" when he returned to live with the Indians, and certainly when he led the sacrifice of the Jesuits. As discussed in the first two chapters, this is a plainly non-Indian view of reality, but one that was becoming increasingly widespread in Europe at that time. I propose a different perspective, also employed in successive chapters, one taking such defined categories as "traditional" and "converted" as heavily qualified statements that thus have much less significance. This perspective goes beyond the question of how conflicting loyalties to both worlds would be resolved, instead placing Don Luis in a liminal position where the two worlds become one, where, for Don Luis, the Spanish Jesuits have been brought into the Powhatan world — and thus there is only one loyalty. Neither world is rejected; rather, they are united.

Several observations are recorded that suggest the sincerity of Don Luis and his continued acceptance of at least some of the Jesuits' teachings. Sacchini wrote: "An older brother of Luis had died, a younger one was ruling. Luis generously returned the rule to him when offered, asserting that he had not returned to his fatherland out of a desire for earthly things but to teach them the way to heaven which lay in instruction in the religion of Christ Our Lord. The natives heard this with little pleasure" (1953:222). Father Quirós had written shortly after arriving at their place of settling: "Don Luis has turned out well as was hoped, he is most obedient to the wishes of Father and shows deep respect for him, as also to the rest of us here, and he commends himself to you and to all your friends" (Quirós and Segura 1953:92). In a similar vein, Lewis and Loomie noted that he had "helped energetically in getting the Fathers adjusted and persuaded Father Segura to send one of the company from the ship six or eight leagues into the interior to baptize his three-year-old brother, who was dying" (1953:44). As already noted, he ensured that the bodies of the Jesuits were given Christian burials (although this may have been prompted by Alonso), and he seems to have been touched by the sacrifice of these men, perhaps even calling them "martyrs." Why, then, did he kill them? Given the small size of the mission and its lack of supplies, the Jesuits were entirely at the mercy of the Indians; they could have been robbed, enslaved, subjected to any form of humiliation — or simply left to starve. Although the question may never be answered, one possibility has not been previously considered: that Don Luis gave the Jesuits what he thought they wanted — martyrdom. This is not as odd as it may seem, and in fact it was apparently a theory among the Spanish colonists in Florida: "The governor, if I recall correctly, or another official of those provinces, used to say (it was a byword there) that these good Fathers seemed to believe that the sole purpose for which His Holiness and His Majesty and their superiors had sent them was to be martyred and cut to pieces by the savages" (Martínez 1953:157). The same attitudes, emphasizing sacrifice and perhaps even seeming to desire mar-tyrdom, were also noted in Jesuits in New France in the seventeenth cen-tury (cf. Ragueneau 1898:139–49). The idea of sacrifice seems to have been pronounced among the fathers; in Father Quirós's first and only letter from Virginia, he wrote

> I am convinced that there will be no lack of opportunity to exercise patience, and to succeed we must suffer much. But it has seemed good to expose ourselves to that risk. . . .
> With the great need of provisions for the entire crew, it has been thought necessary that they leave today, and we will remain here in this lonely region amid the trials mentioned above. (Quirós and Se-gura 1953:90–91)

The sacrifice of Christ for humanity would also have been emphasized in the teachings Don Luis received, with all of its implications as the Christian ideal. This is not to say that the Jesuits were consciously seeking martyr-dom, but their notion of self-sacrifice was extreme by European standards, even for that time, and it would have resonated with the cultural ideals of self-sacrifice evident in many Native American cultures, including the Powhatans and others of the Eastern Woodlands.

Note, too, that these killings took place during the Christian holy season, "the Sunday after the feast of the Purification." This interpretation would also supply meaning to an act that has been considered simply a barbaric misappropriation: the distribution and wearing of the vestments and vessels by the Indians, seemingly by the chiefs (Rogel 1953a:110). There was no attempt to hide this from the Spanish on their return; Rogel described the Indians: "Taking the robes of the dead Fathers, they put them on and walked along the shore, and the rest of the Indians called out that there were the Fathers and to come ashore" (1953b:120). Furthermore, one of the Indians who freely went onto the Spanish ship was wearing the Jesuits' paten; he was immediately taken prisoner (Rogel 1953a:108). There seems to be much more here than one would expect for a simple status object. These actions make sense fully only if one assumes that the Indians — taught by Don Luis — recognized the power of these items and wore them with respect, as a way of maintaining that power. This is not to say that they had converted to the Jesuit faith, but rather that they had absorbed that religion into their own. These Indians accepted the teachings of the Jesuits — received salvation — but they did so in their own terms. From this perspective, the killing of the Jesuits is indeed a sacrifice — the ultimate sacrifice, since the Fathers gave their lives for the redemption of the Indians. The peaceful resignation with which they seem to have met their fates would also meet the native ideal and confirm their inner strength and power; the wearing of the material signs of their power — their vestments, the paten, the chalice — would reflect the conveyance of this power. Indeed, it is suggested that these items were later stored away in the chiefs' "treasure houses" for years to come (Rogel 1953b:121; Oré 1953:182–83) — the same treatment given more traditional powerful goods such as crystals, copper, and beads.

Late in spring 1571 a supply ship was sent to the Jesuit mission from Havana. This ship was not met with the expected signals, the pilot refused to land, and a fight ensued. The sailors managed to return to Havana with at least one captive, from whom they learned that only Alonso survived the February attack (Lewis and Loomie 1953:50). In the summer of 1572 an armed ship with thirty soldiers entered Virginia, killed and captured a number of Indians, and recovered Alonso, who had almost forgotten Spanish. They demanded Don Luis and his two brothers, and, when they were not turned over, executed some of the Indians they had captured. At this time they apparently questioned the Indian prisoners as well as Alonso about the killings, because at least five Indian prisoners were released on the basis of their uninvolvement (Lewis and Loomie 1953:53–54). The ship then returned to Havana.

These events of the 1560s and 1570s helped shape the Powhatans' perceptions of Europeans, and they present some of the same problems of interpretation as the events of the early seventeenth century, when the English arrived. The spread of disease and decline in population undoubtedly affected the developing organization of that population; Powhatan inherited a group of tribes by the 1590s and rapidly expanded his control through the following decade. Powhatan and Opechancanough were both of an age to have witnessed or even been involved in these killings; indeed, various writers have suggested that one or the other of these two was Don Luis himself. These events in Virginia, one peripheral settlement of the Spanish New World, had relatively little impact on the process of Spanish colonization elsewhere. The news of this mission seems not to have reached the English; it is never mentioned in contemporary English documents, nor is it offered as a comparison to later English experiences in Virginia. Although they had explored and fished the coasts of North America, the English colonial precursors to Jamestown were mostly in Ireland rather than in the New World.

EARLY ENGLISH EXPLORATION
AND COLONIZATION

As already mentioned, English explorers had begun to visit the New World by the late fifteenth century, and fishermen made annual trips to the rich coastal fishing areas. By this time, however, their first attempt to conquer the Irish, begun under Henry II in 1171, had long since stagnated: "Failing to conquer Ireland, the Anglo-Normans established not so much a colony as a garrisoned foreign province, the Pale, whose foreignness was proclaimed in law and asserted by violence" (O'Farrell 1971:16–17). The form of the English presence in Ireland was established through the fourteenth and fifteenth centuries, particularly through the second attempt at conquest under Henry VIII and Elizabeth I. Although there are many differences, there are also similarities between the English in Ireland and those in America. Canny (1988:2) summarizes contemporary opinions, noting that both were considered to be primarily acts of civilizing a heathenish people and converting them to the true religion while enriching England with resources not available at home. O'Farrell (1971:17–18) describes the English colonies in Ireland in a less flattering light, as developing into an intermediate group neither Irish nor English, often adopting the language and customs of the Irish, typified by neglect and lack of consistency in leadership, thought, and action. In general the Irish seem to have been considered as more fully human than the Indians were by the English; whereas colonists adopted some Indian foods, ways of dress, hunting, etc., Englishmen only learned Indian languages in order to trade with them. Other characteristics of the English in Ireland, though, also seem to fit the English in America.

O'Farrell (1971:18–19; cf. Brady 1986) has argued that the driving motivation behind the renewed English efforts in the sixteenth century to conquer or colonize Ireland was fear: fear that some foreign enemy might use Ireland as a base from which to attack England, that the Irish themselves might attack, or that the Irish and another enemy might conspire against England. The English foothold in Ireland, though tenuous, was nevertheless seen as essential to the security of England itself. Possible enemies abounded, particularly after the establishment of a separate Church of England by Henry VIII made enemies of all other Catholics. This situation is conducive to a particularly negative character, as O'Farrell observed: "Fear is not a perceptive or magnanimous emotion: it is blind and harsh. The fact that it was fear which impelled English policy towards Ireland does much to explain the nature of the relationship" (1971:19). In the New World of the late sixteenth and seventeenth centuries, this fear had a specific focus on the Spanish. The Spanish were extracting a vast wealth from the New World, and their efforts at exploration and at conversion of the Indians were extensive. This posed a threat to the English not just in terms of political power but from the standpoint of religion as well: the faith that the Spanish were spreading was seen as false by the English, and yet the Spanish successes seemed to suggest the favor of God. The English had a similar fear of the French and of French Catholicism. It was thus essential for them to find heathens of their own to convert to the true belief, and this effort would necessarily be rewarded, as discussed in chapter 2.

This fear-based chauvinism can be seen as motivating English explorations from about the mid–sixteenth century. In 1497 and 1498, when John Cabot crossed the Atlantic for England, it was still thought that the coast reached by such explorers was that of Asia (Quinn 1974), and Cabot was directly competing with Columbus for information and trade routes for the lucrative Asian trade (Quinn 1974:105–11). At the beginning of the sixteenth century several additional voyages took place, but it seems "that Henry VII was not very optimistic of the London-Bristol associates developing a highly profitable trade" (Quinn 1974:123). After Henry VII's death, English exploration was even less encouraged (Quinn 1974:143–44).

Sebastian Cabot would later plan an attempt at a northwest passage under the English flag, but this drew little support from the London merchants, and the attempt was never made. Cabot returned to Spain, where he had been serving for several years (Quinn 1974:146–47). Through the 1520s and 1530s there were occasional English voyages to observe the Spanish New World empire or to seek a northwest passage. No such voyages were recorded between 1536 and 1563, although in 1546 a young Englishman who was later captured by the Spanish sailed with a French squadron that traded with the Indians near the Chesapeake Bay. The Indians who met the French there were prepared to trade, suggesting that they may have previously encountered Europeans (Quinn 1974:189–90). By the time Elizabeth I came to the throne at the end of 1558, the English had been relegated to a minor role in North America.

Martin Frobisher was the next Englishman to attempt to locate a northwest passage, making two trips in 1576 and 1577. These voyages accomplished little; on the first, one Indian man was taken captive, who bit his tongue in two in despite and who later died of a cold in England (Foreman 1943:14). There were a few other voyages of exploration from 1578 to 1583, by Humphrey Gilbert and others; Bartholomew Gosnold even built a small trading post in New England but then abandoned it (Quinn 1974:234–41). The next English effort in North America was the series of attempted colonies on the Outer Banks of North Carolina.

THE LOST COLONY AND ITS AFTERMATH

In 1584 two small ships sailed from England for the Outer Banks of North Carolina. Sir Humphrey Gilbert had obtained a patent from the queen in 1578 to settle in the New World but had never succeeded in that endeavor. His half brother Walter Raleigh was issued a nearly identical patent in early 1584, and under his direction this expedition set out. Although Raleigh is the person most generally associated with these colonies of the 1580s, he never sailed for their shores. This first expedition, led by Philip Amadas and Arthur Barlowe, landed on 4 July 1584 near Roanoke Island (Quinn 1985:3–32). They remained for perhaps a month exploring the islands and sounds and trading with the local Indians. These were an Algonquian-speaking group led by the chief Wingina, although the chief the English met and dealt with at this time was his brother Granganimeo. Relations between the two peoples seem to have been cordial and friendly. When the English departed, they carried with them two Indians: Wanchese, a Roanoke Indian, and Manteo, a Croatoan Indian, from somewhat further south (Quinn 1985:32–39).

Raleigh seems to have learned from the failures of his half brother; he planned an initial expedition of perhaps five hundred men to be increased with successive reinforcements (Quinn 1985:53, 67). Thomas Hariot and John White, respectively trained in the sciences and arts, were to survey, study, and record their environs. Both produced notable records, Hariot in written description (1588), as noted in chapter 2, and White in drawings and watercolors (Hulton 1984). Hariot began studying the Algonquian language from Manteo and Wanchese shortly after they arrived in England, and Raleigh also consulted with them (Quinn 1985:43, 49).

In early April 1585 seven or more vessels sailed from England for Virginia with a complement of about six hundred men, roughly half of whom were to remain in the colony. After being separated by storms, regrouping at Puerto Rico, and engaging in both trade with and piracy against the Spanish, five ships sailed north, including a replacement for a lost pinnace built in their first week on Puerto Rico in mid-May. Anglo-Spanish relations were deteriorating at this time, with the two nations officially trading but with English captains actively preying on Spanish shipping. By early July the English ships arrived on the Outer Banks, where they found and rejoined two of their missing ships, and they began to explore the area by sea and by land. Within a few days of their arrival the English had burned the village of Aquascogoc and its fields in reprisal for the theft of a silver cup, the return of which had apparently been promised by the chief. They then turned north to the location selected for the colony. After sending greetings to Wingina and apparently receiving his welcome to settle, the colony was established on Roanoke Island (Quinn 1985:55–65, 70–72).

Because of concerns about supplies and the available land, only about a hundred men remained as colonists. In early August the first ship returned to England with word of the colony, followed by other ships in later August and early September. One of these ships, returning via Bermuda, captured a straggler from the Spanish treasure fleet, thus providing a profit for investors in the colony and demonstrating an advantage of having a base in the New World. By this time English relations with Spain had further deteriorated and were verging on open warfare. The ships Raleigh had intended for Virginia in June had been ordered to Newfoundland to warn English ships and to capture Spanish and Portuguese fishing vessels, Queen Elizabeth having issued the letters of marque that transformed such piracy into lawful privateering. All of the original ships from Roanoke Island except the pinnace and two smaller boats had returned to England by November, leaving the colony to wait until spring for supplies and reinforcements (Quinn 1985:67–86).

The colonists were not idle over the winter. One party explored northward, entering the Chesapeake Bay and establishing friendly relations with the Chesapeake Indians. This was followed by explorations into the mainland of North Carolina, prompted by stories of an inland sea and of deposits of copper or possibly even gold. Inadequately prepared and unable to exact the food they had expected to get from the Indians, the party was fortunate to return to Roanoke Island (Quinn 1985:106–20). Ralph Lane, a soldier and leader of the colony, reports a dizzying sequence of betrayals by Wingina, their most closely neighboring chief, and by other Indian leaders (Quinn 1985:115, 121–26). These have almost a quality of paranoid ravings, likely based in the colonists' desperate need for food, their increasing demands upon the Indians, who increasingly rejected them, and Wingina's apparent decision in the spring to remove his village from the vicinity of the colony. Lane records that Wingina agreed to assist the colony that spring only at the urging of other chiefs, who had been impressed by Lane's return from that near-fatal exploration up the Roanoke River and who had acknowledged the sovereignty of Elizabeth (Quinn 1985:122–23). After Wingina had constructed fish weirs for the English and had cleared and sown fields for them, he moved his village. Lane reportedly received news that Wingina intended to return with other parties of Indians to exterminate the colony, and based on this information he launched an attack. On 1 June 1586 Wingina was killed and his head returned to Lane (Quinn 1985:124–27). This may have been the first American case of a head taken as a trophy by the English, although they had long been doing so in Ireland and would continue to do so elsewhere in the Americas.

Although this might seem an extreme response, Quinn refers to this attack as a "daring and sanguinary action," believing that it can be defended as an act of "agressive self-defense" that gave the colony "a new lease on life," justified by the hostility Lane felt the colony had received; he admits, however, that "the surprise attack was, in its own way, a parallel kind of treachery to that with which Lane credited Wingina" (Quinn 1985:128). In other words, inhumane practice was excused by political expediency; the end justified the means. This attitude, described in chapter 2, was inherent in the English ideology and is apparent throughout the history of English colonization. Ironically, within a week of this attack, word was received of the arrival of Sir Francis Drake and his fleet, who were to conduct raids against the Spanish and strengthen the colony (Quinn 1985:133–34). Drake had been away from England for some months, engaged in privateering, and was expecting a considerably larger colony. He and Lane together devised a plan to return the weaker colonists to England and leave skilled men and supplies for the exploration of Chesapeake Bay, but this plan was wrecked by a great storm that lasted three days, damaging many smaller boats and driving away others. Lane decided to abandon the colony, and on 18 June the fleet set sail (Quinn 1985:131–38).

The end of the first colony, which Lane had killed Wingina to avoid, had come to pass, although three colonists who were in the interior were left behind. To compound the irony, within days of the colony's abandonment, the supply ship from Raleigh arrived, looked for the colony, and, not finding them, returned to England (Quinn 1985:140–41). Furthermore, another fleet of six ships intended to expand the colony arrived just a few weeks later, after spending some time privateering. In two weeks of reconnoitering, they captured one Indian who spoke a little English, from whom they learned that the colony had been abandoned. This fleet also returned to England, engaging in further privateering en route (Quinn 1985:142–46) but leaving a party of fifteen men to retain possession. It was later reported by the friendly Croatoan Indians that these men had been attacked by a small party assembled from several tribes, with two Englishmen killed and the remainder unaccounted for — "the first 'Lost Colonists' " (Quinn 1985:150–53).

With most of the original colonists and the supplies intended for their replenishment returned to England, Raleigh was confronted with the decisions of planning another attempt. He seems to have gathered full accounts from Lane, Hariot, and White, and probably from others, including Manteo, who had returned with the colonists. Many of these were written accounts, but few have survived. Raleigh decided to reduce the strong military presence represented by Lane and the many soldiers of the first colony and, apparently, to relocate the settlement to the area at the south of the Chesapeake Bay, where the harbors were deeper, the soils were superior, and the Indians not yet alienated. White was chosen as the governor, and approximately one hundred people — including women and children, for the first time — sailed for America on 8 May 1587, arriving in early July.

Immediately there was a rebellion, led by the Portuguese pilot Simão Fernandes, demanding a landing at Roanoke Island rather than continuing into the Chesapeake. They found the island abandoned, the former settlement razed. Within their first month there, some Indians from the mainland, remnants of Wingina's people, found one of the colonists catching crabs, shot him with sixteen arrows, beat him with clubs, and fled to the mainland. White held a council with the still-friendly Croatoans, then returned to his ships. A few days later he led a night attack on the village of Wingina's people, but they had fled. Instead, several Croatoans — who had come to harvest the crops left behind — were injured and one killed before the mistake was recognized. Manteo, himself a Croatoan, had participated in the attack, as unaware as the English, at first; he seems to have helped settle the grievance, and both parties shared in the spoils of the village, returning together to Roanoke Island. Within the week, Manteo was christened in the Church of England, providing the first instance of the religious conversions for which the English promoters had argued. Five days later Virginia Dare, granddaughter of John White, was delivered, the first English child born in the New World (Quinn 1985:265–86).

A few days later, responding to repeated demands by all of the colonists that were prompted by concerns over their supplies, White agreed to return to England and hurry back with supplies; the colony was apparently to move "fifty miles into the main," presumably to the Chesapeake. After a series of hardships and accidents, he arrived in England in November. Through the winter he and Raleigh prepared the resupply, which was to sail as part of a privateering fleet directed against the Spanish in the western Atlantic. The fleet was ready to leave in late March, but, while waiting for favorable weather, orders came through to cancel the trans-Atlantic voyage in order to join the fleet assembling at Plymouth, a fleet that was to prove most effective against the Armada in July. This left the supply ships without an escort. They sailed anyway, in April, but the captains of the two small ships were more concerned with privateering than with the colony. One of these ships was eventually taken, itself, and pillaged; both returned to England by the end of May, having failed to reach Virginia. Through 1588 and 1589 all ships of any size were employed in the wars against Spain and Portugal, so, although merchants and investors were organized in England, no further attempt to reach Virginia could be made until 1590 (Quinn 1985:289–314).

In March 1590 White sailed with an escort of privateers, including Captain Christopher Newport, who would later figure prominently in the

Jamestown colony. After several months of privateering, battles (including one in which Newport lost an arm), and capturing ships, in mid-August the ships reached the Outer Banks, sighting columns of smoke in the direction of Roanoke Island. They were again beset by storms and sighted several brushfires burning. Arriving at the settlement on Roanoke Island, they found it stripped, having been previously fortified, and the word "CROATOAN" carved into one of the posts, without the cross that had been agreed upon as a sign of distress. Inside the palisade they found bars of iron and lead, four light cannons, shot for a heavier cannon, and other heavy objects. Buried chests had been dug up and broken into, the goods scattered about — including the personal possessions White himself had left behind. The weather again turned foul, costing one ship two anchors. A series of forced decisions found White back in England in late October, having visited neither Croatoan nor the Chesapeakes, a victim of having to rely on captains more interested in taking prizes than in seeking the colonists (Quinn 1985:317–33).

The fate of these colonists will probably never be known; no further English ships would enter this area for at least ten years. Quinn (1985:353–60) examined the slim evidence for voyages through 1605, concluding that some word of the survival of the colony had reached England by that time, but there appears to have been no direct contact. In the early years of the Jamestown colony there were several explorations into the mainland of North Carolina and repeated inquiries made to various Indians; these later colonists apparently concluded that there were few surviving descendants, and little effort was made to contact them. Several contemporary authorities assert that Powhatan admitted to having killed the survivors shortly before the arrival of the Jamestown colonists — perhaps even on the day of their arrival — but modern scholars differ over where this took place. Quinn (1985:344–53) argues that the colonists were near the Chesapeake, which Powhatan conquered shortly before the arrival of the English in 1607, and where smoke from great fires was seen as they arrived (Quinn 1985:362–63). Rountree believes that "if any such attack occurred, it was on the Carolina mainland" (1990:21–22), suggesting that Powhatan was not involved; Fausz (1985:241) also feels that Powhatan was wrongly accused.

Given the small size of the colony and the documented survival rate for the later colony at Jamestown, the question is most likely of little consequence: there were probably very few survivors by 1607, and those few would have had little effect on the culture of even their neighboring Indians, much less on more removed groups. Even Quinn, who seems to expect the English culture to have been tenacious and somewhat pervasive even in this situation, notes that "After twenty years, however, their Englishness would be wearing thin, and they would be approaching virtual assimilation" (1985:353). The real effects on the Indians would have been most evident in the spread of disease — noted by Hariot as early as 1588 — and in knowledge of the behavior of the English, with aspects of both good and bad, strengths and weaknesses. For the Powhatans, this knowledge would have been added to their observations of the Spanish in the 1570s and before. The experience seems to have taught the English valuable lessons on the need for regular resupply and on the best-suited size and form for the colony; it also certainly contributed to the English predisposition to see Indians as treacherous, and suggests the English potential (at the least) for opposition to the Indians' very existence.

4 ✦ The Birth of Virginia in Tsenacommacah

When the two races first met on the eastern coast of America, there was unlimited potential for harmony. The newcomers could have adapted to the hosts' customs and values or at least understood and respected them. The discovery could have been the start of a new and better age. But this did not happen. The vast differences in basic beliefs and values of the two groups continually proved that they could not live together in peace. — George Horse Capture, "An American Indian Perspective"

THE NUMBER OF ENGLISH voyages to Virginia between 1590 and 1607 may never be known, and very few details have been found, but there is evidence for increased interest in the early years of the seventeenth century. Thomas Hariot seems to have been involved in a voyage of 1602 (Quinn 1974:407–13), and at least two Indians were present in London in 1603, where some demonstrations were performed (Quinn 1974:419–31), although these may have been voyages to and Indians from further north, around present-day New York or Massachusetts (Beverley 1947:23–24). The peace treaty signed between Spain and England in 1604 (Quinn 1974:450) provided some measure of stability, but the Spanish were still concerned about any attempted English presence in the New World, as the English remained concerned about Spanish attacks at least into the 1620s. There was another voyage to the New York area in 1605, and the possibility of the survival of the Roanoke Island colony had gained sufficient public interest that it was mentioned that year in London in the play *Eastward Hoe* (Chapman et al. 1926); this survival seems to have been one of the justifications for renewed English colonial efforts, for which a charter was granted in April 1606 (Quinn 1974:452). Without further recorded exploratory visits (although Quinn [1974:452–53] suggests these may have taken place), an English colonial force was to sail for Virginia.

At the end of 1606, Captain John Smith was dispatched with three small ships under the command of Captain Christopher Newport to make settlement in Virginia. During the course of the voyage, Smith seems to have crossed Edward Wingfield, one of the gentleman adventurers, who became the first president of the colony after their landing (Barbour 1964:113–14). The accusation was reportedly that "he intended to usurp the government, murder the council, and make himself king; that his confederates were dispersed in all the three ships; and that divers of his confederates that revealed it, would affirm it" (Smith 1986c:207). Smith was arrested and remained under restraint until after landfall in Virginia, when "an oration was made, why Captain Smith was not admitted of the council as the rest" of those appointed by the Virginia Company (Smith 1986c:205). After first exploring the James River,[1] they selected a site on a small peninsula and established the first permanent English settlement in the New World, at Jamestown, in May 1607 (Smith 1986c:205). This was met by two responses from the Powhatans. Immediately on beginning construction of a fort, an English party was sent out on 21 May to explore; this party included Smith (G. Archer 1969:81–95). The party proceeded as far as the falls of the James, visited a number of villages and met several chiefs along the way, including Powhatan's son Parahunt, at the village of Powhatan, and was well-received at every stop. They were able to trade goods, bestow and receive gifts, share meals, and learn some of the language and topography with the help of various individual Powhatans. On 27 May, while at Weyanock on their way home, word was apparently passed to their guide of an attack on Jamestown; he said he would go but little further with them, but would see them at Jamestown three days later. This worried the explorers, who returned home that day, only to find that an attack had occurred the previous day. Reportedly over two hundred men had launched a furious assault on the fort for about an hour but were stopped by small shot from the ship's cannons. Ten colonists were injured and two killed; the number of Powhatans killed and injured was not known, although one was seen being carried off. Two days later, "the savages gave on again, but with more fear, not daring approach scarce within musket shot. They hurt not any of us, but finding one of our dogs they killed him; they shot above forty arrows into and about the fort" (G. Archer 1969:95–96). Just over a week later, of which several days included arrows being shot into the fort or at an individual, two unarmed Indians appeared in the distance, calling that they were friends; they ran off after one of the colonists shot at them. Another week later (14 June), two unarmed Indians again presented themselves and were this time met by Wingfield and Newport. One of the Indians proved to be their guide from the exploration. They told the English that these attacks were by the neighboring groups and that others, closer to Powhatan, would help procure peace for the English (G. Archer 1969:96–98). On 21 June the same messenger was sent by Opechancanough desiring peace, which seems to have been forthcoming (Smith 1986a:33).

After staying five weeks to help establish the colony, the ships left on 22 June to resupply in England, leaving 104 men. A governing council had been established, and as of 10 June Captain Smith had been sworn into it (G. Archer 1969:97), ending his legal restraint, but the council had little effect in controlling the efforts of the adventurers. As Robert Beverley noted in his early history of the colony, the men destroyed the advantages the colony had in trade by competing with each other for the trade with the Powhatans, "by which they not only cut short their own profit, but created jealousies and disturbances among the Indians, by letting one have a better bargain than another; for they being unaccustomed to barter, such of them as had been hardest dealt by in their commodities thought themselves cheated and abused, and so conceived a grudge against the English in general, making it a national quarrel. And this seems to be the original cause of most of their subsequent misfortunes by the Indians" (1947:29–30). As developed in chapter 1, this represents only the English perception of the Powhatans' reactions. They were certainly not "unaccustomed to barter," but rather saw the aggressively dominating form of trade engaged in by the English as improper and unfair. Seen in this sense and not simply as a personal grudge, Beverley's assessment of this difference as one of the roots of the "national quarrel" has some validity.

Smith's relationship with the Powhatans was unique, based on what at first passes for an unusually astute understanding of their culture. Prior to going to Virginia, he had seen military service in Brittany and Transylvania; been captured and sold into slavery there and escaped; traveled extensively through eastern Europe and as far east as Muscovy; and sailed with a French pirate along the West African coast — all by the time he was in his mid-twenties (Barbour 1964:3–73). Barbour (1964:x) described him as "by disposition tolerant of everything but intolerance," lacking the social background and ruthlessness needed for commercial or political success — an assessment that may have overestimated Smith's tolerance and underestimated his ruthlessness. Nevertheless, Smith did repeatedly demonstrate an ability to match wits with the Powhatans in trade, diplomacy, and military affairs in ways that they could appreciate.

In December 1607 Smith was captured by the Powhatans while exploring near the headwaters of the Chickahominy River. His captivity lasted almost a month, and during this time Smith was subjected to a series of rituals, including the well-known incident of his apparent rescue from imminent death by Pocahontas. Four published works by Smith include information on the events of his captivity. The *True Relation* was published in 1608, very shortly after these events occurred (Smith 1986a). It was apparently edited from a letter from Smith and rushed into print; there are many obvious omissions in the text, and the editor moved several passages, in some cases probably changing their intended meanings. The Barbour edition cited here notes these editorial changes, but many of them are not recoverable, since the letter is not known to survive. *A Map of Virginia* (Smith 1986b) and the *Proceedings* (Smith 1986c) were published together in 1612. None of these texts mentions the rescue by Pocahontas, although each provides information on other incidents of Smith's captivity. The fact that no account of the rescue was published prior to his 1624 *Generall Historie* (Smith 1986d) is the principal reason some scholars have questioned the truth of the account, as discussed below. Although in some ways Smith's works are both naive and biased, when used carefully they may be taken as essentially truthful.

When first captured, Smith was brought before Powhatan's war-chief, Opechancanough, whom he impressed with his compass. Nevertheless, a threat to his life was then made — the first of three that would occur during this captivity:

> Much they marvelled at the playing of the fly and needle, which they could see so plainly, and yet not touch it, because of the glass that covered them. But when he[2] demonstrated by that globe-like jewel the roundness of the earth and skies, the sphere of the sun, moon, and stars, and how the sun did chase the night round about the world continually, the greatness of the land and sea, the diversity of nations, variety of complexions, and how we were to them antipodes, and many other such like matters, they all stood as amazed with admiration. Notwithstanding, within an hour after they tied him to a tree, and as many as could stand about him prepared to shoot him, but the king [Opechancanough] holding up the compass in his hand, they all laid down their bows and arrows. (Smith 1986d:147)

Smith was then taken to Rasawek, a hunting town between the Chickahominy and Pamunkey rivers (figure 3), where he was at the center of what seems to have been a ritual dance in three parts:

> Their order in conducting him was thus: drawing themselves all in file, the king in their midst had all their [Smith's and his men's] pieces and swords borne before him. Captain Smith was led after him by three great savages, holding him fast by each arm, and on each side six went in file with their arrows nocked. But arriving at the town (which was but only thirty or forty hunting houses made of mats, which they remove as they please, as we our tents), all the women and children staring to behold him, the soldiers first all in file performed the form of a bisson so well as could be, and on each flank officers as Sergeants to see them keep their order. A good time they continued this exercise, and then cast themselves in a ring, dancing in such several postures, and singing and yelling out such hellish notes and screeches, being strangely painted, every one his quiver of arrows, and at his back a club; on his arm a fox or an otter's skin, or some such matter for his vambrace; their heads and shoulders painted red, with oil and puccoon mingled together, which scarlet-like color made an exceeding handsome show; his bow in his hand; and the skin of a bird with her wings abroad, dried, tied on his head, a piece of copper, a white shell, a long feather, with a small rattle growing at the tails of their snakes tied to it, or some such like toy. All this while Smith and the king stood in their midst guarded, as before is said, and after three dances they all departed. Smith they conducted to a long house, where thirty or forty tall fellows did guard him, and ere long more bread and venison was brought him than would have served twenty men; I think his stomach at that time was not very good; what he left they put in baskets and tied over his head. About midnight they set the meat again before him. All this time not one of them would eat a bit with him, till the next morning they brought him as much more, and then did they eat all the old, and reserved the new as they had done the other, which made him think they would fat him to eat him. (Smith 1986d:147–48)

Smith was being honored here by being given first rights to food. He was kept at Rasawek for several days and there had many conversations with Opechancanough. He also sent a letter to Jamestown to let the colony know that he was well and to keep them from seeking revenge against the Powhatans. The next day an Indian threatened to kill Smith but was

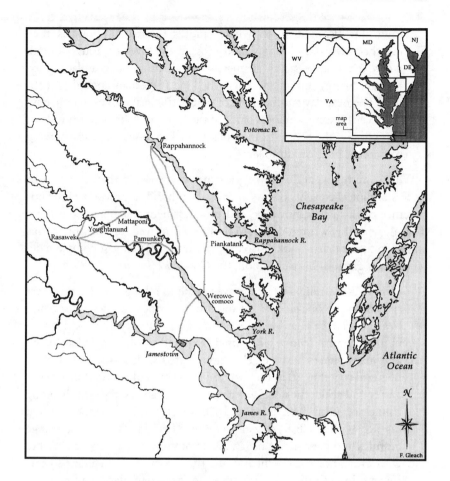

FIGURE 3. Smith's Travels in Captivity

stopped by a guard; Smith was told that this Indian was the father of a man he had killed (Smith 1986a:49). This was the second threat to his life. His peregrinations then began in earnest, and he was to walk well over a hundred miles before he was returned to Jamestown:

> the king [Opechancanough] presently conducted me to another king-dom, upon the top of the next northerly river, called Youghtanund. Having feasted me, he further led me to another branch of the river, called Mattaponi; to two other hunting towns they led me, and to each of these countries, a house of the great emperor of Powhatan. . . . After this four or five days march, we returned to Rasawek, the first

town they brought me to, where binding the mats in bundles, they marched two days journey, and crossed the river of Youghtanund, where it was as broad as Thames, so conducting me to a place called Menapacute in Pamunkey, where the king [Opechancanough] inhabited. The next day another king of that nation, called Kekataugh, having received some kindness of me at the fort, kindly invited me to feast at his house; the people from all places flocked to see me, each showing to content me. (Smith 1986a:49–51)

While Smith was at Pamunkey, a ritual was enacted that is crucial to understanding the events of his captivity. Smith did not recognize the importance of this ritual, however, and its assessment was made even more difficult when his written description of it was moved, presumably by his editor, in Smith's first book (1986a:59, 104 n.141). The most complete description is given in his third book, the *Generall Historie*:

early in a morning a great fire was made in a long house, and a mat spread on the one side, as on the other, on the one they caused him to sit, and all the guard went out of the house. Presently came skipping in a great grim fellow, all painted over with coal, mingled with oil; and many snakes and weasels' skins stuffed with moss, and all their tails tied together, so as they met on the crown of his head in a tassel; and round about the tassel was a coronet of feathers, the skins hanging round about his head, back, and shoulders, and in a manner covered his face; with a hellish voice and a rattle in his hand. With most strange gestures and passions he began his invocation, and environed the fire with a circle of meal. Which done, three more such like devils came rushing in with the like antic tricks, painted half black, half red; but all their eyes were painted white, and some red strokes like mustaches along their cheeks. Round about him those fiends danced a pretty while, and then came in three more as ugly as the rest, with red eyes, and white strokes over their black faces. At last they all sat down right against him, three on the one hand of the chief priest, and three on the other. Then all with their rattles began a song, which ended, the chief priest laid down five wheat corns,[3] then straining his arms and hands with such violence that he sweat, and his veins swelled, he began a short oration. At the conclusion they all gave a short groan, and then laid down three grains more. After that, began their song again, and then another oration, ever laying down so many corns as before, until they had twice encircled the fire. That done, they took a bunch of little sticks prepared for that purpose, continuing still their devotion, and at the end of every song and oration, they laid down a stick between the divisions of corn. Until night, neither he nor they did either eat or drink, and then they feasted merrily, with the best provisions they could make. Three days they used this ceremony, the meaning of which they told him was to know if he intended them well or no. The circle of meal signified their country, the circles of corn the bounds of the sea, and the sticks his country. They imagined the world to be flat and round, like a trencher, and they in the midst. After this they brought him a bag of gunpowder, which they carefully preserved until the next spring, to plant as they did their corn, because they would be acquainted with the nature of that seed. Itoyatan the king's brother invited him to his house, where, with as many platters of bread, fowl, and wild beasts, as did environ him, he bid him welcome. But not any of them would eat a bit with him, but put up all the remainder in baskets. At his return to Opechancanough's, all the king's women and their children flocked about him for their parts, as due by custom, to be merry with such fragments. (Smith 1986d:149–50)

We must question Smith's statement that this was a divination ceremony to determine his intent. According to Smith, the Indians were concerned that he might have been a European captain who had killed the Rappahannock chief a year or two earlier; if this was considered likely, he could have been taken directly to Rappahannock for identification, and if guilty there would have been no question of it. However, he was not taken there until after this ceremony — at which time it was said that the killer had been a large man, which effectively acquitted Smith, who was small.

There are stronger reasons to question this as a divination ritual; this complex and protracted ceremony bears no relation to rites of divination recorded for Native American peoples. In his study of the Naskapi, northern Algonquians of Labrador, Speck (1977:128–73) discussed the distribution and forms of divination, and particularly scapulimancy, throughout the northern hemisphere, finding a variety of bones and other signs being used, but no protracted rituals. In the nearest possible comparison to the Powhatans, the Delawares also used simple mechanical procedures using an object of divinatory power (Newcomb 1956:63). Divination seems to have been performed as needed by shamans or other individuals who needed to know what to expect in a particular situation, such as hunters. The ritual to which Smith was subjected at Pamunkey is not like this. The duration, repetitions, sacrifices, and forms evident here seem more like those of ceremonial creations or renewals of cultural relations, rituals that maintain the world, processes that require the participation of supernatural forces to achieve or maintain significant effects. Although these major ceremonies were more typical at harvesttime, some took place in winter — perhaps most notably the Midwinter Rites of the Iroquois (Speck 1995; E. Tooker 1970). Iroquois Condolence ceremonies, in which a deceased chief is condoled and a new chief installed, would last a full day (see Fenton 1946). The Delaware Big House Ceremony, or *Gamwing*, was a ritual renewal of the world lasting twelve days, although it took place at harvesttime (Speck 1931).

The *Gamwing* may provide the best analogy for understanding this ritual. The Big House itself represented the universe, and representatives of the divisions of mankind sat in their appropriate places on its floor, the earth; carved face images represented the *manitus*. The course followed by participants was the "Good/Beautiful White Path," the "Righteous Path," the proper road of human life, ritually swept clean and followed by the dancers (Speck 1931:22–24). Speck noted the connection between these actions and the reality of the universe: "The symbolism of the harmonized progression of the celestial and terrestrial plane-realms is consistently carried out in thought in every performance and ritual connected with the Big House" (1931:24). Such mimetic processes are typical of rituals constituting reality, where ritually created "maps" can effect change, or maintain the status quo, in the "territory" of the universe (see Bateson 1987:179–84, Gleach 1996b, T. S. Turner n.d.); a reflection of these connections through Native eyes can be seen in Johnston's modern interpretation of the Ojibwa "Pipe of Peace Smoking Ceremony" (1990:134–40).

The ritual to which Smith was subjected lasted "eight, ten, or twelve hours without cease" (Smith 1986b:171) and was repeated three times on successive days, with feasting each evening at the conclusion. The principal action, repeated each day, was the creation of an elaborate diagram. Not simply the presentation of a static map of the Powhatan world, as understood by Smith, this diagram was likely created by a much more complex, active process, like the mimetic processes of the *Gamwing*, where the creation of a "map" has effects in the universe through its use in a ritual context. The intent seems to have been to control the way in which the English (represented by the sticks) entered from beyond, through the boundaries (the grains of corn), into the Powhatan world itself (the cornmeal). Rather than divination, this is better understood as a ritual of redefinition, establishing the forms of the relationship between the colony and the Powhatans.

Given that this all transpired in a language new to Smith, and given his ego- and ethnocentrism, some misunderstanding of such complicated notions is to be expected. This interpretation represents a relatively minor shift from Smith's understanding, which would have been limited by his poor knowledge of the Powhatan language, and restores meaning to what is otherwise an anomalous account. In the Algonquian world, as elsewhere, ceremonial invocations, repetitions, and sacrifices are no more necessary for the explanation of a map than they are for divination — but they are necessary for the kind of creative process suggested here. Although map-making is a mimetic process and divination often has mimetic aspects, neither activity needs or typically employs powerful supernatural forces on a large scale. Complex mimetic processes, sacrifices, tobacco-burning, ritual participant-preparation, feasting in conclusion — all of which are seen here — are elements found in ceremonies involving such supernatural forces. Repetition, in particular, makes things true, brings things into being, and three seems to have been a ritual number for the Powhatans at this time[4]: the priests enter in three groups, first the head priest, then two groups of three; three circles are made around the fire; the ritual is repeated three times, in three days; there are even three threats to Smith's life, among other instances of threes during his captivity.

The details of this ritual demonstrate that the Powhatans were redefining the world to include the English colony. It is significant here that the Powhatan world is represented by cornmeal — processed, culturally modified corn — and the boundaries of the Powhatan world are represented by natural corn. The "raw" kernels of corn are both natural (unprocessed) and cultural (cultivated), bridging these two realms that are often considered to be mutually exclusive; the use of corn to represent the boundaries, and the clustering of those kernels of corn, further suggest that what was being represented by their use was something more than simply "the bounds of the sea." Given the context, it is likely that they represented surrounding groups of non-Powhatan people, possibly including the varieties of spirit-beings that Hallowell (1976a) glossed as "other-than-human persons." The sticks representing the English are completely outside of this system; one is left to wonder whether they were simply natural sticks or were carved into some particular form, although the fact that they were "prepared for that purpose" suggests that they were worked in some way.

Having been brought into the Powhatan world through this ritual,

Smith was then taken to Rappahannock, where he was exonerated of the killing of the chief, and then on to Werowocomoco: "From hence this kind king [Kekataugh] conducted me to a place called Rappahannock, a kingdom upon another river northward. . . . The next night I lodged at a hunting town of the Powhatans, and the next day arrived at Werowocomoco upon the river Pamunkey, where the great king is resident" (Smith 1986a:51–53). Note that there was a change during the stop at Pamunkey: instead of being led by Opechancanough, Powhatan's war-chief, responsible for relations with outsiders, Smith is now being conducted by Kekataugh, a brother of Powhatan, and a *werowance*, but not a war-chief. This further suggests that he was no longer viewed as an outsider. The meeting at Werowocomoco was the first time Smith met Powhatan, although he had been trying to do so for months, and in this first account he described their conversation concerning the reasons for the English presence in Tsenacommacah, and their search for the western sea (1986a:53–55). While at Werowocomoco Smith was rescued by Pocahontas, although there is no published account of this incident until the *Generall Historie*:

> Before a fire upon a seat like a bedstead, [Powhatan] sat covered with a great robe made of raccoon skins, and all the tails hanging by. On either side did sit a young wench of sixteen or eighteen years, and along on each side of the house, two rows of men, and behind them as many women, with all their heads and shoulders painted red; many of their heads bedecked with the white down of birds, but every one with something, and a great chain of white beads about their necks. At his entrance before the king all the people gave a great shout. The queen of Appomattox was appointed to bring him water to wash his hands, and another brought him a bunch of feathers, instead of a towel, to dry them. Having feasted him after their best barbarous manner they could, a long consultation was held, but the conclusion was, two great stones were brought before Powhatan. Then as many as could laid hands on him, dragged him to them, and thereon laid his head, and being ready with their clubs to beat out his brains. Pocahontas, the king's dearest daughter, when no entreaty could prevail, got his head in her arms, and laid her own upon his to save him from death. Whereat the emperor was contented he should live to make him hatchets, and her bells, beads, and copper. (Smith 1986d:150–51)

This is perhaps the most famous incident in the history of Virginia. Pocahontas has frequently been supposed to have instantly fallen in love with

Smith and to have saved his life for that reason — an interpretation that has served as the basis for children's books, historical novels, epic poems, at least one romance novel, and a film from Disney Studios. The debate over whether this incident even happened has raged for over a hundred years; given its articulations with the ritual complex described here, however, it likely happened much as described. Smith has been accused of inventing or at least embellishing the incident, either for reasons of self-glory, as the arguments ran in the mid–nineteenth century (see Barbour 1986b:lxiii–lxiv), or as a conventionalized form of English appropriation of the other (e.g., Hulme 1992:136–73). Although these arguments based in Smith's English cultural tradition are interesting, and the biases proceeding from that culture certainly must be considered, the events described here and the larger ritual context in which they occur can be better understood in terms of the Powhatan culture, without resorting to such arguments. Like the articulation of this incident in the larger ritual context described here, the details Smith reported also support his account; they fit with the Powhatan world-view too well to be made up by an outsider. Washing Smith's hands and drying them with feathers is a cleansing act typical of Algonquian rituals; the formal organization and attire of the Powhatans also supports this view. Pocahontas was acting in an important cultural role as mediator (cf. Kidwell 1992), symbolically saving Smith's life so that he could effectively be reborn into a new world of cultural relationships.

The final episode in this ritual complex took place two days later:

> Powhatan having disguised himself in the most fearfulest manner he could, caused Captain Smith to be brought forth to a great house in the woods, and there upon a mat by the fire to be left alone. Not long after, from behind a mat that divided the house, was made the most doleful noise he ever heard. Then Powhatan, more like a devil than a man, with some two hundred more as black as himself, came unto him and told him now they were friends, and presently he should go to Jamestown, to send him two great guns, and a grindstone, for which he would give him the country of Capahowasick, and forever esteem him as his son Nantaquoud. (Smith 1986d:151)

That this arrangement included not only Smith, but the colony as well, is given more clearly in the *True Relation*: "He desired me to forsake Paspehegh, and to live with him upon his river, a country called Capahowasick. He promised to give me corn, venison, or what I wanted to feed us; hatchets and copper we should make him, and none would disturb us" (Smith

1986a:57). The "great house in the woods" in which this took place was most likely a temple; this liminal setting, neither domesticated cultural space, like a village, nor utter wilderness, is the usual setting for such a sacred place. The ritual implications of red, black, and white — colors used throughout each ritual in this series — should be noted, with the Powhatans painted black here; the gifts to be given in return further suggest that this was a continuation of the protracted ritual described. Like the redefinition ritual, this began with Smith being left alone by a fire, and the other participants in the ritual came to him there; the rescue episode inverts this pattern, with Smith being brought to the assembled Powhatans.

A number of scholars have suggested that some part of this series of rituals, most typically his rescue by Pocahontas, may have been an adoption of Smith (e.g., Barbour 1970:23–26). As already mentioned here, beginning in the nineteenth century, others have questioned whether the rescue even happened. Two recent writers have differed on this point. Lemay argues from a critical reading of the original texts that the rescue probably happened as described; as he suggests (1992:72–79), the acceptance of the story by Samuel Purchas, who knew Smith and talked with several Powhatans, including Pocahontas, argues strongly for its veracity. In contrast, Rountree (1990:38–39) believes the rescue never happened, following the nineteenth-century argument that Smith invented the story for his own glory. She then asserts that "the rescue of John Smith by Pocahontas does not bear scrutiny from an anthropological viewpoint, either. We are expected to believe that Powhatan welcomed and feasted a powerful guest whom his astute brother and his most trusted priests had tested and approved, and then suddenly, after 'a long consultation,' he tried to have that guest's brains clubbed out on an altar stone — a quick death normally meted out to disobedient subjects, not to captured foreigners. . . . This scenario simply does not ring true" (Rountree 1990:39). Rountree is certainly right in questioning the literal nature of the rescue, but her dismissal of it "from an anthropological viewpoint" is mistaken; lacking a larger framework as developed here, she dismisses the entire event as ritual. After describing the successive gathering with Powhatan and his men painted black, she writes:

> This incident, along with the "rescue," has been taken by some historians to be a formal adoption procedure. The incident by itself (conference, decision, announcement) may have been something of the sort, since it approximates descriptions of adoption procedures in

other Indian groups (e.g., Iroquois), and Powhatan is known to have placed his real sons in ruling positions and expected them to send him tribute. However, Smith did not write of the "rescue" itself as though it were part of a ritual, and no identical sequence of events is recorded as an adoption procedure for any other native American group. (Rountree 1990:39)

Rountree does not explain why she trusts Smith to recognize a ritual from a foreign culture when she does not trust his account of the rescue. Furthermore, Smith's interpretations of meanings and reasons are far more likely to be wrong than the simple facts he chose to record. Any observer — or even participant — can misunderstand or only partly understand the meanings of and reasons for an event; this is particularly true of ritual events and is even more likely if the observer is unfamiliar with the culture in which the event is embedded. But if Smith, or any other observer from another culture, completely fabricated an incident, we would not expect it to fit with other observations from the culture being described. Smith consistently misunderstood things that happened to him in his interactions with the Powhatans, but it is still possible to reconstruct some of those meanings from the detailed accounts he published. It is worth remembering, as Sahlins (1995:42) notes in defense of a different set of colonial European records, that the truth of an idea depends not on the character of its proponent but on the substance of the idea itself, and that one cannot assume "that an author who may be suspected of lying on grounds of interest or ideology therefore *is* lying." Insofar as Smith's accounts are not contradicted, and make sense *within the context in which they are based* — as demonstrated here — they can be accepted.

Different Algonquian and other eastern cultures included a variety of ceremonies for adoption, although none is known to match this in elaboration. The only recorded ceremonies are for the adoption of individuals, however, and I would argue that this ritual was part of something much larger. Flannery (1939:127–28) provides references for the adoption of prisoners in several eastern cultures; although she writes that the practice is "unrecorded for the Virginia-Maryland region," she also provides another example recorded from the Powhatans by Smith. The threat of death by clubbing may seem excessive for a ritual of adoption, but structurally it is precisely what one might expect: a symbolic ending of one existence and the beginning of a new one. In this sense, the threat of death was intended to be perceived as real; the end of the prior state must be marked, dramatically and finally.[5]

The rescue and the final ritual with Powhatan must be considered together, and together with the protracted redefinition ritual and the procession through Tsenacommacah that preceded them, as a rite of passage "adopting" the English colony. The structure of this ritual complex follows the classic pattern of rites of passage (van Gennep 1960). Separation is marked by Smith's capture; the liminal phase includes the procession and redefinition ritual and ended with the rescue; the final ritual in the temple marked his incorporation. Liminality is obviously emphasized here; the point of the ritual complex is the redefinition of the English colony as part of Tsenacommacah — the transition from English outsider to Anglo-Powhatan. The elaboration of different phases in rites of passage, and indeed the possibility that one or more phases of a rite of passage could themselves be structured as rites of passage, was recognized by van Gennep (1960:11) in his original description. Victor Turner (1967, 1969, 1977) has further examined the liminal phase, emphasizing its "relatively unstructured, undefined, potential (rather than complete or realized) qualities" (T. S. Turner 1977:54). Turner referred to this structure of potentiality in ritual as "anti-structure" (V. Turner 1969), although that term suggests a binary opposition to the structure of the everyday that need not pertain. The structure of ritual, including that of the liminal phase, can be better seen as another expression of the structure of the everyday, with rituals of the liminal phase manipulating potentials within that overarching structure (see T. Turner 1977), often employing the kind of mimetic processes noted above. The structural relationships between this ritual complex and the cultural relations it engendered are obvious and clearly involve the boundaries of the Powhatan world and Smith's transition across those boundaries.

Further support for this interpretation of the Powhatan understanding of the arrangement made here comes from Pocahontas herself. Years later, while visiting England with her husband, John Rolfe, she had an opportunity to meet with Smith. After a period of silence, in which she seemed angry at Smith, she said to him, "You did promise Powhatan what was yours should be his, and he the like to you; you called him father being in his land a stranger, and by the same reason so must I do you" (Smith 1986d:261). Smith interjected that he could not permit this because she was "a king's daughter" and he was only a commoner — which seems to have further irritated her. She replied, "Were you not afraid to come into my father's country? — and caused fear in him and all his people (but me)? — and fear you here I should call you father? — I tell you then I will, and you shall call me child, and so I will be for ever and ever your countryman"

(Smith 1986d:261). After almost ten years, Pocahontas recalled the terms of this arrangement that Smith never understood. Through this ritual process, he and the English colony had become fellow countrymen of the Powhatans, with all due responsibilities.

This perspective elucidates the events of Smith's captivity. The ritual complex apparently began with the very act of capturing Captain John Smith. He was captured by a large party, variously reported as two to three hundred bowmen, led by the Powhatan war-chief Opechancanough. They may have been on a collective deer hunt, as Barbour suggests (Smith 1986d:147n), but there is a sense of purposefulness in the actions of the capturing party, which comes through even in Smith's accounts of his capture, that suggests that his capture was more than incidental (Smith 1986a:45–47, 1986c:213, 1986d:146–147). He was immediately taken before Opechancanough, whose duties as war-chief would include dealing with outsiders, and his life was threatened — the first of three times during this captivity. He was then taken to the seasonal village of Rasawek and treated as a captive chief; the three dances at Rasawek were centered on Smith and Opechancanough, and after the dances Smith was feasted. He was kept there close to a week, during which time his life was threatened a second time.

A few days after this second threat, the next phase of his captivity began: a physical transition from the margins of Tsenacommacah to its heart, the village of Powhatan, and a metaphysical transformation from English to Anglo-Powhatan. Smith was first taken to a series of smaller, peripheral villages, returned to Rasawek, and then taken to Menapacute, one of the main villages of Pamunkey. The redefinition ritual took place while he was there, creating a place for the English in the Powhatan world. Having done this, the Powhatans returned Smith to the periphery of Tsenacommacah by taking him to Rappahannock, and from this outside position he was then brought to Werowocomoco, Powhatan's principal residence at this time. With Smith's old life ended, Pocahontas spared him from death, allowing him to begin his new life as a Powhatan, and two days later the ritual was completed, giving Smith and the colony a specific place in Tsenacommacah.

Powhatan's intention at the end is clearly to have the English settle within his territory, as his subordinates. In exchange for their furnishing Powhatan with the goods he desired, the English would be permitted to remain, with Smith as their chief, safe in their own territory within Tsenacommacah. The move from Jamestown was not made, however, nor were the "two great guns, and a grindstone" given over. This would not necessarily have negated the terms created through this ritual complex, but tensions would have been increased by the lack of completion, and the Powhatans could be expected to apply pressure of various sorts to induce the colony to meet their obligations, even if in another form.

Whereas the Powhatans adopted the English into Tsenacommacah in good faith, Smith and the colony never recognized what had transpired in this ritual complex. Smith was returned to the colony but continued to travel in explorations through Powhatan territory. Although it would be contested through much of the rest of the seventeenth century, Virginia had come into being as a colony.

Imagine all that to be England where Englishmen, where English people, you with them, and they with you, do dwell. (And it be the people that makes the land English, not the land the people.) So you may find England, and a happy England too, where now is, as I may say, no land, and the bounds of this land of England, by removing of yourselves and others the people of this land, to be speedily and wonderfully removed, enlarged, and extended into those parts of the world where once the name of England was not heard of and whereon the foot of an Englishman till of late had not trodden.
— Richard Eburne, *A Plain Pathway to Plantations*

THE FIRST FIFTEEN YEARS of the colony would see continuous turmoil in its concerns, both in Virginia and in England. Leadership in the colony changed repeatedly, particularly in the earlier years, and there were continued problems of supply and a high mortality rate. Relations with the Powhatans were constantly being reassessed as English demands of food, land, and trade goods continued to conflict with their goal of converting and civilizing the Powhatans. The leadership of the Powhatans also changed during this period, as Powhatan stepped down as chief in favor of his brothers.

These leadership changes make useful markers for the division of time in this period, because the nature of the relationship between these peoples seems to have been closely tied to the individual personalities involved; and because the major leaders of this period — Captain John Smith and Powhatan in particular — are so well known, there is popular recognition of such divisions, as well. With considerable scholarship already devoted to the complexities of this period, I do not attempt to detail the entire history but rather focus on the same issues emphasized in previous chapters in order to develop the argument of opposing understandings of the relationship by the Powhatans and the English.

CAPTAIN JOHN SMITH IN VIRGINIA, 1608–9

Captain Christopher Newport and his two ships constituted the first supply from England, arriving the same day Smith was returned to Jamestown. Smith had described Newport during his meeting with Powhatan as his "father" (Smith 1986a:55), the "king of all the waters" (1986a:57): "The president and the rest of the council they knew not, but Captain Newport's greatness I had so described, as they conceived him the chief, and the rest his children, officers, and servants" (1986a:63). As suggested in chapter 1, this was likely perceived by the Powhatans as an institution of dual leadership, like their own; in this case, with Newport as the peace-chief and Smith as the war-chief. Once the English had been brought into Tsenacommacah through the rituals of Smith's captivity, it would be appropriate for Powhatan and Newport to meet, and after Newport had sent the presents he brought for Powhatan, Powhatan expressed a desire to do so. Smith then escorted Newport and a company of men to Werowocomoco to meet Powhatan. Smith went ahead, at which Powhatan asked, "Your kind visitation does much content me, but where is your father, whom I much desire to see; is he not with you?" (Smith 1986a:65). Smith assured Powhatan that he was following and would be there the next day.

When Newport went ashore the next day, Powhatan seems to have been pleased to meet him. They all feasted for several days, and an English boy named Thomas Savage was sent to stay with Powhatan in exchange for Powhatan's servant Namontack. After considerable trading, feasting, and giving of gifts, the English eventually were taken to Pamunkey to meet Opechancanough, Itoyatan, and Kekataugh (Smith 1986a:69–79). While they were trading at Werowocomoco, an exchange took place between Powhatan, Newport, and Smith[1] that reveals something of each man's character. It began with Powhatan addressing Newport:

> 'Captain Newport, it is not agreeable to my greatness, in this peddling manner to trade for trifles, and I esteem you also a great *werowance*. Therefore lay me down all your commodities together; what I like, I will take, and in recompence give you what I think fitting their value.'
>
> Captain Smith being our interpreter, regarding Newport as his father, knowing best the disposition of Powhatan, told us his intent was but only to cheat us; yet Captain Newport thinking to out-brave this savage in ostentation of greatness, and so to bewitch him with his bounty, as to have what he listed, it so happened, that Powhatan having his desire valued his corn at such a rate that I think it better cheap

in Spain, for we had not four bushels for that we expected twenty hogsheads. This bred some unkindness between our two Captains, Newport seeking to please the unsatiable desire of the savage, Smith, to cause the savage to please him; but smothering his distaste to avoid the savage's suspicion, glanced in the eyes of Powhatan many trifles, who fixed his humor upon a few blue beads. A long time he importunately desired them, but Smith seemed so much the more to affect them, as being composed of a most rare substance of the color of the skies, and not to be worn but by the greatest kings in the world. This made him half mad to be the owner of such strange jewels, so that ere we departed, for a pound or two of blue beads he brought over my king for 2 or 300 bushels of corn, yet parted good friends. (Smith 1986d:156)

Each man was trying to get what he considered to be a fair trade, but had different ideas of what that meant and of how to go about getting it. It is reasonable to assume that Newport, not having to stay in the colony, wanted to please Powhatan to keep him friendly. For his part, Smith sought to get the most he could, knowing how the colony depended on trade with the Powhatans for their survival. And Powhatan sought goods worthy of his position, giving liberally in return for things he wanted–even if that desire was kindled by Smith.

The Jamestown settlement burned about the time Smith and Newport's party returned, with the loss of much of the colony's provisions. This made trade even more important for the colony, whose situation was compounded by one of the ships that remained in the colony, resulting in additional people to be fed, and that engaged in private trade that undercut the official trade of the colony. Indeed, the ship remained fourteen weeks, well into March 1608, before leaving. It was also at this time that some in the colony were consumed with gold-fever, which Smith also opposed. Newport returned to England in the spring; Smith was busy first with rebuilding the fort and maintaining trade with the Powhatans and then with exploring the Chesapeake Bay, going as far as what is now Maryland, trading and battling different groups along the way (Smith 1986d:157–80).

Following this, and after the short and troubled terms of two gentleman-presidents, Captain John Smith was elected to the council presidency in September 1608. By his own account, his actions saved the colony, and there are accounts that support that assessment. His account also has been validated by history; the early colonial historian Robert Beverley described this period in terms that most would still agree with, noting that "Smith was the only man among them that could manage the discoveries with success, and he was the only man, too, that could keep the settlement in order" (1947:31). The Jamestown colonists did, however, harvest their first crop of corn of their own planting that year, having barely survived the first winter on provisions supplied by the Indians. Of the 104 men left in June 1607, only 38 had survived the winter, 46 having died before the end of September 1607 (Earle 1979:97). In September 1608, when Smith was elected president, there were only perhaps 130 colonists alive, despite the arrival between January and September of 100 to 120 new immigrants (Earle 1979:106). This severe mortality rate was typical of the early years at Jamestown, due to disease propagation largely resulting from lack of fresh water flow and poor waste disposal (Earle 1979).

In October 1608, Powhatan again demonstrated that he saw himself as the superior in this relationship between natives and colonists. Captain Newport had arrived with the second supply from England in September, and King James had sent with him presents for Powhatan, with instructions that Powhatan should receive a crown — and granting Newport the authority to overrule Smith if necessary. Smith seems here genuinely concerned with the interests of the colony and not only with his own; he accused Newport of misleading the company and council to obtain a private commission, seeking gold or a passage to the western sea, and of devising the coronation, which Smith considered a mistake (Smith 1986d:181). Their differences came to a head in the council, when Smith argued that the supplies were inadequate for the colony, much less for Newport's voyage, but he was outvoted (1986d:182). Nevertheless, Smith agreed to convey Newport's message to Powhatan,[2]

> Whereunto the subtle savage thus replied:
>   If your king have sent me presents, I also am a king, and this [is] my land. Eight days I will stay to receive them. Your father is to come to me, not I to him; nor yet to your fort: neither will I bite at such a bait. (Smith 1986c:236)

The presents were taken to Powhatan, "but a foul trouble there was to make him kneel to receive his crown. He, neither knowing the majesty nor meaning of a crown, nor bending of the knee, endured so many persuasions, examples, and instructions, as tired them all. At last, by leaning hard on his shoulders, he a little stooped, and Newport put the crown on his head" (Smith 1986c:237). Powhatan clearly knew the significance of being given a crown and of kneeling to receive it, and he was not going along with it. Only by force was he placed in the subordinate position by the English, a metaphorical repetition of their general relationship that the English apparently did not recognize.

Newport's voyage was a failure, recovering only false ore, getting no help from the Monacans in finding the Lost Colonists or a route to the west, and unable to either trade for or steal any quantity of corn. Immediately following the return of this party, Smith increased discipline and set everyone to work; he describes the capacity of the harder working colonists — even the oft-maligned gentlemen — to perform even heavy labor without being forced or impressed, but simply from the pleasure of doing a job properly, acting from a sense of moral rightness grounded not in the individual but in the community (Smith 1986c:238–39). He continued, however, to note how exceptional this community spirit was in the colony, with most of the men engaging in their own private trade with either the Indians or with the English sailors — using supplies that belonged to the company, while still drawing their shares of food and drink, and pay. One sailer was recorded to have taken £30 worth of furs back to England while the colony had not managed to obtain any (Smith 1986c:239–40). In the early years of the colony, most property was held communally, and so this private trade was doubly troublesome for the colony: it meant both the loss of needed goods and the loss of the controlled-market trade that Smith and the other officials could have otherwise waged with the Powhatans. For the good of the colony, Smith was determined to reduce such activities.

The winter of 1608, with Smith as leader, saw a dramatic improvement in survival rates, with no more than 21 of the 130 colonists dying between October 1608 and the summer of 1609, including 11 by drowning. This improvement seems to be largely attributable to the efforts of Captain John Smith, who, having observed the seasonal movements and subsistence patterns of the Powhatans, applied what he had learned. Apparently recognizing that Jamestown was an unhealthy site, particularly in spring and summer, he dispersed the colonists into the countryside. In August 1609 supply ships from a nine-ship flotilla began to arrive in Jamestown, but the ship carrying the three new joint governors (Sir Thomas Gates, Sir George Summers, and Captain Newport) was wrecked in the Bermudas, in the storm immortalized by Shakespeare in *The Tempest*. The passengers and crew survived but were unable to reach Virginia for some time. The arrival of these supply ships brought another 185 to 270 colonists, with a new charter. Despite the absence of the three governors, and partly due to burns received from an accidental gunpowder explosion, Smith was removed from power and returned to England in October 1609 (Beverley 1947:33–34; Smith 1986c:272–73).

By the end of his time in Virginia, Smith may have become taken with his own successes (and bravado); he certainly seems to have used every opportunity to demonstrate his personal dominance of the Indians and of the colony. He wrote (Smith 1986c:273) that his actions were motivated by a concern for the benefit of the colony, not for his personal benefit, but not everyone believed this. Percy wrote of his "being an ambitious, unworthy and vainglorious fellow attempting to take all men's authorities from them" and "rule all and engross all authority into his own hands" (1922:264). Smith also failed to consider Powhatan's carefully constructed place for the colony in his plans. In early 1609, as part of his plan to disperse the colony, Smith had a settlement founded at the falls of the James, very near Powhatan's home village. Although such dispersal, and particularly removal from Jamestown, was good for the physical health of the colonists, it directly opposed Powhatan's expressed desire to have all of the English living in one area within his territory, the arrangement made at the end of Smith's captivity. By mid-1609, even before Smith's departure, the Powhatans were attacking the English wherever they found them in small groups (Percy 1922:262–69).

Smith's departure constituted a loss for the colony and removed their principal liaison with Powhatan. It also appreciably weakened our knowledge of the following period; despite the controversy over parts of Smith's accounts, they remain among our principal sources for the early years of the colony. He wrote about the later period in his *Generall Historie*, but those accounts, written from the descriptions of others, lack the force and authority of firsthand experience. Smith perhaps exaggerated his own importance, and inflated accounts of "his conquests of war and love," but "the important thing is the evidence substantiating, in the main, both the *Historie* and his claim to have rendered significant services to the colony" (Craven 1970:72–73). These contributions to the colony were many, not the least being the sharply lowered mortality rate he achieved by emulating the native cyclic population movements for harvesting food resources. His successes in securing from the Powhatans the food that the colony so badly needed and in negotiating directly with Powhatan were also crucial. Despite the paucity of supplies sent from England, with Smith's leadership the colony had survived; "But as soon as he had left them to themselves, all went to ruin; for the Indians had no longer any fear for themselves, or friendship for the English" (Beverley 1947:35–36). In fact, Smith was partly responsible for the ruin, as he had never recognized his and the colony's obligations to Powhatan; but none of the colonists ever did, and Smith had, at least, been able to engage Powhatan, maintain friendly relations, and prevent serious repercussions for the colony's lack of upholding its obligations.

POWHATAN AGGRESSION AND ENGLISH EXPANSION, 1609–17

The winter following Smith's return to England, the winter of 1609–10, was the infamous "Starving Time," which only 100 out of the 220 remaining colonists survived (see Earle 1979:106–8). Starvation was not necessarily the primary cause of death, however. Earle (1979) has described the effects of a variety of diseases, including typhoid, dysentery, and salt poisoning, and their contributions to the high mortality rate of the Virginia colony. The Powhatans also continued to prey upon the colonists, particularly when they left their settlements seeking food.

Fausz (1977:267–91) has described the first half of this period as "the First Anglo-Powhatan War (1609–1613)" because of the protracted violent encounters, asserting that it began because Powhatan had decided that there was not sufficient profit in trading with the English to warrant the difficulties they caused, and that they should simply be exterminated: "The probationary period in Anglo-Powhatan relations was over; the Indians' revenge against the English had begun in earnest" (Fausz 1977:253–54). If the actions of this period are to be considered war, it is not in these terms, which represent only an English understanding of Powhatan motivations — and even the term "war" seems too strong to be applied here. This period was marked by regular but sporadic violence in which neither side recognized the terms under which the other was fighting; the actions of each were interpreted in the frameworks of the other. Powhatan's motivations must be considered in light of his own culture, not of English perceptions. The goal was not to "exterminate" the colony; a message recorded from Powhatan himself makes this clear. In July 1610 Lord De La Warr, freshly arrived as the new governor of the colony, sent messengers to Powhatan to demand that he return any Englishmen held captive, and the arms and goods he reportedly had. "Unto all which Powhatan returned no other answer, but that either we should depart his country, or confine ourselves to Jamestown only, without searching further up into his land or rivers, or otherwise he would give in command to his people to kill us, and do unto us all the mischief which they at their pleasure could, and we feared" (Strachey 1906:65). The colonists clearly knew at this time, as did Powhatan, that if he had sought to exterminate the colony, he easily could have done so. The inability of the colonists to feed themselves would have been a potent weapon for the Powhatans. That the English were aware of this weakness is evident from part of the 1609 instructions to the governor, which noted that "if they may destroy but one harvest or burn your towns in the night they will leave you naked and exposed to famine and cold" (Virginia Council 1933a:18). To avoid that possibility, the colony was instructed to "keep good watches" on their settlements, fields, and cattle. But no such attack was made; Powhatan did not attempt to exterminate the colony. He wished the English either to keep to the territory he had allowed them (although apparently this had already shifted from Capahowasick to Jamestown) or to leave; violence would be used in response to violation, as corrective punishment. The English, apparently reneging on an agreement entered into by Smith and Powhatan, had to be brought into compliance. Any "probationary period" was only in terms of this agreement.

During this period, any small group of colonists leaving the settlement in search of food risked being killed. Many tried to flee to the Indians, "but they were served according to their deserts, for not any of them were heard of after" (Percy 1922:265). One party that went out was found "slain, with their mouths stopped full of bread, being done, as it seems, in contempt and scorn, that others might expect the like when they should come to seek for bread and relief amongst them" (Percy 1922:265). This again reflects the violent application of irony so typical of Algonquian warfare. The intention was to humiliate the English into appreciating their position of dependency on the Powhatans. Instead, such actions simply reaffirmed their perception of the Indians as barbarous.

When Lord De La Warr arrived in June 1610, he met the remaining colonists in the process of abandoning the colony. When he left for England in March 1611 — due to illness — he left the colony under the guidance of Captain George Percy, one of the surviving original colonists, himself in poor health. At the same time, the Virginia Council in London was meeting to decide if the colony was worth further expenditures. Despite the numbers of men and ships and the amounts of supplies and money expended, there had been virtually no return for the company. Sir Thomas Gates persuaded them to continue, and Sir Thomas Dale was dispatched with three hundred men, the title of High Marshall, and the *Lawes Divine, Morall and Martiall* (Strachey 1969), most likely prepared by Dale, Gates, and De La Warr (Flaherty 1969:xxiii–xxiv). As high marshall, it was Dale's responsibility to implement and enforce these laws.

The title of High Marshall and the nature of the laws suggest that the Virginia Company was trying to introduce military discipline in order to save the colony. The title was used in the Elizabethan army, and the company's laws were similar to English military code for troops serving in the Netherlands (Flaherty 1969:xvii, xxv–xxvi). Furthermore, Percy, Gates, De La Warr, and Dale had all served in the military forces in the Netherlands (Flaherty 1969:xviii, xxvi; see Neill 1878:40n on Dale). The selection of this series of leaders with military experience supports the idea that the Virginia Company was trying to institute strict discipline and organization in the colony.

When Dale arrived in Jamestown, in May 1611, he found the colony again falling into disorder, having failed to plant for the spring. He relieved Percy as acting governor and set the colonists to planting and building. Despite — or perhaps because of — the harsh laws imposed, several rebellions took place that summer (Campbell 1860:104; Stith 1865:123). The men who tried to run away to join the Indians rather than work for the colony were severely punished: "divers of his men being idle and not willing to take pains did run away unto the Indians. Many of them, being taken again, Sir Thomas in a most severe manner caused to be executed. Some he appointed to be hanged, some burned, some to be broken upon wheels, others to be staked and some to be shot to death. All these extreme and cruel tortures he used and inflicted upon them to terrify the rest for attempting the like." (Percy 1922:280). As discussed in chapter 2, the necessity of such discipline was questioned by some at the time and has been since, but several of the ranking men in the colony agreed that it was the only way to ensure that enough work was accomplished to keep the colonists alive.

Dale had instructions to found a new settlement near the falls of the James (Land 1938:459), the old settlement begun by Smith near the village of Powhatan having been abandoned. During the summer of 1611 he surveyed up the river seeking good locations and made plans for settlement (Dale 1975). Arriving in August with an additional 300 men, Sir Thomas Gates relieved him of the responsibilities of being governor. In early September he sailed upriver with 350 men and began construction of the settlement of Henrico, suffering several attacks from the Powhatans led by the war-chief Nemattanew,[3] "commonly called amongst us Jack of the feathers, by reason that he used to come into the field all covered over with feathers and swan's wings fastened unto his shoulders as though he meant to fly" (Percy 1922:279–80). The English population at that time totaled 682 men. During the construction of Henrico, which housed about half the population by May 1613, the death rate was probably 50 percent or more, leaving only 305 to 350 men (Earle 1979:111–12).

A letter by the Reverend Alexander Whitaker, who had arrived in the colony with Dale in May (Porter 1979:379), provides an interesting glimpse of this time. In this letter he wrote of an expedition Dale took up the James River to its falls; Powhatan had specifically prohibited this trip, demanding also the return of two Indians who had been taken captive, and threatening that he would make the English drunk and kill them if they disobeyed. Dale did not return the prisoners, and did go to the falls, "where one night our men being att praiers, in the Court of guard a strainge noise was heard comeing out of the Corne towards the trenches of our men, like an Indian *hup hup* wth ann *oho oho*, some say that they saw one like an Indian leape over the fier and runne into the Corne with the same noyse, Att the which all our men were confusedly amazed" (Whitaker 1611:ff 192^{v}). Disoriented and senseless, they began to attack each other but seemed not to know how to work their arms; this state lasted about five minutes when they seemed to wake as from a dream, and while several men were knocked down none were injured, and no Indians were found in the vicinity. This passage reveals Dale's lack of respect for Powhatan's wishes and his lack of concern for the threat posed by the Powhatans. It also provides another example of the Powhatans' approach to war, and of the importance of magical means of attack.[4] Again, Powhatan plainly considered himself superior to the English and demonstrated this in Powhatan cultural terms; just as plainly, the English saw the situation very differently.

At the same time Henrico was being developed,[5] Dale took revenge for "treacherous injury" by seizing an Appomattox Indian village and their corn, killing "some few of those Indians, pretending our hurt," and settled what Hamor described as "our next and most hopeful habitation," the settlement at Bermuda Hundred (Hamor 1615:31). This, like Henrico, was defended by a palisade, two miles long in this case, cut from river to river, securing "some eight miles circuit of ground, the most part champion, and exceeding good corn ground" (Hamor 1615:32). These were the two most important of several such palisaded settlements established in this area along the James River.[6]

These palisades were not primarily to defend against the Indians; by 1611–12 the threat of the Spanish was probably uppermost in Dale's mind.

Shortly after Dale's arrival in 1611, a Spanish caravel sailed into Chesapeake Bay and requested a pilot. The caravel then sailed off with the pilot, leaving behind the three men the English had made prisoner in exchange. These three were Spanish spies, including Diego de Molina (Land 1938:458–59). A series of letters written by Sir John Digby from Madrid reveals the level of Spanish interest in the English colony. He wrote in June 1612 of their displeasure with the English but considered it unlikely that they would take quick action against the colony (Digby 1612a:ff 307^v–8). Five months later he reported a rumor in the court that was interpreted as an intention by the king to remove the colony, and on the next page of the same letter reported news that the Spanish had already destroyed the colony, but he considered these unfounded (1612b:f 223) — a correct assessment, since no such attack seems to have taken place. One of the mutinous incidents Dale had to quell in 1611 involved five colonists who tried to flee to a Spanish settlement they wrongly thought was nearby (Stith 1865:123), in further evidence of the Virginia colonists' considerations of the Spanish. Based on a papal bull, Spain held claim to the entire eastern coast of North America (Land 1938:455). Although the English did not recognize the Pope, they were aware of this claim and knew that the Spanish had colonies on the North American coast. Dale's new settlements were intended to be more easily defended against the Spanish than was Jamestown (figure 4).

Already worried about the Spanish, in the summer of 1613 the Virginia colonists became aware of a new French colony, located near Bar Harbor, in what is now Maine. An English ship commanded by Samuel Argall, blown off course and lost in thick fog, came to shore near the French settlement. They saw a French ship, entered the harbor, and attacked (Jouvency 1896b:227). Argall then captured the settlement and commanded all to return to France. The French suffered various storms and other problems, with some being driven to the Azores and some having their ships swamped during their return. Argall returned to Virginia, where he received orders from Dale to destroy the French settlement; he returned and did so (Jouvency 1896b:229–35). The leaders of the Virginia colony at this time clearly felt that any other European colonial presence on the American coast constituted a threat.

A further purpose for the upriver settlements was to broaden the footing of the colony, reinventing and elaborating the plan Smith had tried implementing in 1608–9. Dale's settlements included a great deal of fertile ground for food production, which had been a weak point since the founding of Jamestown. The population would be dispersed in order to make it

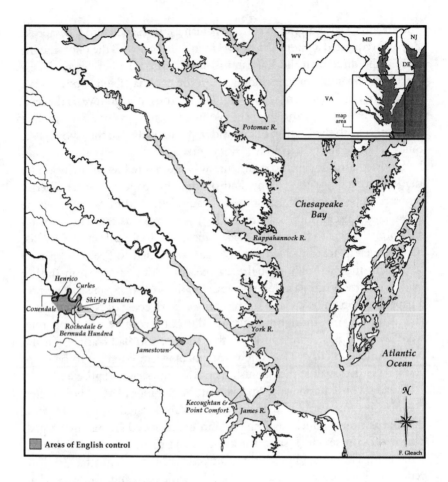

FIGURE 4. English Settlements to 1613

more difficult for the colony to be completely destroyed, particularly by
outside attack such as threatened by the Spanish. Dale (1975:34) also hoped
that a stronger English presence would lead Powhatan to seek greater alliance.

In early April 1613 Pocahontas, the favorite daughter of Powhatan, was
betrayed by the Potomac Indians, with whom the English had established
more or less peaceful relations, and taken captive by the English. Their
hope was to ransom her to Powhatan for the men and goods he had taken.
After three months of consideration he returned seven captives, each with
a damaged musket, and promised that when Pocahontas was returned "he

would make us satisfaction for all injuries done us, and give us five hundred bushels of corn, and for ever be friends with us" (Smith 1986d:244). The English responded that "his daughter should be well used, but we could not believe the rest of our arms were either lost or stolen from him, and therefore till he sent them, we would keep his daughter" (Smith 1986d:244) — an attempt to force Powhatan to behave as the English desired. The colonists refused to negotiate, making inflexible demands of Powhatan and ignoring his efforts to come to a negotiated agreement. Powhatan had agreed to cede an advantage to the English at this point, again offering to allow them to live in peace in Tsenacommacah. But again, the offer was ignored by the English.

A year later, at the beginning of April 1614, Pocahontas married the Englishman John Rolfe, having converted to Christianity while living in the household of Reverend Alexander Whitaker. Two of her brothers and an uncle attended the wedding on behalf of Powhatan (Hamor 1615:55–56; Smith 1986d:245–46). In May 1614, Dale tried to purchase a second of Powhatan's daughters for marriage (Hamor 1615:40–42), an arrangement Powhatan flatly refused, saying

> I desire no firmer assurance of his friendship, than his promise which he has already made unto me. From me, he has a pledge, one of my daughters, which so long as she lives shall be sufficient, when she dies he shall have another child of mine, but she yet lives. I hold it not a brotherly part of your king, to desire to bereave me of two of my children at once. Further give him to understand that if he had no pledge at all he should not need to distrust any injury from me, or any under my subjection; there have been too many of his and my men killed, and by my occasion there shall never be more; I which have the power to perform it, have said it. No, not though I should have just occasion offered, for I am now old, and would gladly end my days in peace, so as if the English offer me injury, my country is large enough, I will remove my self farther from you. (Hamor 1615:42)

This rebuff indicates the nature of the peace obtained at this time. The English saw themselves as victors and saw Christianity as having triumphed over barbarism (Fausz 1977:285–90). In "defeat" the Powhatans had given to the English what they had twice previously offered: the right to exist peacefully within Tsenacommacah. There was perhaps some loss of relative position, and the English were occupying more territory than had been offered, but the Powhatans could still see themselves as at least equals to the English.

The Powhatans were not the only group to make peace with the colony at this time. The Chickahominies, still independent of Powhatan, sought peace with the colony shortly after the wedding of Pocahontas and John Rolfe, in the best-documented negotiation from this period:

> these people hearing of our concluded peace with Powhatan, as the noise thereof was soon bruited abroad, sent two of their men to us, and two fat bucks as a present to our king (for so Sir Thomas Dale is generally reputed and termed among them), and offered themselves and their service to him, alleging that although in former times they had been our enemies, and we theirs, yet they would now if we pleased become not only our trusty friends, but even King James's subjects and tributaries, and relinquish their old name of Chickahominies, and take upon them, as they call us, the name of *tassantasses*, and because they have no principal commander or *werowance* they would entreat Sir Thomas Dale as King James's deputy to be their supreme head, king, and governor, and in all just causes and quarrels to defend them, as they would be ready at all times to aid him; their only desire was to enjoy their own laws and liberties, and because he, by reason of his many other employments, beside the charge he has of his own people, may not always be present among them, to be governed as formerly by eight of the elders and principal men among them, as his substitutes and counsellors, and this was the sum and effect of their embassy. Sir Thomas Dale appointed a day to send some men to their river, to propose certain conditions to them, whereunto if they assented he would gladly accept of their proffered friendship, and be himself their *werowance*; and with this answer, offering them copper for their venison, which they refused to take, dismissed them. (Hamor 1615:11–12)

The Chickahominies first approached the colony with a proposal of terms. The colony implemented most of these terms in a generous manner and agreed to approach the Chickahominies to complete the agreement. These negotiations were clearly between equal sovereign entities and were conducted in a way that fit with both cultural understandings of how such should be conducted, although the symbolism of gift-giving, among other points, had differing meanings. The Chickahominies were seeking to align themselves with the English in order to retain self-government, whereas the English were attempting to guarantee peaceful relations.

When the appointed day came, Sir Thomas Dale himself and Captain Argall with fifty men in a barge and frigate, well appointed lest any treachery might be intended, set forward to Chickahominy, an arm of our river some seven miles from Jamestown, where we found the people according to promise expecting our coming, assembled and met together, who after their best and most friendly manner bade us welcome, and because our business at home would permit us but small time of stay with them, they presently sent for their principal men, some of whom were then absent, who hastened to us, and the next morning very early assembled, and sat in council about this business. Captain Argall (supplying Sir Thomas Dale's place amongst them, who though present there for some respects, concealed himself and kept aboard his barge) after long discourse of their former proceedings, Captain Argall told them that now, since they had entreated peace and promised their love and friendship, he was sent to them from the great *werowance* to conclude the same, all former injuries on both sides, set apart and forgotten, which he would do upon these conditions. (Hamor 1615:12–13)

As with the earlier negotiations between the Powhatans and the colony, where Smith could be seen as the war-chief acting in external relations and Newport as the peace-chief acting in internal affairs, the colony was here represented by an apparent dual leadership, with Argall making the negotiations on behalf of Dale, who was simply "present there for some respects." Unfortunately, we are not told precisely what his actions here were, but their actions in these multiple contexts suggest that the English themselves might have been aware of and acting to meet the Powhatans' and the Chickahominies' understanding of the proper people to perform negotiation.

The English stipulated a series of conditions for the agreement, but these were essentially elaborations of the terms proposed by the Chickahominies. The Chickahominies were to be called Englishmen (*tassantasse*s) and were to be loyal subjects of King James; they would not kill English colonists or cattle and could seek legal recourse for any trespass; they would supply three or four hundred soldiers if needed to fight the Spanish; they would not damage any property, nor enter a settlement without proper announcements; and they would supply to the colony each year two bushels of corn for every adult male Chickahominy as tribute, receiving in return iron hatchets (Hamor 1615:13). These first conditions put relatively minor constraints on the Chickahominies, establishing a relationship of relative equality: they were to be King James's subjects, but so, too, were the colonists. The list of conditions concludes:

> Lastly, the eight chief men which govern as substitutes and counsellors under Sir Thomas Dale, shall at all times see these articles and conditions duly performed, for which they shall receive a red coat or livery from our king yearly, and each of them the picture of his majesty, engraved in copper, with a chain of copper to hang it about his neck, whereby they shall be known to be King James's noblemen; so as if these conditions, or any of them be broken, the offenders themselves shall not only be punished, but also those commanders, because they stand engaged for them. (Hamor 1615:14)

The colors and materials of these gifts seem to have been carefully chosen to appeal to the Algonquian system of symbolism as discussed in chapter 2. The terms and conditions are thus an interesting combination of points suggested by the Chickahominies and others added by the colonial government to appeal to them. The Chickahominies were giving up very little by this agreement, and there seems to have been little if any dissent among them; the provision for them to retain their leadership by the council was particularly well received (Hamor 1615:14). They had never entered into such an arrangement with Powhatan, preferring to keep their independence; presumably he would have insisted on placing a *werowance* over them. By allying with the colony, which was also allied with the Powhatans, they could secure their independence from Powhatan, and they relinquished very little freedom to the English. The Chickahominies could also expect to reap benefits in the form of trade goods. Although the English clearly felt that they were subjugating the Chickahominies, they, like the "defeated" Powhatans, could equally clearly feel that they were in control. As with the Powhatan case, however, this peace would not last more than a few years.

English mortality rates had dropped dramatically in 1613 with the population movement away from Jamestown to the new settlements. When Dale returned to England in 1616 with Pocahontas and John Rolfe, leaving Deputy-Governor George Yeardley in charge, he could be confident that the colony would survive (Earle 1979:113–14). The 1615 harvest had been very poor, and the Powhatans and Chickahominies alike had been forced to buy food from the colony. When Yeardley sent for the corn due from the Chickahominies the next year, he was told that they had allied with

Dale, not him, and the colony responded with military force. Opechancan-ough intervened at this point to assure the English that he had matters in hand and that the Chickahominies were under his control (Rountree 1990:61–62; Smith 1986d:257). This was not the only difficulty of Yeardley's term, and he was soon replaced. He had not seen to the proper maintenance of the colony and had neglected farming for food in favor of tobacco, from which monetary profit was to be made. He also apparently tolerated more free interaction with Indians in the settlements, including allowing them to be armed and employed to hunt for the settlers (Beverley 1947:44–45).

Yeardley's successor was Governor Samuel Argall, one of the leaders who had objected to Smith's dispersal of the colonists in 1609; newly returned from England, he reversed some of Yeardley's policies. He began to realign settlement to Jamestown, which he personally preferred and where the mortality rate again increased (Earle 1979:115). The dispersed settlements were not abandoned, but their populations decreased relative to the pop-ulation at Jamestown. This pattern continued through the dissolution of the Virginia Company in 1624 (Earle 1979:115–20) and probably contrib-uted to the weakness of many of the settlements in the face of the 1622 attack. Argall, however, was replaced as governor in 1618 — by the newly knighted George Yeardley, returned to favor.

The turn to tobacco noted by Beverley above was then a recent phenom-enon. John Rolfe was the first Englishman to breed and grow tobacco in Virginia, in 1612, and by 1617 it already dominated the economy of external trade with England. Although production increased at a prodigious rate, prices quickly began to fall (McCusker and Menard 1985:120–21). Virginia-grown tobacco was considered inferior to Spanish-imported tobaccos, and a series of Royal Proclamations were issued beginning in the early 1620s in an attempt to protect the Virginia planters from Spanish competition (Craven 1964:39; Johnson 1946:12–23). At the same time, the Virginia Company in London repeatedly demanded that the settlers desist from planting tobacco in favor of corn so that they would not be dependent on the Indians for their subsistence (Smith 1986d:327); there were also many in England opposed to the use of tobacco, including King James himself (Craven 1970:139–40).

Pocahontas spent some time in London with Dale and her husband. She was presented to the king and met many others of London society. Meeting with Smith, she reported to him that they had been told he was dead (Smith 1986d:261). Shortly before the time they were to leave England, in early 1617, Pocahontas died (Smith 1986d:262), dissolving the bond of marriage between the two peoples. Her young child Thomas Rolfe stayed there, after becoming sick on the short voyage by ship from Gravesend to Plymouth. His father wrote from Virginia, upon his return: "My wife's death is much lamented, my child much desired, when it is of better strength to endure so hard a passage, whose life greatly extinguishes the sorrow of her loss, saying all must die, but 'tis enough that her child lives" (Rolfe 1933:71). The reactions of Powhatan and Opechancanough were similar: "Powhatan goes from place to place visiting his country, taking his pleasure in good friendship. With us, laments his daughter's death but glad her child is living. So doth Opechancanough. Both want to see him, but desire that he may be stronger before he returns" (Argall 1933b:92). In the spring of 1617, Powhatan "left the government of his kingdom to Opechancanough and his other brother [Itoyatan]" (Argall 1933a:73–74).

A NEW CHIEF IN TSENACOMMACAH, 1617–22

At least as early as 1608, the question of Powhatan's successor as paramount chief seemed to have been settled. Smith wrote: "Powhatan has three brothers, and two sisters; each of his brothers succeed other. For the crown, their heirs inherit not, but the first heirs of the sisters, and so successively the women's heirs" (1986a:59–61). He gave the brothers by name in 1612: "His kingdom descends not to his sons nor children, but first to his brothers, whereof he has three, namely Itoyatan, Opechancanough, and Kekataugh, and after their decease to his sisters. First to the elder sister, then to the rest, and after them to the heirs male and female of the eldest sister, but never to the heirs of the males" (Smith 1986b:174). According to this description of the order of inheritance, the Powhatans reckoned descent through the matriline. The sequence is problematic, however; Itoyatan is given as the first heir, despite the fact that he was apparently younger than Opechancanough. Beverley (1947:45) recorded that Opechancanough was said "by some" to be Itoyatan's elder brother; inference from Strachey (1953:69), where the territory governed by Powhatan's three brothers is named after Opechancanough and he is the first named of the three, supports this statement. Barbour (1986a:xliv) and others have agreed that Opechancanough was older than Itoyatan; Fausz (1977:324), however, described Itoyatan as older.

Beverley (1947:45) tried to explain the change in order by political differences, stating that Opechancanough was "then king of Chickahominy;

but he having debauched them from the allegiance of Powhatan, was disinherited by him." But Beverley's perception of the rift between Powhatan and Opechancanough is mistaken. Although generally allied, the Chickahominies had never been under the authority of Powhatan's paramount chiefdom; Opechancanough had, however, seized control of the Chickahominy village of Ozinies in 1616 and entered into an agreement with the English to live in mutual peace (Smith 1986d:257); this apparently brought the Chickahominies and the Powhatans together, rather than the reverse. Even had this action caused any rift, however, it could not have been a contributing factor in Powhatan's decision, since the designation of Itoyatan as his successor (in 1612) was clearly made prior to this action (in 1616).

Opechancanough was noted as a great and powerful chief by all of the early writers. Beverley summarizes those descriptions: "This Opechancanough was a man of large stature, noble presence, and extraordinary parts. Although he had no advantage of literature (that being nowhere to be found among the Indians), yet he was perfectly skilled in the art of governing his rude countrymen. He caused all the Indians far and near to dread his name, and had them all entirely in subjection" (1947:61). Little is known of Opechancanough's history, but he seems to have been in a position to exercise a certain independence from Powhatan. Seizing control of Chickahominy had demonstrated his power, and by entering into treaty with the English himself he effectively undercut Powhatan's relations with them. Very little is recorded regarding Itoyatan aside from the fact that, like Opechancanough and Powhatan's third brother Kekataugh, he was originally a chief of Pamunkey, one of the districts inherited by Powhatan. Beverley (1947:45) described him simply as "a prince far short of the parts of Opechancanough"; Purchas (1617:957) described him in 1617 as "decrepit and lame," although his source for this statement is unclear; he had never been in Virginia but had interviewed the Powhatans brought to England and others who had been in the colony.

If there were personal differences between Opechancanough and Powhatan, there may also have been structural reasons why Opechancanough was not the first heir to Powhatan, even though he was older than Itoyatan. A number of scholars have noted that they need not have been "brothers" to have been called by the term of address the English would gloss in that way; they could equally well have been "cousins," by the English manner of reckoning (see Feest 1966a:77). Beverley notes "this king [Opechancanough] in Smith's *History* is called brother to Powhatan, but by the Indians he was not so esteemed. For they say he was a prince of a foreign nation, and came to them a great way from the southwest. And by their accounts, we suppose him to have come from the Spanish Indians, somewhere near Mexico, or the mines of St. Barbe" (1947:61). Furthermore, Hamor (1615:13) indicates that Powhatan's father had been driven by the Spanish from the West Indies. Note here that the English term "father" as translated from Powhatan could refer to either father or uncle; particularly since Powhatan had been the heir of his maternal uncle, that relationship would likely be glossed as "father" by the English.

Lewis and Loomie (1953) were the first to suggest the possible relationships between Powhatan, Opechancanough, and Don Luis, the Virginia chief who had been captured by the Spanish, taken to Spain, and then returned to Virginia in the attempt to establish a Jesuit mission in 1571; these possible relationships were elaborated by Feest (1966a:77). It seems most likely that Opechancanough was a parallel cousin of Powhatan's, rather than a brother, and this is why Itoyatan was Powhatan's first successor as paramount chief. Figure 5 shows a likely kinship diagram for these relationships. The identity of the common maternal uncle for Powhatan and Opechancanough represented in figure 5 is speculative, but having Don Luis in that position would help explain both their strong positions and the apparent ease with which they adjusted to the English presence.

Beverley also misunderstood the nature of chiefly authority of the Powhatans, as have historians to this day. Where the English and Euro-American historians have generally seen a single chief, the actual Powhatan structure was most likely dual, with a peace-chief and a war-chief (see chapter 1). Fausz, for instance, recognized that both Opechancanough and Itoyatan had chiefly power, but he still could not reconcile that with the traditional Euro-American notion of a single chief. He cites the greater visibility and activity of Opechancanough and the fact that the English called both him and Itoyatan "great king" to suggest that "by the early 1620s, if not before, Opechancanough was said to have the effective power of government, while [Itoyatan] only the dignity of office" (Fausz 1977:324). This paraphrase of Pory's awkwardly written comparison to the chiefs of Accomac (Smith 1986d:290–91) misses the subtlety of the dual nature of Powhatan chiefdom. When Powhatan gave up his position as paramount chief, Opechancanough did not seize "all the empire to himself" (Beverley 1947:45); Powhatan "left the government of his kingdom to Opechancanough and his other brother [Itoyatan]" (Argall 1933a:73–74). Itoyatan did more than hold "only the dignity of office" (Fausz 1977:324); he was the paramount chief, the head of council. Opechancanough as

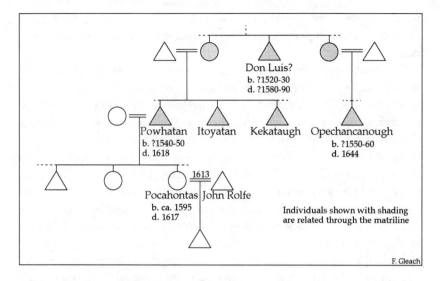

Don Luis?
b. ?1520-30
d. ?1580-90

Powhatan
b. ?1540-50
d. 1618

Itoyatan Kekataugh

Opechancanough
b. ?1550-60
d. 1644

1613

Pocahontas John Rolfe
b. ca. 1595
d. 1617

Individuals shown with shading
are related through the matriline

F. Gleach

FIGURE 5. Hypothetical Kinship Diagram for Powhatan

the war-chief acted in issues of the "outside"—an important councilor. He had presented himself to Thomas Dale, "saying he was a great captain, and did always fight" (Hamor 1615:54). Because he was more visible in interactions with the English, it is understandable that his role as chief is more extensively recorded in the histories than is Itoyatan's. Both clearly served chiefly roles, however, and continued to do so, as even the English were aware (Smith 1986d:265, 308; Virginia Co. 1906b:483; Pierce 1629?:f 69ᵛ).

During this period the English had continued their expansion in Tsenacommacah and their attempts to diversify their economic foundations. As early as 1610, efforts had been made to establish an ironworks in Virginia, where ore had been discovered in the vicinity of Falling Creek (Craven 1970:85). In 1620 a second attempt was made, involving 150 people and considerable expenditure of money. This was an effort to broaden the production of the colony, help achieve self-sufficiency, and provide a variety of products for exchange in England. There were also efforts at shipbuilding and at producing glass beads for the Indian trade (Craven 1970:141). Despite such efforts, the economy remained tied to tobacco production: "Paradoxically, Virginia became a relatively stable, permanent plantation with a secure future only when it began to build upon smoke" (McCusker and Menard 1985:118). The first slaves in Virginia, twenty men and women, were brought in the summer of 1619 at the order of Samuel Argall (Neill 1885:112–16); the importation of slaves in quantity did not begin until mid-century, however.

One final project attempted by the Virginia Company was the foundation of a college for the religious and technical education of native youths (Land 1938). Various individuals, both in the colony and in England, donated land, money, and books to this effort. The conversion of Pocahontas to Christianity in 1613–14 indicated to the English that this was a viable hope and fueled their efforts (Fausz 1977:291–305). The key individual in this activity was George Thorpe, who had taken into his care a Powhatan boy brought back to London by Sir Thomas Dale in 1616. Known as "Georgius Thorpe" or "Homo Virginiae," this boy was educated by Thorpe. The boy was baptized on 10 September 1619, probably because of serious illness; he died seventeen days later (Gethyn-Jones 1982:55–58). George Thorpe arrived in Virginia in 1620 to oversee the college, and he actively proselytized among the Powhatans, trying to win the favor of Opechancanough so that he would allow Indian children to live among the English to be converted. Thorpe was later criticized as being far too kind to the Powhatans; when he received complaints about the fierceness of the settlers' dogs he had some of them killed in the Indians' presence, and he gave many presents to the Powhatans, presenting Opechancanough with "a fair house [built] according to the English fashion, in which he took such joy, especially in his lock and key, which he so admired, as locking and unlocking his door a hundred times a day" (Waterhouse 1933:552). At the time, however, having the Powhatans living among the colonists was seen as an important step towards their conversion, "seeming to open a fair gate for their conversion to Christianity" (Waterhouse 1933:550). Thorpe, a favorite of Governor Yeardley and Gentleman of the King's Privy Council and of His Majesty's Council for Virginia (Gethyn-Jones 1982:173–74, 68–69), has been described as a "culture hero" for the English (Fausz 1979a:116), engaged in work of the utmost spiritual significance. This might have made him impressive to the English — or at least modern historians — but to the Powhatans he was simply another Englishman trying to take their children away.

Council records from 1619 cast further light on both English and Powhatan attitudes towards such projects:

At the same consultation, November 11th, the governor demanded the opinion of the council concerning a project revealed unto him by Nemattanew, an Indian commonly called by the English name of Jack-with-the-Feathers, at Charles Hundred the 25th of October; as from the part of Opechancanough, who by the mouth of the same Indian required from the governor some eight or ten English with their arms to assist him in battle against a people dwelling about a days journey beyond the falls . . . , to be revenged of him for murdering certain women of his, contrary to the law of nations; offering to furnish our people with Indian shoes to march, and to carry their armor for them till they should have occasion to use it; as likewise to share all the booty of male and female children, of corn and other things, and to divide the conquered land into two equal parts between us and them.

This project those of the council embraced, because they found the war to be lawful and well-grounded, the aid required to be very small and not of consequence enough for Opechancanough to put any treacherous disaster upon, this the only way to oblige Opechancanough, who ever since Sir George Yeardley's coming in has stood aloof upon terms of doubt and jealousy and would not be drawn to any treaty at all, notwithstanding all the art and endeavor the governor could use. The children taken in their war might in time serve as well for private uses of particular persons as to furnish the intended college, this being a fair opportunity for the advancement of this blessed work, seeing those Indians are in no sort willing to sell or by fair means to part with their children. Lastly, this course, at least for the present, might win amity and confidence from Itoyatan the great king, from Opechancanough his brother, and likewise from their subjects of these three rivers of Roanoke, Powhatan and Pamunkey. (Virginia Council 1933b:228)

This action seems never to have been undertaken, but the transaction is nevertheless informative. It establishes the fact that Nemattanew served as an intercessor in at least this instance, after leading Powhatan forces against the English at Henrico in 1611, and it discloses English awareness of the dual leadership positions of Itoyatan and Opechancanough. It is plain here that the Powhatans were intent on employing the English for their ends, just as the English sought to take advantage of the Powhatans. The Indians whose conquest Opechancanough has here proposed, however, were one of the piedmont groups, not part of the Powhatan paramount chiefdom. The education of their children would be of no use in the English attempt to convert the Powhatans — they even spoke a completely unrelated language — and would cost the Powhatans nothing; what Opechancanough has offered here is a plan that would gain for them land, goods, and people, while the English took all the risks of war. Perhaps Opechancanough even intended that the English portion of the conquered land be a new home for them, eliminating the problems of having the colonists living in Powhatan territory.

At some time in 1621, Opechancanough took the name Mangopeesomon, and Itoyatan took the name Sasawpen (Virginia Council 1933c:584).[7] This indicates a change in position and probably reflects the beginning of their plans to attack the English (cf. Fausz 1977:349–50). In the summer of 1621 Opechancanough reportedly sought a supply of poison from an Eastern Shore *werowance* to use against the English, but that chief turned him down (Waterhouse 1933:556). Because this was not reported until after the coup, it may represent an attempt by this Eastern Shore *werowance* to revalidate his ties with the English. On the other hand, the Nanticokes of the Eastern Shore were widely and specifically known for their witchcraft and for the production of a very powerful poison (Heckewelder 1876:92; Zeisberger 1910:126), and other Eastern Shore groups may have shared the same reputation.[8] The same *werowance* had warned of a plot by Opechancanough "to set upon every plantation of the colony" following "the taking up of Powhatan's bones," presumably a reburial ceremony (Virginia Council 1935a:10); watches were reportedly kept in the colony, while Opechancanough denied the allegations. No evidence of such a plot was found (Virginia Council 1935a:10). There was also a sudden change, in late 1621, in Opechancanough's stated attitude towards Thorpe and the prospect of Powhatan children going to live among the English:

> Opechancanough gave him very good hope of their entertaining of some of our families to live amongst them, and of their sending [children] to cohabit with us. . . . Captain Thorpe found by discoursing with him that he had more motions of religion in him than could be imagined in so great blindness, for he willingly acknowledged that theirs was not the right way, desiring to be instructed in ours, and confessed that God loved us better than them, and that he thought the cause of his anger against them was their custom of making their children black boys [referring to the *huskanaw*]. (Virginia Council 1933c:584)

Waterhouse notes the same confession by Opechancanough: "that our God was a good God, and much better than theirs, in that he had with so many good things above them endowed us" (1933:552). This statement can be read in three ways in light of the attack that soon followed: Opechancanough was sincerely won over to the English faith, but then rejected his new faith to kill the colonists; he was lying, in an attempt to allay English suspicions; or he was expressing his acceptance of the English god without repudiating his traditional beliefs. The last seems most likely, since this was common among native groups, and the first two possibilities are oversimplistic. Seeing the superiority of English material goods as evidence of the potency of their god might well have prompted Opechancanough to search for the cause of this god's anger towards his people, without causing him to change completely his understanding of the organization of the universe.

The plan for a college died with Thorpe in the coup, but this religious effort was much more than the superficial "missionary racket" that Jennings (1975:53–56) asserts was designed to encourage the "gullible English faithful" to make donations to the Virginia Company. Although the encouragement of donations may have been an effect of the plans for the college — and perhaps the intention of some individuals — others were acting from a deep faith, in a program they felt was truly beneficent. They were seeking to destroy the native culture, but that cynical view does not properly describe their motivation, and to understand English policy in Virginia it is essential to recognize the religious as well as the economic aspects.

> Wild as they are, accept them, so were we;
> To make them civil, will our honor be.
> And if good works be the effects of minds
> That like good Angels be, let our designs
> As we are Angli, make us Angels too;
> No better work can Church or statesman do.
> (Strachey 1953:6)

6 ✦ "The Great Massacre of 1622"

When Sol exalted, surmounts the Ram with his hot rays: Mars if need urges, esteems phlebotomy as wholesome. And are not medicines, if they be skillfully applied, dangerous as they prove, when they be willfully taken?— Daniel Browne, *A New Almanacke and Prognostication*

I N E A R L Y 1622 T H E great warrior Nemattanew was killed by the English.[1] According to the historical accounts, he went to the private settlement of an Englishman named Morgan and persuaded him to go to Pamunkey to exchange some goods he had that Nemattanew wanted. This Morgan was never again heard from. Within a few days, Nemattanew returned to Morgan's house, where he met two young men, servants, who asked after Morgan. Nemattanew was wearing Morgan's cap, which the boys recognized, and he told them Morgan was dead. The two tried to take Nemattanew to the authorities: "But he refused to go, and very insolently abused them. Whereupon they shot him down, and as they were carrying him to the governor, he died" (Beverley 1947:53). This governor was Sir Francis Wyatt, who had replaced Yeardley in November 1621. As Nemattanew was dying, he asked the boys not to tell how he was killed; he also asked to be buried among the English. The English viewed this event as the cause of the 1622 coup (Beverley 1947:53).

When Opechancanough received word of this murder, he reputedly "much grieved and repined, with great threats of revenge; but the English returned him such terrible answers, that he cunningly dissembled his intent, with the greatest signs he could of love and peace" (Smith 1986d:293). On 22 March 1622, less than two weeks after Nemattanew's death (Smith 1986d:293), the coup took place (Beverley 1947:51–55; Virginia Council 1933d:612; Waterhouse 1933:550–56). That morning the Indians went into the English settlements, even using their boats to cross the rivers, as had become usual. Presents of food had been taken the previous evening, and on that morning some joined the colonists in their breakfasts, and worked alongside them in the fields. Having entered the settlements unarmed, when the time came they picked up the colonists' tools and weapons and killed them all, men, women, and children, old and young alike, "so sudden in their cruel execution that few or none discerned the weapon or blow that brought them to destruction" (Waterhouse 1933:551). The bodies of some of the slain were also mutilated. This attack fell as a single stroke across much of the colony, without successive attacks: "whatever was not done by surprise that day, was left undone, and many that made early resistance escaped" (Beverley 1947:51). According to the official counts, 347 colonists were killed; a "true list of the names of all those that were massacred" was included in the printed account by Waterhouse (1933:564–71), but there were no reports from some settlements, such as Bermuda Hundred, so the total number killed could have been higher. After its dissolution, the Virginia Company stated that "about 400 of our people were slain" in this attack (Virginia Co. 1935:524). Many isolated settlements, decreased in size by the company policy of concentrating population in Jamestown, were completely wiped out. At the Falling Creek ironworks, for example, "no soul was saved, but a boy and a girl, who, with great difficulty, hid themselves" (Beverley 1947:55).

Some settlements, on the other hand, emerged unscathed, either fighting off the attackers or not being attacked in the first place (figure 6). According to tradition, Jamestown was saved by a warning from a Christianized Indian boy named Chanco, but there is no first- or even secondhand account of an attack taking place there. One would expect to have descriptions of the successful defense against the Indians, if such occurred, particularly since accounts of other such defenses are given. The only mention is in a letter from Joseph Mead, a biblical scholar at Christ College, Cambridge, to another Christ College scholar:

> it chanced in the place near which the governor himself lived, that an Indian youth asked another Indian youth (who was baptised and served an English gentleman of the colonies and had been in England), if he knew what they must do at this feast? What saith the other? Why, quoth he, we must cut all the Englishmen's throats, and I hope thou wilt cut thy master's. The Christian Indian presently informed his master, and he the governor, who presently with all the speed he could dispatched messengers to every place to give them warning. But it

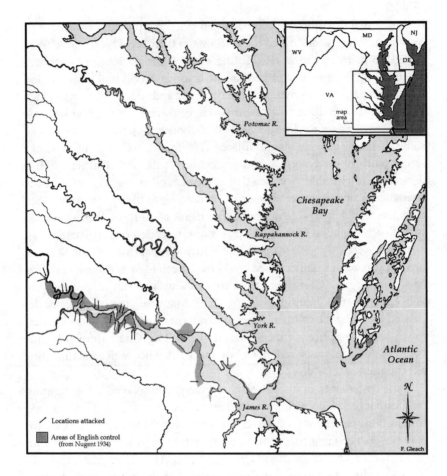

FIGURE 6. English Settlements and Locations Attacked in 1622

came too late to one place, the massacre being committed before it came; to all the rest, God be thanked, it came in time enough, and to Jamestown at the very instant when the Indians, between 3 or 400, were come to fetch them to their feast. Whereupon, in stead of other complements, they fell upon them and beat out their brains, scarce any escaping, and so expiated in some sort the blood of their brethren which they slew in other places as aforesaid. (Mead 1963:408–9; cf. Beverley 1947:52; Waterhouse 1933:550–56)

This is not mentioned in the official account of the coup (Waterhouse 1933:555–56). Furthermore, the governor was at Jamestown at the time

(Waterhouse 1933:555), so the warning could not have come from him to Jamestown "at the very instant" of the attack. The only known letter Mead had received regarding this event said simply, "an Indian boy, the night before, discovered it to his master, who all night sent about to give notice. Yet in Martin's Hundred, too far off to have notice, almost all were slain" (Mead 1963:408). Mead's description of this attack at Jamestown, then, would seem to provide an excellent example of the extent to which the coup thrived in the English rumor-mills, but lacking any other account one is left to draw the conclusion that there was no such attack at Jamestown.

A brief comparison with the Irish Rebellion[2] of 1641 is enlightening regarding the interpretation of such acts within the English culture: official English accounts reported that

> on the 23d of October 1641, a rebellion broke out in all parts of Ireland, except Dublin, where the design of it was miraculously discovered the night before it was to be executed . . . but that, in the other parts of the kingdom, they observed the time appointed, not hearing of the misfortune of their friends at Dublin . . . a general insurrection of the Irish spread itself over the whole country, in such an inhuman and barbarous manner that there were forty or fifty thousand Protestants murdered before they suspected themselves in any danger, or could provide for their defense, by drawing together into towns or strong houses. ("A Brief Account" 1747:22–23)

The parallel of the miraculous discovery of the planned attack at the most important settlement is striking. Later investigations also demonstrated that there were actually very few, if any, Englishmen killed at the beginning of the rebellion; that it was primarily confined to Ulster; and that it was largely due to abuses of the Irish by the English settlers, including unfair seizures of land ("A Brief Account" 1747:25–35, 6–10, 35–45) — very much akin to the situation in Virginia. Also, as with the Natives in the Virginia coup, the Irish "neither began that tragedy, nor committed a murder that was not returned upon them, at least four-fold" ("A Brief Account" 1747:47). Violence on the part of the English settlers preceded the Irish attacks ("A Brief Account" 1747:49–53) as well as the Powhatan attacks. Clearly, the English reactions were based on severely skewed or even factually incorrect interpretations of the events.

Returning to Virginia, the Chanco story itself is somewhat questionable. There is first the question of his identity, and second that of his motivation. The name "Chanco" for the Indian boy who warned Pace seems to have entered popular historical usage by the nineteenth century, but its origin is unknown. Contemporary accounts do not name the boy. Only one document gives a form of the name: a letter from the council in Virginia to the Virginia Company in London, referring to an incident that took place over a year after the coup. The relevant portion is here, in direct transcription: "since our laste Lre, there cam two Indians to m[artins] Hundred, . . . one of which Called (Chauco) who had lived much amost the English, and by revealinge yt pl[ot] To divers vppon the day of Massacre, saued theire lives"[3] (Virginia Council 1935b:98). Kingsbury is notorious for her mistakes in transcription, and Rountree wisely checked the spelling against a microfilm copy, noting that the text plainly reads "Chauco" (1990:303 n.68). The manuscript itself, however, is almost certainly a contemporary copy (like most early Virginia documents now archived), and the parentheses around the name suggest a copyist's question, later filled. In seventeenth-century hands, "n" and "u" are frequently indistinguishable, and even though this copyist was careful, the original might not have been clear. Because the available information yields no compelling reason to revise a long-standing traditional usage, I have retained the spelling "Chanco," *contra* Rountree. Rountree (1990:303–4: n.69) believes that this is not the boy who warned Pace. Seeing them as two individuals is one way to resolve the conflict, and, like Rountree, I have no difficulty envisioning several Indians "caught in the middle," but "a fit of conscience about his own people" (Rountree 1990:303–4: n.69) is not the only possible motivation for Chanco's behavior. Perhaps Chanco's warning was not a betrayal of the Powhatans at all, but was part of their plan; if so, then his acting as a trusted messenger the next year makes perfect sense, as he had already proven himself as an intermediary. I do not raise this argument for the sake of parsimony, but as an interpretation based in the cultural understandings presented here.

Chanco's betrayal of his people due to religious conversion and received kindness should be surprising, given the ways Indians accepted Christianity, but it was accepted by the English at the time in wish-fulfillment and has been accepted since for similar reasons: this view demonstrated that an Indian could be a good Christian, that he could be civilized, and ultimately that the English were right in asserting the superiority of their culture. The most detailed contemporary account (Waterhouse 1933:550–56) offers a more confusing version of the Chanco incident, giving the number saved as "thousands of ours" (1933:555) — which would have been difficult, since there were only about 1,240 in the colony at the time (Earle 1979: table 4);

as noted above, such exaggeration is typical of contemporary English accounts of attacks against their colonies.

The greatest questions regarding Chanco and his warning are the intent of the warning and the depth of Chanco's conversion. Just over a year later, he again appears[4] in the historical record, as an emissary sent to Martin's Hundred with a message from Itoyatan, "that blood enough had already been shed on both sides, that many of his people were starved, by our taking away their corn and burning their houses, and that they desired they might be suffered to plant at Pamunkey and their former seats, which if they might peaceably do they would send home our people (being about twenty) whom they saved alive since the massacre, and would suffer us to plant quietly also in all places" (Virginia Council 1935b:98). Chanco was sent back with an acceptance of these terms, and returned within a week "with Mrs. Boise, the chief of the prisoners, sent home appareled like one of their queens, which they desired we should take notice of" (Virginia Council 1935b:98). Chanco continued to travel between the two peoples as a negotiator (Virginia Council 1935b:98–99), his position among the Powhatans not damaged by his supposed betrayal of the coup; indeed, he would seem to have held an improved position, since he was not noted in the records at all prior to this time.

Finally, the conversion of Chanco to English beliefs should not be casually accepted; as discussed in chapter 1, Native American acceptance of the English God was generally in addition to but did not replace their traditional beliefs. Father Biard described the results of such conversions among the Algonquians of New France, noting that the unbaptised seemed to understand the sign of the cross as well as those baptised as Christians, and that their understanding of the baptism was simply that it made them like the French; even so, they continued to take multiple wives, and "the same customs, ceremonies, usages, fashions, and vices remain, at least as far as can be learned; no attention being paid to any distinction of time, days, offices, exercises, prayers, duties, virtues, or spiritual remedies" (Biard 1896b:163–65). Chanco had not received intensive, long-term training and education, as Don Luis had in Spain, and even Don Luis's conversion must be qualified. There is no reason to assume that Chanco had been any more completely converted than any of these Indians, so some other motivation for his warning must be found if it is to be accepted.

As at Jamestown, there was no attack recorded in the Corporation of Elizabeth City, at the mouth of the James River. The Indians of this area were among those only recently conquered by the Powhatans, and it has traditionally been assumed that they simply did not go along with the coup (e.g., Fausz 1977:399). The distribution of attacks can be interpreted in that way; many more attacks occurred west of Jamestown than to the east, which reflects the historical orientation of Powhatan control. It could also reflect the intentions of the Powhatans, however.

In those areas attacked, not only were the colonists killed, but scalping and other acts of degradation were also committed:

> not being content with taking away life alone, they fell after again upon the dead, making as well as they could a fresh murder, defacing, dragging, and mangling the dead carcasses into many pieces, and carrying some parts away in derision, with base and brutish triumph. (Waterhouse 1933:551)

> Captain Nathaniel Powell, another of the council, who had some time been governor of the country, was also killed. He was one of the first planters, a brave soldier, had deserved well in all ways, was universally valued and esteemed by all parties and factions and none in the country better known among the Indians. Yet they slew both him and his family, and afterwards haggled their bodies, and cut off his head, to express their utmost height of scorn and cruelty. (Stith 1865:212)

Given the Powhatans' aesthetic of war (see chapter 1), an attitude of "derision" or "scorn" is probably a reasonably accurate partial description; the point in acts such as these was to humiliate the defeated opponent, to demonstrate his relative weakness. But at the same time, if he was a worthy individual his strength was desired. Either way, the application of skill, shrewdness, and wit were of utmost importance. George Thorpe seems to have received particular attention: "And both [Opechancanough] and his people for the daily courtesies this good gentleman did to one or another of them, did profess such outward love and respect unto him, as nothing could seem more; but all was little regarded after by this viperous brood, as the sequel showed: for they not only willfully murdered him, but cruelly and fiercely, out of devilish malice, did so many barbarous despites and foul scorns after to his dead corpse, as are unbefitting to be heard by any civil ear" (Waterhouse 1933:552–53). As developed in chapter 7, Thorpe's estate would later suffer abuses at the hands of his fellow Englishmen, who were simply exercising greed; these "barbarous despites and foul scorns" inflicted by the Powhatans probably demonstrated an element of respect for Thorpe as an individual, as well as derision of the English and their culture.

By means of such acts the attackers demonstrated their superiority —
from the Powhatan perspective. The English reaction, however, was just
the opposite: "these miscreants, contrariwise in this kind, not only put off
humanity, but put on a worse and more than unnatural brutishness"
(Waterhouse 1933:551). The Powhatans reduced themselves to a state below
that of wild beasts, in the colonists' perception. Although there would be
calls from England to continue the attempts to convert them, the English
colonists in Virginia would pursue a harsh policy of aggression: "Because
the way of conquering them is much more easy than of civilizing them by
fair means, for they are a rude, barbarous, and naked people, scattered in
small companies, which are helps to victory, but hinderances to civility"
(Waterhouse 1933:557). The English perceived the Powhatans as defeated,
but the Powhatans themselves consistently acted to maintain their position
of superiority in the relationship, and they clearly saw themselves as dominating the English. This is evident from their exchanges, beginning with
those between Powhatan and Captain John Smith, and up to and including
the coup itself. The Powhatans had absorbed the English into their own
culture, although the English refused to see it that way.

This coup has been interpreted by Fausz (1977:345–49) as an "uprising,"
founded in a revitalization movement which had Nemattanew as its
leader — after only fifteen years of interaction. The killing of Nemattanew
then produced a state of "desperation" in Opechancanough (Fausz
1977:356) and prompted him to attack immediately. The political and social
reasons why this should not be viewed as an uprising have already been
noted; there is also another misunderstanding of Powhatan world-view
involved in such a characterization. Again, for the Powhatans a defeat represented a lack of sufficient support by spiritual powers. An attack in desperation would not be an appropriate response. Two quotations recorded
by the Indian captive Oliver Spencer in the late eighteenth century illustrate
the attitudes of Indians to the Europeans' expansion in America. The first
is a speech by a Shawnee elder:

> He spoke (as Mr. Ironside afterward informed me) of the distinguish-
> ing favor of the Great Spirit to his red children, the first and most
> honorable of the human race, to whom he had given the vast country
> stretching from the sun's rising place in the far east to where it sets in
> the great waters beyond the Rocky Mountains. . . .
> He then spoke of the "palefaces," whom he represented as the first
> murderers and oppressors; ascribed their own sad reverses to the anger

of the Great Spirit for affording these murderers an asylum on their shores; of their duty to exterminate if possible these intruders on their soil, at least to drive them south of the Ohio. He said that their late victories over the whites, particularly their signal defeat of St. Clair, were evidences of the returning favor of the Great Spirit. (Spencer 1907:103–4)

These attacks, however, were taking place decades after contact, not immediately; note, too, that the context of this address was a gathering of warriors. The second quotation is from a conversation with a Mohawk woman living with the Shawnees:

She spoke of the first landing of the "palefaces" from their monstrous canoes with their great white wings, as seen by her ancestors; of their early settlements, their rapid growth, their widely spreading population, their increasing strength and power, their insatiable avarice, and their continued encroachments on the red men; who, reduced by diseases, thinned by civil wars, and diminished by their long and various struggles, first with the British (Met-a-coo-se-a-qua) then with Se-mon-the (the Americans or Long-knives), were no longer powerful; and that they would not be satisfied until they had crowded the Indian to the extreme north to perish on the great ice lake; or to the far west until, pushing those who should escape from their rifles into the great waters, all would at length be exterminated. She spoke of the anger of the Great Spirit against the red men, especially those of her own nation, nearly all of whom had perished; and that herself and her children, the remnant of her race, would soon sleep in the ground, and that there would be none to gather them at the feast of the dead or to celebrate their obsequies. (Spencer 1907:127)

This sort of resigned acceptance, perhaps with hope for a future reversal, would be the most likely immediate response of the Powhatans to perceived successful challenges to their primacy by the English, not an attempted genocide. But first the Powhatans would have to perceive themselves as defeated, as inferiors in their relationship with the colony, and this was not the case here.

The coup had probably been in planning since at least the previous year, when Opechancanough and Itoyatan took on new names, reflecting new positions or status; Rountree (1990:66–73) believes that it had been in planning for several years. The murder of Nemattanew was supposed the proximate cause of it, although the English recognized another long-term factor: "that in time we by our growing continually upon them, would dispossess them of this country" (Waterhouse 1933:556). The English, who had originally informed Powhatan that they intended to stay only long enough to repair their boat (Smith 1986a:54–55), and who had twice been offered their own lands in which to live in peace, continued to take over lands beyond what was offered, often killing the inhabitants to do so. Such a killing by an inferior generally had to be revenged, or paid off, within the Powhatan culture (cf. Warren 1984:198), although the *Mamanatowick* could excuse a killing, in effect accepting the responsibility for the act. Nemattanew was an important war-chief, but as Opechancanough had assured the English the previous year, the death of "but one man should be no occasion for the breach of the peace" (Virginia Council 1935a:11). A single murder might need to be revenged, but it need not start a war.

The killing of Nemattanew was thus but one element in determining the attack against the English. Even before that event, the coup was probably planned for this time of year. Food supplies for the English and the Powhatans alike were at their shortest in the late winter and early spring, but whereas the English repeatedly had to rely on food obtained from the Powhatans to get through the winter, Smith had noted in January 1608 "the plenty he had seen, especially at Werowocomoco, and . . . the state and bounty of Powhatan (which till that time was unknown)" (Smith 1986d:152). The assumption by the English of barely adequate stores for the Powhatans was more likely a projection of their own situation. The English would thus be at their weakest at this time and in a worse position than the Powhatans. The timing is also strikingly close to the quarter moon, which, according to an English almanac for that year, was on 23 March (Browne 1622:n.p.); the lunar quarters were a time marker of native significance, as recorded for the neighboring Delaware Indians: "They distinguish the phases of the moon by particular names; they say the 'new moon,' the 'round moon' (when it is full), and when in its decline, they say it is 'half round' " (Heckewelder 1876:308). Furthermore, the Indians, including Opechancanough, were probably aware that this was a holy season for the English, falling between Ash Wednesday and Easter. This assertion is based on the fact that George Thorpe often conferred with Opechancanough "and intimated to him matters of our religion" (Waterhouse 1933:552). This would give the sacrifice of the English colonists an ironic religious overtone as a physical instantiation of their rejection of the English Church as it was being forced on them.

Fausz (1977:359–60) suggested that this was a dangerous time for the Powhatans to go to war, because "in March . . . the Powhatan economy afforded little or no corn surplus from the previous autumn's harvests, and planting for the next season would not begin until late April." As already suggested, this was a misperception, and the Powhatans' ability to survive later colonial attempts to starve them out reinforces my previous observations. The question is moot, however, since food supplies were not critical for the Powhatans: they were not planning an extended campaign. This was to be a coup, not a protracted war. The Indians suffered no significant losses during the attack — and yet they did not continue beyond that single simultaneous stroke across the colony. There was no further assault on the colonists until 9 September 1622, when four laborers were reportedly killed (Smith 1986d:312).

The destruction could have been much greater — if that had been the plan. Contrary to the English perception, however, this was plainly no attempt at extermination. Neither was it intended to drive the colonists back to England, as Rountree (1990:75) suggests; the colonists were valued for the material goods they could provide, as the original negotiations between Smith and Powhatan make clear. But they were unruly; they refused to live as they were supposed to. When viewed from the perspective of the history of interactions, when considered in the context of traditional native forms of war, and when taken into consideration with other aspects of the attack, it seems clear that the Powhatans' goal was not to remove the English but rather to confine them in a small territory, put a halt to their local Christianization efforts, and demonstrate the Powhatans' superiority over the English. The warning of the colonists near Jamestown, seen in this light, was but one step toward that goal: the desired result was to get the settlers to remove from their scattered, indefensible settlements to the comparative safety of Jamestown — and thus to return them to a single location, in which they could be more closely controlled. Farther outlying settlements were destroyed to ensure they would not be reoccupied and to make clear that such settlements were inappropriate for the English colonists. This coup was intended to be "a bold and effective strike, which would long be remembered, and keep their enemies in fear and check" (Warren 1984:127, writing on Ojibwa warfare).

Our hands, which before were tied with gentleness and fair usage, are now set at liberty by the treacherous violence of the savages, not untying the knot, but cutting it. So that we, who hitherto have had possession of no more ground than their waste, and our purchase, at a valuable consideration to their own contentment, gained, may now by right of war, and law of nations, invade the country, and destroy them who sought to destroy us: whereby we shall enjoy their cultivated places, turning the laborious mattock into the victorious sword (wherein there is more both ease, benefit, and glory) and possessing the fruits of others' labors. Now their cleared grounds in all their villages (which are situated in the most fruitful places of the land) shall be inhabited by us, whereas heretofore the grubbing of woods was the greatest labor.
— Waterhouse, "A Declaration of the State of the Colony"

AFTER THE COUP, the Powhatan warriors presumably returned to their homes, exulting in the glory of their successful attack. Having defeated the English settlers in almost every location attacked, the Powhatans would have expected the English to return to their settlements that had not been destroyed, to cease trying to buy or steal Powhatan children for their projects, and perhaps to plot or work towards someday being able to seek revenge. That "someday" came very soon, since the colonists were not appropriately humiliated, and the coup resulted in an immediate self-righteous offensive designed by the English to exterminate the Powhatans.

Not only were the Powhatans persecuted following the coup, but it seems that a small group of some of the more important colonists conspired to appropriate goods of value from some of the slain colonists — and particularly from the estate of George Thorpe, whose family was still in England. There seems to have been some enquiry about this: John Smyth of Nibley, one of the main supporters of Berkeley Hundred in England, had copies made of all mentions in the Virginia General Court records of claims against Thorpe's estate. In most cases the original court records survive (McIlwaine 1979) and can be compared to the extracts prepared by the clerk of the court, Benjamin Harrison, for Smyth (Smyth of Nibley n.d.). The first claims against Thorpe's estate were recorded in early March 1623, less than a year after the coup. At that time an inventory of the estate was ordered by Yeardley, who, as former governor, was a senior member of the court. The inventory was prepared 10 April 1624[1] and is notable for its omissions: there are no books, no smaller pieces of furniture, and only a relatively small amount of silver and other tablewares. The statement that the four barrels of wine in Thorpe's estate were consumed during the preparation of the inventory (Smyth of Nibley papers, no. 43) suggests the fate of his valuable goods. Analyzing these documents, Gethyn-Jones (1982:206–19) has found several instances of misrepresentations in the claims against Thorpe's estate, particularly in the claims of George Yeardley. The claims made by Edward Blany and Abraham Piersey also are questionable. No news of the manner of Thorpe's death or the disposition of his estate was reported to his family, as demonstrated by his son's letter of 1634 asking for any information concerning his death and estate (Smyth of Nibley n.d., no. 44). Note here that Blany, with the certification of the governor and council of Virginia, had occupied the estate of Nathaniel Powell, who, like Thorpe, had been killed in the coup (Gethyn-Jones 1982:207), and that Yeardley and Piersey held the largest numbers of African slaves in the colony; slaveholding was still considered a morally questionable act at that time (Neill 1885:116).

Whereas the dealings of these ranking English colonists among themselves was morally and legally questionable, their reprisals against the Powhatans carried widespread and open approval. Since the English perceived the coup as an attempt at annihilation, a response in kind was widely accepted both in the colony and among the sponsors in England. What they believed the Indians had intended for them, they determined to execute against the Powhatans — but this protracted war had to be weighed against their economic interests.

"A POLICY OF PERPETUAL ENMITY," 1622–32

Because of the effectiveness of the attacks on outlying settlements, the fact that Jamestown had survived, the perceived threat of a second attack, and the company policy reinstated under Argall five years earlier to focus settlement in Jamestown, the colony's immediate response was to withdraw to a small number of defensible settlements (Beverley 1947:54; Earle 1979:115–16) — essentially the response the Powhatans desired. The English also tried to take revenge on the Powhatans, but the latter were able to escape easily into the woods. The colonists then allowed the Powhatans to return to their villages and plant their fields; when it was too late for another planting they attacked the villages and destroyed the crops (Beverley 1947:54).

It is ironic, of course, that the English resorted to an attempt to starve the Powhatans, since they had relied for so long on food supplies obtained by trade. This tactic is what Fausz has referred to as a "feedfight" (1977:457ff), where the primary mode of attack was the prevention of successful planting and harvesting of crops by the Powhatans. Captain John Martin[2] described the methods and rationale of such an attack, noting that it was also essential to prevent their trading for food. The English were to conduct winter raids to destroy towns and fish weirs as well as summer raids to destroy the crops, using foot soldiers and boats; this would permit the seizure of furs and taking of prisoners as well as preventing Powhatan harvests and inhibiting their trade. Disrupting the Powhatans' trade with the Eastern Shore tribes also permitted the English to exploit that trade. Martin gave two reasons for not exterminating the Indians: for practical purposes, to keep the wild beasts of the forests under control, and for the religious cause of their conversion — which also had a practical side: they could be employed as servants, since "natives are apter to work than yet our English are, knowing how to attain great quantity of silk, hemp and flax, and most exquisite in the dressing thereof, for our uses, fit for guides upon discoveries into other countries adjacent to ours, fit to row in galleys and frigates, and many other pregnant uses too tedious to set down" (Martin 1933:704–6).

The English concerns for food and trade are evident here; Indians were to be allowed to live only for the benefit of the English colonists. The war against the Powhatans was unlike typical European warfare in that the attacks were against villages and fields of crops, not against organized fighting forces. Powhatan counterattacks seem to have been limited and few. The term *war*, again, can only be used here with some caution; this should be understood as a protracted series of brief attacks followed by withdrawal, against an opponent whose response was limited to occasional quick reprisals, with goals of revenge and the prevention of future threat more than of military conquest.

Perhaps the most bizarre incident of the colonists' war against the Powhatans occurred in the spring of 1623, when they tried to poison a number of Indians. A party of twelve colonists, sent to conclude a peace with Opechancanough and return with some English prisoners, took a cask of poisoned sherry for toasting, and pretending to taste it first gave it to Opechancanough and the other Powhatan leaders to drink. All became drunk, and the colonists fired on the Indians before leaving, reportedly killing "the two kings and many others" (Bennett 1922:507). The council reported to the Virginia Company in London that "we have by a successful stratagem not only regained our people but cut off some kings and divers of the greatest commanders of the enemy, among whom we are assured that Opechancanough is one" (Virginia Council 1906:486). This seemingly unlikely incident is the most vivid example of the ways in which this English war against the Powhatans was more like native warfare than like traditional European warfare. Note that the English were mistaken in at least one particular: Opechancanough was not killed in this attack — he lived another twenty years. It is entirely possible that most of these people were not killed but perhaps only rendered unconscious for a time.

The pursuit of this war was put in the charge of former governor George Yeardley by Governor Wyatt, who was given "leave, and absolute power, either to make peace or war with any of them as it shall seem most behooving and necessary for the present estate of this our Commonwealth, as also peaceably to trade for furs, corn or any other commodities with such as shall be friends, and forcibly to take such or the like from those that dare be our enemies" (Wyatt 1933:657). Note that at this time the option of war or peace was to be evaluated in each instant, although the decision lay in the hands of a person who had repeatedly demonstrated a tendency to serve his self-interest; the privilege to trade for or seize goods was zealously protected by the colony's leaders. Soon official policy would eliminate the option of making peace, but even so trade was never completely stopped; war simply seems to have been both easier and more profitable, as noted by Waterhouse (1933:557). Yeardley's commission also authorized him to attack virtually any European forces that he encountered[3] (Wyatt 1933:657), indicating that even after the Powhatans' coup this was a major concern. The colony may indeed have been more vulnerable following this attack, although the consolidation of settlements should have improved their defensibility, but it seems that obtaining supplies — by whatever means — and avoiding attack by other Europeans was more important than waging war against the Powhatans. The possibility of further attack by the Indians was still a concern — but not the sole or even the most important one.

The abandonment of the more isolated interior settlements may have made the settlement more readily defensible, against both Indians and potential incursions by other Europeans, but it also resulted in an increased mortality rate due to disease. An additional 350 or more individuals died within the next year, of the same diseases that had plagued the colony from the start: typhoid, dysentery, and salt poisoning (Earle 1979:116–20). In February 1624, the English population was at essentially the same level as it was immediately prior to the coup (1,275, as compared with 1,240), despite the arrival of 1,100 new settlers during the intervening two years (Earle 1979: table 4).

In 1623 the English government launched an investigation of the Virginia Company. The only profitable staple being exported from Virginia continued to be tobacco; all other efforts had either failed outright or been curtailed by the loss of lives, time, and capital inflicted by the coup. The royal (and popular) opposition to tobacco in England thus caused difficulties for the Virginia Company, particularly since the company had to negotiate monopolistic control of the English market to keep from being driven out by the superior product imported from Spanish colonies. This monopoly caused further tension between the Virginia and Bermuda adventurers. In 1624, the Virginia Company was dissolved, and the Virginia settlements became a royal colony (Craven 1970:147–49).

In March 1624 the General Assembly in Virginia met for the first time after the coup. Among the various laws pertaining to taxes, ministers, public stores, and general defense were several regarding the colony's relationship with the Powhatans:

> 4. That the 22d of March be yearly solemnized as holiday, and all other holidays (except when they fall two together) betwixt the feast of the annunciation of the blessed virgin and St. Michael the archangel, then only the first to be observed by reason of our necessities. (Hening 1823, 1:123)
>
> . . .
>
> 17. That all trade for corn with the savages, as well public as private, after June next shall be prohibited. (Hening 1823, 1:126)
>
> . . .
>
> 23. That every dwelling house shall be palisaded in for defense against Indians.

24. That no man go or send abroad without a sufficient party well armed.

25. That men go not to work in the ground without their arms (and a sentinel upon them). (Hening 1823, 1:127)

. . .

32. That at the beginning of July next the inhabitants of every corporation shall fall upon their adjoining savages as we did the last year, those that shall be hurt upon service to be cured at the public charge; in case any be lamed to be maintained by the country according to his person and quality. (Hening 1823, 1:128)

This may be seen as the normal state of affairs for this period: regular attacks against the Powhatans, maintenance of defenses in case of a counterattack, and government attempts to control the trade with the Indians, which seems to have been rampant.

The only pitched battle recorded in this "war" took place in the summer of 1624, described in an account — probably exaggerated — in a letter from the Virginia Council begging supplies, particularly gunpowder:

It has pleased God this year to give us a great victory over Itoyatan and the Pamunkeys, with their confederates, by a handful, being in all not above sixty fighting men (whereof twenty-four were employed only in the cutting down of corn) conducted by the governor, in which it was shown what the Indians could do, having maintained fight two days together, and much thereof in open field, the young men being beaten up by the elder, many slain, and as much corn cut down, as by the estimation of men of good judgement was sufficient to have sustained four thousand men for a twelve-month, who were so discouraged that they gave over fighting and dismayedly stood most ruefully looking on while their corn was cut down. And had we been well furnished with powder, the governor would have proceeded further to Mattaponi River, whereby he could have hazarded the starving of all those nations. In this expedition sixteen of the English were hurt the first and second day, whereby nine of the best shots were made unserviceable for that time, yet never a man slain, nor none that miscarried of those hurts, since when they have not greatly troubled us, nor interrupted our labors. The Indians were never known to show so great resolution, either encouraged by the paucity of ours or their own great numbers, there being of the Pamunkeys 800 bowmen, besides divers nations that came to assist them, fighting not only for safeguard of their houses and such a huge quantity of corn, but for their reputation with the rest of the savages, which we now hope they have lost, it depending much upon the success of this action, the Pamunkeys having made great brags of what they would do, among the northern nations, of whom the king of Patuxent sent an Indian to us expressly to be an eye-witness of the event. (Virginia Council 1935c:507–8)

Although this may be largely a propagandistic account designed to encourage shipments of gunpowder, it is the only description of one of these raids by the colonists on the Powhatans. It would seem to describe not a single pitched battle but a series of calculated retreats by the Pamunkeys, who harried the colonists as they destroyed field after field of corn, perhaps trying to deflect them from villages, religious sites, or storehouses, rather than trying to destroy the English party outright. A force the size of that described for the Pamunkeys should have been able to inflict much more damage in such an effort.

The 1624 law prohibiting private trade with the Indians was repeatedly reissued, along with the exhortation to keep 22 March as a holiday. There was officially sanctioned trade with certain more distant groups, however. The statements from the 28 July 1626 court book are typical:

3. It is ordered that a commission be granted to Captain John Stone to trade with those Indians on the Eastern Shore, which Captain Epps shall inform him to be our friends, either for corn, furs, or any other commodities, provided he exceed not the ordinance rate for corn.

. . .

6. It is ordered that a proclamation be renewed concerning private parley with the Indians. (McIlwaine 1979:104)

The nature of these repeated commissions and proclamations suggests that there was a great deal of profit to be had through trade with the Indians, that certain ranking members of the colony were seeking to keep that profit to themselves, and that others were willing even to trade with the neighboring Powhatans, their avowed enemies, in order to secure some of that profit. Former Governor George Yeardley, in particular, was thought to pursue the war against the Powhatans only so far as to ensure a continued return of confiscated corn for his personal profit (Fausz 1977:476–78).

This discussion should not suggest that relations with the Indians were the principal concern within the colony. They reflect only a small part of the court records and statutes of the time, the majority of which concern interpersonal claims and differences within the colony and the need to have all colonists actively participating in the church — by force, if necessary. Statutes were passed requiring church attendance and specifying the forms of such services (Hening 1823, 1:123ff). As already noted, there was also concern over the possibility of foreign invasion. This concern was held at least as late as 1629, when the construction of a fort at the mouth of the James River was proposed and discussed (Harvey 1629?:f 65v); it was again mentioned in an overview of the condition of the colony presented that year in London by William Pierce[4] (Pierce 1629?:ff 69–70v).

Pierce's account places little emphasis on the Indians, perhaps because it seemed that peace had been obtained at that time; it does record, however, that Itoyatan ("Sasapen") is recognized as the chief, not Opechancanough. The colony had sufficient small arms for approximately half the population, but the lack of fortifications is again noted. A peace treaty mentioned by Pierce does not survive, but it was short-lived; it was dissolved by the council on 31 January 1629:

> At this court was taken into consideration the treaty of peace with the Indians which has been continued since the beginning of August last, and finding that upon this treaty the people and planters of the colony have grown secure and utterly neglected either to stand upon their guard or to keep their arms fit and ready about them to defend themselves upon any occasions wherein the treacherous Indians might attempt anything against us, which mischiefs are by no means to be prevented (the condition of our people being so wretchedly negligent in this kind), that neither proclamations nor other strict orders have remedied the same, and also on the other side the Indians have been extremely false and altogether neglected the conditions of the treaty and offered some injuries in divers of our plantations, the governor and council therefore, upon serious deliberation concerning the same, have thought fit and are of the opinion that in their judgement it is a safer course for the colony in general to prevent a second massacre utterly to proclaim and maintain enmity and wars with all the Indians of these parts. And do thereupon order that all the people and planters within this colony do take notice that all the former treaties of peace be utterly extinct and disannulled. And that hereafter they do strictly and precisely stand upon their guard. And that hereafter they do keep the Indians off from their plantations, without any parley or converse

with them, but for the better safety of some of our weaker plantations, and that all in the colony may have in the meantime intelligence of the proceedings herein. It is thought convenient that if it may be possible they fail to shoot or kill any of them until the 20th of February next, but after that time to esteem them utter enemies and to take the best advantages they can against them. (McIlwaine 1979:184–85)

The "mischiefs" committed by the Indians seem to have been very few throughout this period, primarily consisting of continued visits to the English settlements, against the commands of the council (McIlwaine 1979:190). The Powhatans were blamed for two additional killings of colonists, one in 1623 (McIlwaine 1979:51) and one in 1627 (McIlwaine 1979:153); there were also "many of our hogs and cattle" killed (McIlwaine 1979:190) and hoes stolen (McIlwaine 1979:198).[5] Even these cannot all be certainly assigned to the Powhatans, or any other Indians, of course. Violence between the two peoples seems to have markedly declined between 1625 and 1629. Studying the minutes of the courts, one is left with the conclusion that the council's main concern in their legal actions was to control the individual colonists' ability to interact with the Indians, and in particular their ability to conduct trade. The ideological, moral outrage of the English in England (Fausz 1977:404–42) was heavily tempered by economic pragmatics in Virginia.

Legal records demonstrate that during this period everyday life for the colonists continued almost unchanged from the years prior to the coup, with the greatest change being the loss of daily interaction with individual Powhatans, but this loss of interaction results in a near-complete absence of information on the Powhatans at this time. Itoyatan died sometime around 1629; the last mention of him is in a relation probably dating to 1629 (Pierce 1629?:f 69ᵛ), and the killing of five colonists in that year (McIlwaine 1979:198) might be related to his death, although there is no obvious connection. Although some Powhatans were recorded as killed during English raids to destroy their crops, it seems likely that there were few other casualties due to these actions. The majority of such English attacks were conducted by men delivered by boat and were concentrated on the fields near the rivers. There was little apparent incentive for long overland expeditions, since Powhatan villages and their fields were traditionally concentrated near the rivers. There was extensive arable land in the interior, however, and new fields were probably located in these areas. There were also stores of food, as were occasionally noted by the English.

The colonial "feedfight" thus probably did not cause the widespread starvation the settlers expected. There is certainly no record of desperate defenses, abandoned villages, or pleas for food in trade from the colonists by the Powhatans, the kinds of results one might expect from people under severe dietary stress in this context. The results of these actions were more likely changes in the annual routine of population movement and diet, an increase in value for the trade goods that would be increasingly more difficult for the Powhatans to obtain, and an increased flow of valuables out to other neighboring groups in trade for needed goods.

But perhaps the most important change was in the Powhatans' perspective towards the English. It would be at this time, not the earlier period postulated by Fausz, that the Powhatans would begin to see the English colonists as perhaps being able to dominate them, and they would become increasingly reliant on English goods obtained by trade or raid. I have suggested here and elsewhere that in many ways the Powhatans, as a group, never viewed the English as their superiors, but simply as being able to dominate them in terms of political power (Gleach 1990b, 1992b). In the period following the 1622 coup, such domination begins to be evident.

In October 1629 three expeditions each year against the Indians were authorized by the General Assembly (Hening 1823, 1:140–41), partly in response to the killing of five colonists earlier that year. These acts of war were ordered to be maintained in 1630 (Hening 1823, 1:153), but in February 1632, and repeated in September, the statutes were changed. Speaking with any Indian was permitted, with restrictions, rather than completely prohibited (Hening 1823, 1:167, 192), and restrictions were placed on the killing of Indians: "And because we hold the neighboring Indians our irreconcilable enemies, it is further thought fit: That if any Indians do molest or offend any plantations in their cattle, hogs, or anything else, or that they be found lurking about any plantation, then the commander shall have power by virtue of this act to raise a sufficient party and fall out upon them, and persecute them as he shall find occasion" (Hening 1823, 1:193). Although still declared enemies, the Indians had to act to provoke English attack under this law, rather than being subject to attack without immediate provocation, as they were previously. Finally, peace with the Pamunkeys and Chickahominies was enacted on 30 September 1632, with the same proclamation "not to parley with or trust them" (McIlwaine 1979:480). The documents pertaining to this peace do not survive, but there is no indication of a substantial treaty like that negotiated following the 1644 coup. It was more likely simply an agreement to engage in warfare no longer.

ENGLISH EXPANSION, TRADE, AND WATCHFULNESS, 1632–44

As early as the mid-1620s the English colonists had begun to return to some of the settlements they had abandoned following the coup, and numerous land patents were issued for these territories (see Nugent 1934:2–14). There were also increases in the total English population in Virginia. There had been about 1,275 colonists in February 1624 and 4,914 by 1634, in large part due to the spreading of settlements away from the Jamestown area (Earle 1979:121–22). By 1640 the colonial population had grown to approximately 8,000 (McCusker and Menard 1985:136). The population was still largely white and male; in 1625 it is estimated to have included only 10 percent women, and there were only about 100 blacks as late as the 1640s (McCusker and Menard 1985:135–36). Not until well into the 1670s did the "slave society" (Kulikoff 1986) really begin to take shape, as the black slave population, which had been around 5 percent or less of the colonial population from the 1620s through the 1660s, reached 7 percent in 1680 and surpassed 10 percent in the 1690s (McCusker and Menard 1985:136).

Rountree (1990:79) has estimated Powhatan population to be "probably less than 5,000" for the 1620s and 1630s. By 1669 it had fallen to a more reliably estimated 2,900 (Rountree 1990:96). These figures are in comparison to the approximately 13,000 to 15,000 estimated for the Powhatans at the early years of the colony (Feest 1973; E. R. Turner 1982). Sometime in the late 1630s the colonial population surpassed that of the Powhatans, and by the mid-1640s it was probably twice the Powhatan population. Neither the peace treaty nor the growth of the colony brought confidence in their security, however. In March 1643, a decade after the peace treaty and almost twenty years after the coup, the General Assembly was still reiterating that 22 March "be yearly kept holy in commemoration of our deliverance from the Indians at the bloody massacre," and heads of family were required to carry guns, powder, and shot even to church (Hening 1823, 1:263).

After the 1632 peace treaty there was a great increase in the territory the English were occupying. Not only were there more settlements, but they were spread over an increasingly large area. In 1634, when counties were established, the areas settled included both banks of the James River from its mouth to the fall line, both banks of the lower Chickahominy River, and the south bank of the York River, as well as the lower part of the Eastern Shore peninsula (figure 7). These areas were effectively closed to the Indians. The Middle Peninsula, the land between the James and York Rivers, was sealed off by a palisade running from river to river in 1634 (Hunter et al. 1984:58–60). This construction was to help keep the colonists' livestock, which were allowed to range freely, from falling to the Indians, and to make the Middle Peninsula effectively an "Indian-free" zone. Unlike some of the earlier palisades of Sir Thomas Dale, the Middle Peninsula palisade had no utility in protecting from attack by other European powers. "Young freemen" were required to settle in the Chickahominy area in 1637, presumably because of its frontier nature; this requirement was repealed in 1642 (McIlwaine 1915:xxxvi). The York River no longer marked the northern boundary of the colony; even the Rappahannock River was intended for official settlement in 1643, and colonists settling there were "commanded to compound with the native Indians there, whereby they may live the more securely" (Virginia General Assembly 1901:53). The nature of the arrangements with the neighboring Indians is indicated in another act of settlement of that year: "Provided . . . that an agreement be made . . . with Opechancanough for their peace by the payment of fifty barrels of corn this year, at or before the last day of April, and fifty barrels of corn more the next year. . . . But if upon profer made upon this composition Opechancanough shall refuse to accept thereof, then it may or shall be lawful to seat there with the aforesaid strength notwithstanding his refusal, but Opechancanough's first refusal shall not hinder his after acceptance" (Virginia General Assembly 1901:54). The grant to settle the Rappahannock was then revoked in June 1642, however, and the revocation repeated in 1643 (Hening 1823, 1:274). Although authorization for settlement on the Rappahannock was denied at this time, references to prior settlers in these acts demonstrate the ways in which such far-flung settlements could be begun, to be ratified at later date by the assembly. Purposeful, legislated expansion was not the primary form of growth for the colony; rather, individuals took the risks, secured a territory, and then gained the endorsement of the government — and the profits in land and resources (cf. Rountree 1990:82).

Trade with the Indians was another easy source of profits, and one that was employed throughout this period. A case in point is that of Henry Fleet. Fleet had lived with Indians on the Potomac for several years, after being captured in 1622. When he returned to England, around 1626–27,

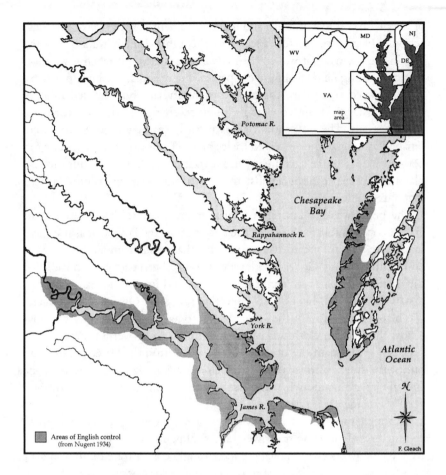

FIGURE 7. Areas of English Settlement in 1634

he was reported to have forgotten his own language, but he soon induced English merchants to outfit him for the fur trade. He made trading voyages to Virginia in 1627 and again in 1631 (Neill 1876:10–15); he was also later an important figure in the colony's response to the coup of 1644. Fleet and the other Virginia traders gained a reputation for unsavory business practices, which were, however, condoned or even abetted by Governor Harvey.

Fleet's journal for his 1631–32 voyage survives as one of the few documents for this period other than legal records, describing the competition between traders for the Indian trade, deception of the Indians, the use of bribery with colonial officials, and the involvement of the governor in these actions (Fleet 1876:19–36). Fleet and the other Indian traders worked within the law when it was to their advantage, skirting it when it was not. Lying, cheating, and stealing were part of their regular business practices. They pursued trade with the more distant Indians but also led military expeditions against the Powhatans, often receiving the Indians' corn and land as spoils. The governors of this period, Yeardley and Harvey, were satisfied as long as they received their share. This form of trade had begun before the 1632 peace agreement, and it continued afterwards, but the regular military expeditions against the Powhatans were discontinued with that agreement.

The peace was not entirely popular; many colonists had been able to extract considerable profits from the raids against the Powhatans, and these raids were a useful means to remove the inhabitants from lands that were desired for settling. Governor Harvey, who had been partly responsible for the treaty, was removed from office in 1639 and imprisoned as a result of dissatisfaction with his policies (Beverley 1947:60). One of these policies was a 1633 restriction of the Indian trade to agents approved by the governor: the trade in cloth was prohibited unless the governor approved it, because "great quantities of cloth, baize, and cotton [had been] bought up out of the stores of this colony by such as have traded the same with the Indians, at such time when the inhabitants have been in great want and need" (Hening 1823, 1:219).

Although important to the colonists who were seeking to line their pockets, such restrictions on trade were a critical issue for the Powhatans, who were trying to survive. They were increasingly concentrated into a smaller area — largely unable to move north, south, or west because those territories were already occupied — and cut off from free access to the seasonally necessary resources of the estuarine areas the English were occupying. They had suffered the devaluation of many valued goods; they had to expend those goods to compensate other tribes for their help in attacking the English; and then they had their access to such goods restricted. The Powhatans had a need for trade that was stronger than ever. Although they probably were not desperate for food, their situation at this time is reminiscent of that described by Loskiel for the Delawares in later times: "Detached Indian families living among the white people on the banks of rivers, and on that account called River-Indians, are generally a loose set of people, like our gypsies. They make baskets, brooms, wooden spoons, dishes, &c. and sell them to the white people for victuals and clothes" (1794:130).

Having been forced from their active fields, the Powhatans may, at times, have even faced a shortage of food, although certainly not to the extent planned by the English in their foodfights. Through the 1630s and 1640s the colonial economy also became increasingly self-supporting, reducing their need to trade with the Indians to obtain food. The result was an Indian population facing increased pressure — political, commodity-economic, and even subsistence-economic — to engage in trade, and a co-lonial population with less of a need to trade with them.

Certainly partly in response to this pressure, the Powhatans developed an enterprise that they continued to employ well into this century: hunting or leading hunts for their white neighbors. Testimony entered in 1624 in-dicates that a number of Indians had been given guns, instructed in their use, and even supplied with powder and shot as early as 1611–15, and sug-gests hunting parties authorized by, if not organized for, the colonists (McIlwaine 1979:28). Such activities were, of course, suspended following the coup, but by 1633 the council deemed it necessary to pass a new law prohibiting the trade of any arms or ammunition to the Indians (Hening 1823, 1:219). In 1642 this was reiterated, with elaborations that demonstrate by their presence the nature of the Indian trade that the council was trying to suppress. An act concerning runaway servants included the death penalty for their carrying guns, powder, or shot to the Indians; any other person trading guns or ammunition to the Indians would forfeit his estate, with half going to the informer; anyone trading other commodities would be imprisoned "at the discretion of the governor and council"; and any Indian carrying arms — even if employed for hunting — would have them confis-cated, and the person who lent the arms was to be fined two thousand pounds of tobacco for a first offense and would forfeit his entire estate for a second offense (Hening 1823, 1:256).

The repeated and detailed regulation of Indian trade and hunting is ev-idence of the growth of their importance to the Powhatans. Increasingly restricted in lands and rights by the growth of the Virginia colony, they sought means to live within or slip through their imposed restrictions. Trade and the conduct of hunting parties continued with varying degrees of success for over three centuries. But in the early 1640s the continued expansion of the colonists into territories the Powhatans had believed to be granted to them and the efforts to regulate these activities prompted Opechancanough to launch his final attack.

8 ✦ The Coup of 1644 and Its Aftermath

Opechancanough was a savage, and with no justice can he be judged by the rules of Christian morality. If he was revengeful, he had wrongs to revenge; if he hated the whites, he loved his own people, whom he believed to be their victims. If he made war with the darkest perfidy, it was the manner of his race, and not a crime peculiar to himself. Indian valour would avail little in the open field against European science, and Indian wiles alone could compensate the disparity. He was faithful to his own countrymen, among whom he ruled for many years with the sway of a superior mind; and the circumstances of his death affixed another blot upon our escutcheon, already stained with the blood of thousands of native Americans.

— Howison, *A History of Virginia*

DOCUMENTS PERTAINING TO the 1644 coup are all but non-existent, and records for the period afterward are as sparse as those for the 1630s. Two accounts, each written years after the attack, provide our principal sources for the coup: an anonymous account published in 1649 (*Perfect Description* 1963:11), and Robert Beverley's history (1947:60–61), originally published in 1705. Both consist principally of speculations on the Powhatans' motives and make the now familiar assumption that this was another failed effort to exterminate the colony, but Beverley does give a brief description:

> by the direction of Opechancanough their king [the Powhatans] laid the ground-work of another massacre, wherein by surprise they cut off near five hundred Christians more. But this execution did not take so general effect as formerly, because the Indians were not so frequently suffered to come among the inner habitations of the English, and therefore the massacre fell severest on the southside of James River, and on the heads of the other rivers, but chiefly of York River, where the emperor Opechancanough kept the seat of his government. (1947:60–61)

The anonymous account adds that the Powhatans had again attacked and withdrawn rather than pressing their opportunity (*Perfect Description* 1963:11).

The "near five hundred Christians" killed in this attack — more likely "near four hundred," as noted by the General Assembly just months afterwards — were part of a population probably in excess of 10,000 (McCusker and Menard 1985:136), in comparison to the 1622 toll of about 350 killed from a population of 1,240. Once again, the attack was coordinated in its timing at the various sites and took place as a single stroke, rather than a protracted series of engagements. Again, the brunt of it fell on the outlying areas of the settlement. As Beverley observed, these areas were closest to the Powhatan settlements, but they were not attacked simply because they were conveniently located. The Powhatans may have been "not so frequently suffered to come among the inner habitations" as in 1622, but the territories at the heads of the rivers, and particularly the York River, were the areas that were in contention between the two groups in 1644, with the English threatening to expand even further into these areas. Even at the time, there seems to have been little effort to portray the 1644 coup as a serious threat to annihilate the English colonists; the colonists were advised that "in places of danger it shall not be lawful for any to seat or inhabit without ten sufficient men at the least, and arms and ammunition accordingly" (Hening 1823, 1:286), but there was no major reorganization of the colony.

The 1644 coup had so little effect in the colony that even its date, 18 April, would be unknown had it not been enacted as a holiday (Hening 1823, 1:290), in the same way that the date of the 1622 coup was ordered observed as a holiday. Beverley dates the event only generally, in relation to the terms of governors (Beverley 1947:60–61), and the early Virginia historian John Burk (1805:54) mistakenly dated it to the winter of 1641–42. Like the coups of 1570 and 1622, this was during a Christian holy season, taking place three days before Easter, apparently a few days after the full moon.[1]

Like his earlier attack, the 1644 coup can best be understood as an attempt by Opechancanough to correct the colonists' inappropriate behavior and to stay their ceaseless expansion. The Powhatans' perception of the colony is less clear at this time, but it would seem that Opechancanough must no longer have perceived the colonists as an inferior power at this time. His attack indicates that he still believed the relative positions of the two peoples to be subject to adjustment — in short, that he could apply a corrective to colonial encroachment — but it was not the crippling effort of the earlier coup.

It is quite likely that other, younger Powhatans had a different view of their relationship to the colony and even of their own identity, than Opechancanough. The culture in which they had grown up, in constant contact and near-constant conflict with the colony, subject to all its acculturative attentions, differed significantly from that of the late sixteenth century, when Opechancanough came of age. We may never know just how much it had changed at this time or how this change had affected the younger people, but we know that Opechancanough retained his dignity and convictions. His actions after he was captured demonstrate that he still claimed a moral superiority over the English. Being then in prison, "he heard one day a great noise of the treading of people about him, upon which he caused his eyelids to be lifted up; and finding that a crowd of people were let in to see him, he called in high indignation for the governor; who being come, Opechancanough scornfully told him that had it been his fortune to take Sir William Berkeley prisoner he should not meanly have exposed him as a show to the people" (Beverley 1947:62). Opechancanough was still "scornful" and "indignant" towards the colony, but the translation of this moral superiority into victory was even less effective in 1644 than it was in 1622.

The colonists again launched war against the Powhatans in the summer of 1644. The Virginia General Assembly met in June 1644, less than two months after the coup, and their first act of that session considers the war, which was to be fought as after the 1622 coup. The act continues with the details of the attacks to be launched (Virginia General Assembly 1915:230–34). Private trade with the Powhatans was again terminated, under penalty of death, because it was seen as "the cause of their enabling and furnishing themselves with such necessaries whereby they may be strengthened and fitted for their defense and subsistence, and that it is generally suspected under the color of license for commerce the natives have been furnished both with guns, powder, and shot, and with other offensive instruments, thereby tending to our utter ruin" (Virginia General Assembly 1915:236). By early 1645 authorized agents of the colony were permitted to trade with other Indian groups, for corn only, however, since otherwise it was feared the colony would starve (Virginia General Assembly 1915:239); self-sufficiency seems to have still eluded them.

Attacks were made on Pamunkey and Chickahominy, as documented by a public levy to defray their expenses (Hening 1823, 1:287–88). Other attacks were authorized south of the James (Hening 1823, 1:292–93). At least one tribe, the Weyanocks, moved south to get away from the English, buying land south of the Blackwater Swamp from the Tuscaroras; they later had to move on several other occasions because of wars with other Indians, as testified by several Weyanocks, Meherrins, and Nottoways in later legal depositions ("Indians of Southern Virginia" 1900:349–52, 1900:4–11). Three forts were ordered built, at Pamunkey and at the fall line on the James and Chickahominy Rivers (Hening 1823, 1:293). Another fort, for the protection of the southside of the James River, was ordered constructed at the falls of the Appomattox River (Hening 1823, 1:315). Again, however, as in the later 1620s and in the 1630s, everyday life for the majority of the settlers seems to have rapidly returned to normal; the majority of the acts of the General Assembly still concerned such issues as taxes, adultery, the sale of wine and liquor, coinage, inns, ministers, and so forth (Hening 1823, 1:288–323). Whereas the acts of the February 1645 session of the General Assembly are dominated by those related to the Powhatans, those from November 1645 and March 1646 show no such precedence.

In March 1646 the General Assembly authorized a force to find Opechancanough and press for peace (Hening 1823, 1:317–19). This force was to be headed by Lieutenant Francis Poythers and was advised and fitted out by Captain Henry Fleet (Hening 1823, 1:318). In addition to his trading background and general knowledge of the Virginia Indians, Fleet had previous experience in negotiating land claims with Opechancanough (Virginia General Assembly 1901:54). It must have been about this time that Opechancanough was captured, since he is mentioned by name in the March 1646 order, and was no longer "king of the Indians" by October 1646, when a peace was concluded (Hening 1823, 1:323). Opechancanough was reckoned to be near one hundred years old ("A Perfect Description" 1963:7) and "was now grown so decrepit that he was not able to walk alone, but was carried about by his men wherever he had a mind to move. His flesh was all macerated, his sinews slackened, and his eyelids became so heavy that he could not see, but as they were lifted up by his servants" (Beverley 1947:61). Poyther's force had no success finding Opechancanough, and when Governor Berkeley learned that Opechancanough was traveling, he resolved to capture him, himself; Opechancanough was taken alive, probably between the falls of the James and Appomattox rivers, and returned to Jamestown as the governor's prisoner (Beverley 1947:61–62; "A Perfect Description" 1963:7; Plantagenet 1963:6; Neill 1886:193). Berkeley hoped to gain some prestige by this action, but was cheated of the possibility:

> Sir William had a mind to send him to England, hoping to get reputation by presenting his Majesty with a royal captive, who at his pleasure could call into the field ten times more Indians than Sir William Berkeley had English in his whole government. Besides, he thought this ancient prince would be an instance of the healthiness and long life of the natives of that country. However, he could not preserve his life above a fortnight, for one of the soldiers, resenting the calamities the colony had suffered by this prince's means, basely shot him through the back, after he was made prisoner, of which wound he died.
>
> He continued brave to the last minute of his life, and showed not the least dejection at his captivity. (1947:61–62)

The meeting noted above at which Opechancanough expressed his indignation to Governor Berkeley took place shortly before he was killed.

The new chief who signed the peace treaty with the colony in 1646, Necotowance, seems not to have entered the English historical record previously. There is no reference in the treaty providing the first record of him to suggest that he was known to the colonists by another name, and there is no earlier record of that name. The process by which he became chief is also unknown, but by October 1646 he was "king of the Indians" (Hening 1823, 1:323).

On 5 October 1646 he entered into treaty with the colony, in the first such treaty to survive in full. This treaty was the first act of the General Assembly in that session:

ACT I.

Art. 1. *Be it enacted by this Grand Assembly*, that the articles of peace following between the inhabitants of this colony and Necotowance king of the Indians be duly and inviolably observed upon the penalty within mentioned as follows:

Imp. That Necotowance do acknowledge to hold his kingdom from the king's Majesty of England, and that his successors be appointed or confirmed by the king's governors from time to time, and on the other side, this assembly, on the behalf of the colony, does undertake to protect him or them against any rebels or other enemies whatsoever, and as an acknowledgement and tribute for such protection the said

Necotowance and his successors are to pay unto the king's governor the number of twenty beaver skins at the going away of geese yearly.

Art. 2. That it shall be free for the said Necotowance and his people to inhabit and hunt on the north side of York River, without any interruption from the English. *Provided* that if hereafter, it shall be thought fit by the governor and council to permit any English to inhabit from Poropotank[2] downwards, that first Necotowance be acquainted therewith.

Art. 3. That Necotowance and his people leave free that tract of land between York River and James River, from the falls of both rivers to Kecoughtan, for the English to inhabit on, and that neither he, the said Necotowance, nor any Indians do repair to or make any abode upon the said tract of land, upon pain of death. And it shall be lawful for any person to kill any such Indian. And in case any such Indian or Indians being seen upon the said tract of land shall make an escape, that the said Necotowance shall upon demand deliver the said Indian or Indians to the Englishmen, upon knowledge had of him or them, unless such Indian or Indians be sent upon a message from the said Necotowance.

And to the intent to avoid all injury to such a messenger, and that no ignorance may be pretended to such as shall offer any outrage, *It is thought fit and hereby enacted*, that the badge worn by a messenger, or, in case there shall be more than one, by one of the company, be a coat of striped stuff,[3] which is to be left by the messenger from time to time so often as he shall return at the places appointed for coming in.

Art. 4. *And it is further enacted*, that in case any English shall repair contrary to the articles agreed upon to the said north side of York River, such persons so offending, being lawfully convicted, be adjudged as felons. *Provided* that this article shall not extend to such persons who by stress of weather are forced upon said land. *Provided also* and it is agreed by the said Necotowance, that it may be lawful for any Englishman to go over to the north side having occasion to fell timber trees or cut sedge, so as the said persons have warrant for their so doing under the hand of the governor. *Provided also*, notwithstanding anything in this act to the contrary, that it shall be free and lawful for any English whatsoever between this present day and the first of March next to kill and bring away what cattle or hogs that they can by any means kill or take upon the said north side of the said river.

Art. 5. *And it is further enacted* that neither for the said Necotowance nor any of his people, do frequent, come in to hunt, or make any abode nearer the English plantations than the limits of Yapin, the Blackwater, and from the head of the Blackwater upon a straight line to the old Monacan town, upon such pain and penalty as aforesaid.[4]

Art. 6. *And it is further ordered enacted* that if any English do entertain any Indian or Indians or do conceal any Indian or Indians that shall come within the said limits, such persons being lawfully convicted thereof shall suffer death as in case of felony, without benefit of clergy, excepted such as shall be authorized thereto by virtue of this act.

Art. 7. *And it is further enacted* that the said Necotowance and his people, upon all occasions of message to the governor for trade, do repair unto Fort Royal [at Pamunkey] only on the north side [of the colony], at which place they are to receive the aforesaid badges, which shall show them to be messengers, and therefore to be freed from all injury in their passage to the governor, upon pain of death to any person or persons whatsoever that shall kill them, the badge being worn by one of the company. And in case of any other affront, the offense to be punished according to the quality thereof, and the trade admitted as aforesaid to the said Necotowance and his people with the commander of the said fort only on the north side.

Art. 8. *And it is further thought fit and enacted*, that upon any occasion of message to the governor or trade, the said Necotowance and his people the Indians do repair to Fort Henry *alias* Appomattox Fort, or to the house of Captain John Flood,[5] and to no other place or places of the south side of the river, at which places the aforesaid badges of striped stuff are to be and remain.

Art. 9. *And it is further thought fit and enacted*, that Necotowance do with all convenience bring in the English prisoners, and all such negroes and guns which are yet remaining either in the possession of himself or any Indians, and that here deliver upon demand such Indian servants as have been taken prisoners and shall hereafter run away, in case such Indian or Indians shall be found within the limits of his domains, provided that such Indian or Indians be under the age of twelve years at their running away.

Art. 10. *And it is further enacted and consented*, that such Indian children as shall or will freely and voluntarily come in and live with the

English may remain without breach of the articles of peace provided they be not above twelve years old.

Art. 11. *And it is further thought fit and enacted*, that the several commanders of the forts and places as aforesaid unto which the said Indians as aforesaid are admitted to repair in case of trade or message do forthwith provide the said coats in manner striped as aforesaid. (Hening 1823, 1:323–26)

A further act of this session provided that land grants made on the north side of the York River prior to the coup be maintained until "the time of leave granted to seat upon the north side" (Hening 1823, 1:328–29).

This treaty is useful in our understanding the attitudes of the colonists towards the Indians at this time. Note that the reference throughout is to a generic "the Indians" rather than to a specific tribe or group of tribes. There seems to be an implicit assumption that Necotowance would be — could be — responsible for all neighboring Indians, despite the colony's earlier recognition and exploitation of the fact that they could gain contact with Indian groups not allied with the Powhatans. This would seem to be the basis for the blame and retribution against Powhatan Indians that would be exacted in response to the violent actions of other Indians in the 1670s. There were also, by treaty, specific separate territories (figure 8) where the Powhatans were to retain all authority and others where the colony would have authority, although the acknowledgment of the sovereignty of the king could be used to require the Powhatan chief to accede to later English expansion; the second article even specifically noted an area where later expansion would take place. Article 6, making it a felony to entertain or conceal an Indian, and the various restrictions placed on messengers and traders suggest that the General Assembly was concerned with controlling access to the Indian trade and that other colonists were willing to face lesser charges in order to participate in that trade. It is also apparent, from Article 9, that there were those in the colony who would choose to live with the Indians: specifically, black slaves, and most likely other servants. An act of March 1643, noting that runaway servants were a common problem, made it a felony for them to carry guns, powder, or shot to the Indians, implying that it was not unusual for runaways to live with the Indians (Hening 1823, 1:254–55). Even in the early years of the colony there had been colonists who preferred to live with the Indians; these were usually harshly punished if captured, as discussed in chapter 5 (see also Percy 1922:265, 280). It is also possible that the English "prisoners" mentioned

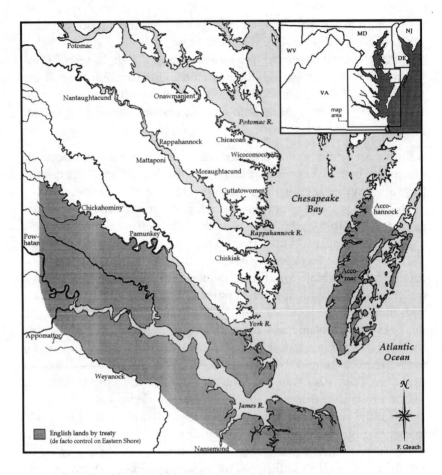

FIGURE 8. Powhatan and English Territories in 1646. *Sources:* 1646 Treaty; Nugent 1934; Rountree 1990, map 4

here, and in many other instances through the early years of the colony, included those who had gone over voluntarily. The second part of Article 9 and Article 10 also demonstrate the treatment of Indian children who went to live with the English; despite their having come "freely and voluntarily" they were subject to being returned by Necotowance should they return to their people before they were twelve, and they apparently lived as servants. This does follow a certain logic: they were treated as indentured servants, paying with their services for the lodging, food, and "civilizing" they were supposed to receive from the colonists. After they were twelve they were expected to return to their people to help spread the benefits of their "civilizing." Nevertheless, that provisions for runaways to be returned were necessary indicates that at least some — and perhaps many — found any benefits not worth the conditions.

These, then, were the conditions of relations between the Virginia colony and the neighboring Indians as the colony entered its fifth decade. Through the effects of disease, warfare, and the appropriation of their lands the Powhatans had been forced to agree to terms that included recognizing the sovereignty of the English king. But despite their losses, the fact that the colony felt it necessary to negotiate with Necotowance as representative of a sovereign nation and the terms of the treaty defining the territories of the two peoples indicate the continued strength of the Powhatans and demonstrate both the colonists' and their own perception of the Powhatans as a sociopolitical entity. The 1646 peace treaty can thus be seen as the foundation for all successive negotiations between these two peoples.

9 ✦ A Survey of Virginia Indian
   Relations after 1646

The Indians had learned, by fatal experience, that they contended in vain with the whites. Their spirits were broken; their bouyancy was gone; they had no alternative, except to suffer their savage habits to be moulded into civilized forms, or to be wasted by the resistless march of the new power in their land. Few, too few, we fear, chose the wiser part. The greater number could not yield, and the result need scarcely be told. They have faded away and gradually disappeared, never more to return. Happily relieved from fear of the savages, the people of Virginia addressed themselves to their duties with great vigor and success. — Howison, *A History of Virginia*

ONLY THREE YEARS AFTER the October 1646 peace treaty it was felt necessary to revise some of the legal obligations of the colony because of abuses by colonists against the Indians. There was concern that the provision allowing the killing of any Indian found in the colony's territory without the appropriate badge was subject to too great abuse, so it was restricted to only "such Indian shall be taken in the act of doing trespass or other harm," but even so the only evidence of offense needed was the oath of the person who "discovered or killed" the Indian (Billings 1975:64). There was obviously still great potential for abuse, but at least some effort was made towards protecting the Indians. There were similar, but stronger, acts designed to protect Indian children brought to the English for education and to prohibit their sale (Billings 1975:64–65). Perhaps most importantly, in terms of historical precedent, patents of land were formally made to three Powhatan chiefs, Ascomowett, Ossakican, and Tottopottomoy, with the stated goal of encouraging their progress toward civility and Christianity. These leaders had acknowledged the sovereignty of the English and requested lands for their people to "inhabit and enjoy the privileges of range and hunting free from the molestation and encroachments of any person, whether Indians or English" (Billings 1975:65–66). The patents for these lands do not appear to have survived, but other patents for English colonists suggest that lands for Tottopottomoy, at least, were actually granted. A patent of 7 June 1650 is described as "bounded NNE upon land of Totapotama" (Nugent 1934:194), and another patent, of 1 July 1653, is described as "on the S side [of] the freshes of York Riv. right against Totopottomoy['s] Fort called Asiskewincke" (Nugent 1934:235). Note that each of these three chiefs was treated separately and that there was no mention of Necotowance, who disappears from the record after 1646; this suggests that the Powhatan paramount chiefdom was disintegrating into smaller units at this time. Tottopottomoy's grant was confirmed in 1653, when colonists were ordered to remove from his lands (Hening 1823, 1:380).

These patents represent the beginning of the formal legal process of moving the Indians onto restricted plots of land. This was at least partly a positive step, at this time, since otherwise they would have been pushed out of their native lands entirely, as was done later to other tribes by the Federal Government. The relatively beneficent nature of these grants is emphasized by an act of the 1650 General Assembly:

> Be it enacted by the governor, council, and burgesses of this present Grand Assembly that there be no grants of land to Englishmen *de futuro*; until the Indians be first served with the proportion of fifty acres of land for each bowman, the proportion of each particular town to lie together, to be surveyed, as well woodlands as cleared ground, and to be land not before patented, with liberty of all waste and unfenced land for hunting for the Indians.
>
> Be it further enacted, and confirmed by the authority aforesaid, that when the land of any Indian or Indians be found to be included in any patent already granted for land at Rappahannock or the parts adjacent, such patentees shall either purchase the said land of the Indians or relinquish the same. (Billings 1975:68)

As the last clause indicates, English settlement of the north bank of the Rappahannock River had begun in 1649, with the approval of the assembly granted in October 1648 (Hening 1823, 1:353–54). This followed a November 1647 order to have removed the few settlers in the Rappahannock and Potomac areas and to establish in their stead what amounted to a military outpost in that area to control trade (Virginia General Assembly 1915:249–54). Within four years of the treaty granting to the Indians territories north of the York River, the colony had crossed both the York and Rappahannock Rivers; but at the same time, the Indians of those areas were assigned land grants for their living and hunting (Hening 1823, 1:382). The sudden rapid growth of the colony at this time made reserved territories for the Indians essential to their survival (figure 9).

This concern over the Indians' lands was matched by some concerns for other aspects of their well-being in this period. The acts protecting Indian children were maintained, the lending of guns to Indians was reduced from a felony (Hening 1823, 1:382), and Indians in the employ of colonists were allowed to carry guns, with a permit "from the county court where they live or from the governor and council" (Hening 1823, 1:391). Anyone with permission from either the county court or at least two justices of peace was allowed to "entertain" (meet or trade with, or employ) an Indian or Indians, instead of only those persons designated in the 1646 treaty (Hening 1823, 1:410), and Indians were employed to kill wolves, which "of late years . . . [had] multiplied and increased throughout the colony exceedingly, to the great loss and decrease of cattle and hogs" (Billings 1975:69). On the Eastern Shore, Indian land sales were to be acknowledged by the commissioners (Hening 1823, 1:391), providing at least some measure of regulation to a class of transactions in which advantages were regularly taken of Indians. A 1656 plan "for civilizing the Indians by introducing among them the idea of separate property" even noted in its preamble that "whereas we have been often put into great dangers by the invasions of our neighboring and bordering Indians, which humanely have been only caused by these two particulars: our extreme pressures on them and their wanting of something to hazard and loose beside their lives" (Hening 1823, 1:393–94). As part of this plan, Indians' lands as granted by the assembly were made inalienable, to avoid the need to allot new lands continually and to give the Indians confidence, both in the assembly and in ownership (Hening 1823, 1:396).

By 1656, however, movements of "western and inland Indians" to the fall line had begun to be of some concern to the colonists (Hening 1823, 1:402). It is likely that the acts of the colony to secure the goodwill of the Powhatans were based on a perception that they could serve as a useful buffer between the colony and these other Indians or even as allies against them. The act pertaining to these Indians of 1656 certainly suggests such reasoning:

> Whereas information has been given that many western and inland
> Indians are drawn from the Mountains and lately set down near the

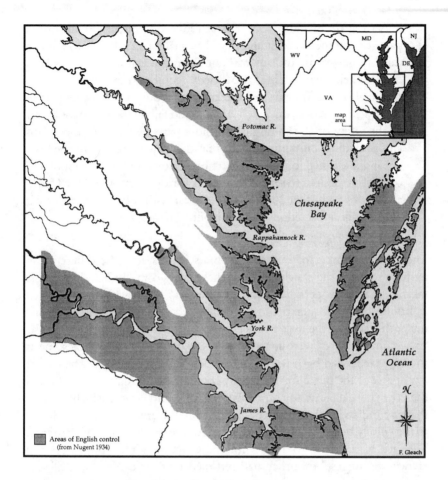

FIGURE 9. Areas of English Settlement in 1652

falls of James River, to the number of six or seven hundred, whereby upon many considerations being had it is conceived great danger might ensue to this colony, this assembly therefore do think fit to resolve that these new-come Indians be in no sort suffered to seat themselves there, or any place near us, it having cost so much blood to expel and extirpate those perfidious and treacherous Indians which were there formerly. It being so apt a place to invade us, and within those limits which in a just war were formerly conquered by us, and by us reserved at the last conclusion of peace with the Indians, in pursuance whereof therefore and due respect to our own safety, *Be it enacted by this present Grand Assembly*, that the two upper counties, under the command of Col. Edward Hill, do presently send forth a party of 100 men at least and that they shall first endeavor to remove the said new-come Indians without making war if it may be, only in case of their own defense, also strictly requiring the assistance of all the neighboring Indians to aid them to that purpose, as being part of the articles of peace concluded with us, and failing therein to look duly to the safety of all the English of those parts by fixing of their arms and providing ammunition, and that they have recourse to the governor and council for further direction therein. And the governor and council are desired to send messages to Tottopottomoy and the Chickahominies and other Indians and to treat with them as they in their wisdoms and discretions shall think fit. (Hening 1823, 1:402–3)

There are a number of interesting points in this act. The difference in attitude towards the Powhatans and these "new-come Indians" is unmistakable. Formerly "perfidious and treacherous," the Powhatans were seen as having been conquered and were expected to help defend the colony under the terms of the 1646 treaty — as now constructed by the colony. The "new-come Indians" were apparently expected to be just as troublesome as the Powhatans had been to the colony before their conquest. The closest any article of the peace treaty actually comes to requiring the assistance of the Powhatans against any other group is the third article, which requires that any Indian inhabiting the designated English area is to be turned over to the colony by the chief — which is far from requiring military assistance. The lack of reference to a chief for the Chickahominies, both here and elsewhere, suggests that they had returned to their earlier form of self-government by council, without a chief. Finally, the governor and council, not members of the assembly or other commanders, are empowered to contact Tottopottomoy and the Chickahominies. This again demonstrates the sovereign status of the Powhatan tribes, as second to and dependent on only that of the king of England; heads of the Powhatan tribes were to be contacted by heads of the colony.

If the Powhatans were to protect the colony in this matter, they were also to receive a few benefits in return. Where the March 1656 assembly had specified the neighboring Indians' duties against the "new-come" Indians, the first act of the December 1656 assembly greatly liberalized the colony's relations with their neighboring Indians. The law that had allowed killing any Indian found committing a trespass was repealed, and enacted in its place was a new law prohibiting the killing of Indians "in our protection" unless they were caught in a felony; other offenses could be punished, "but not to death or maiming," and at least two witnesses to the original offense were required (Hening 1823, 1:415). Furthermore, any of the "Indians in amity" were permitted to enter the colony to hunt fowl, fish, or gather wild fruits, as long as they were not on a fenced plantation, provided they picked up a "ticket" from designated persons at the heads of the rivers, and "any freeman" was permitted to "repair to the said houses or Indian marts and to truck with the said Indians for any commodity not prohibited by the laws of this country" (Hening 1823, 1:415). The securing of these fundamental protections was a great step towards fairness in colonial relations with the Powhatans, but it also demonstrates the increased control of these relations by the colony and the consequent dependence of the Powhatans. Rights were now being granted by the colony, rather than asserted by the Powhatans.

But fight for the colony they did. Sometime between March and December 1656, the force led by Edward Hill, complemented by a hundred Indians led by Tottopottomoy, engaged a party of western Indians. These Indians, variously referred to as "Ricahecrians" (Hening 1823, 1:422), "Mahocks and Nahyssans" (Lederer 1672:7), or simply "enemy Indians" (Mathew 1963:14), defeated the combined Powhatan and colonial force, apparently due to the poor leadership of Hill (Hening 1823, 1:422); Tottopottomoy and most of his men were killed (Lederer 1672:7; Mathew 1963:14). Since the charges against Hill did not mention numbers of colonists killed, the impression is that the Indians were placed in a position to bear the brunt of the attack, whereupon the colonists retreated, leaving the Indians to die. Tottopottomoy is noted in English colonial records for a period of less than ten years but was sufficiently well known to figure in Samuel Butler's *Hudibras*, first published in 1674 but probably written in the 1650s (Nash 1835:vi–vii):

> As lately 't happen'd: in a town
> There liv'd a cobler, and but one,
> That out of doctrine could cut use,
> And mend men's lives as well as shoes.
> This precious brother having slain,
> In times of peace, an Indian,
> Not out of malice, but mere zeal,

> Because he was an infidel,
> The mighty Tottipottimoy
> Sent to our elders an envoy,
> Complaining sorely of the breach
> Of league, held forth by brother Patch,
> Against the articles in force
> Between both churches, his and ours;
> For which he crav'd the saints to render
> Into his hands, or hang th'offender:
> But they maturely having weigh'd
> They had no more but him o' th' trade,
> A man that serv'd them in a double
> Capacity, to teach and cobble,
> Resolv'd to spare him.
> (*Hudibras* part 2, canto 2, ll. 413–33)

Regardless of whether the event occurred or not (and it seems possible, at least, that it did), Butler had an awareness of Tottopottomoy and of who he was; this awareness was completely lost by the 1790s, when Dr. Nash wrote in his notes to *Hudibras*, "I don't know whether this was a real name, or an imitation only of North American phraseology: the appellation of an individual, or a title of office" (Nash 1835:322).

The loss of Tottopottomoy and his warriors may have helped to further the liberalization of colonial policy toward the Powhatans at this time, but it became almost a nonevent in the colony, seldom mentioned in contemporary or later documents. It remained a sore point for the Powhatans for years, however, providing an excellent example of what Fogelson recognized as the "differential recognition of what is considered eventful" (1989:142). About twenty years later, when Cockacoeske, the "queen of Pamunkey" was asked to assist against further "enemy Indians,"

> she after a little musing, with an earnest passionate countenance as if tears were ready to gush out, and a fervent sort of expression, made a harangue about a quarter of an hour, often interlacing (with a high shrill voice and vehement passions) these words, "Tatapatamoi Chepiack," i.e., "Tottopottomoy dead." Col. Hill being next to me, shook his head. I asked him what was the matter. He told me all she said was too true, to our shame, and that his father was General in that battle, where diverse years before Tottopottomoy her husband had led a hundred of his Indians in help to the English against our former

enemy Indians, and was there slain with most of his men, for which no compensation (at all) had been to that day rendered to her, wherewith she now upbraided us.

Her discourse ending, and our morose chairman not advancing one cold word towards assuaging the anger and grief her speech and demeanor manifested under her oppression, nor taking any notice of all she had said, neither considering that we (then) were in our great exigency supplicants to her for a favor of the same kind as the former, for which we did not deny the having been so ingrate, he rudely pushed again the same question, "What Indians will you now contribute, etc.?" Of this disregard she signified her resentment by a disdainful aspect, and turning her head half aside, sat mute till that same question was pressed a third time. She not returning her face to the board, answered with a low slighting voice in her own language, "six," but being further importuned, she sitting a little while sullen, without uttering a word between, said "twelve," though she then had a hundred and fifty Indian men in her town, and so rose up and gravely walked away, as not pleased with her treatment. (Mathew 1963:14–15)

This account shows not only the importance of Tottopottomoy's war party to the Powhatans and its lack of importance to the colony, but also the considerable strength of character retained by Powhatan leaders even at this late date. Although this "queen" might have depended on the English for many things, technically including even her sovereignty, she still saw herself in a position of power, able to take (or refuse to take) significant action independently of the wishes of the colony (see McCartney 1989).

In the late 1650s, however, the colonists were still showing respect for and rewarding the position of the Powhatans as "Indians in amity," at least officially. Whereas the General Assembly of March 1658 kept the sale of guns and ammunition to Indians as a crime, the other earlier acts protecting Indian children and prohibiting their purchase, employing Indians for hunting wolves, and providing for land grants based on the number of bowmen were all reenacted (Hening 1823, 1:441, 456–57, 481–82). Furthermore, the protection of Indians' lands was greatly expanded:

Whereas many complaints have been brought to this assembly touching wrong done to the Indians, in taking away their land and forcing them into such narrow straits and places that they cannot subsist either by planting or hunting, and for that it may be feared they may be justly driven to despair, and to attempt some desperate course for themselves, which inconveniences, though they have been endeavored to be remedied by former acts of assembly made to the same purpose, yet notwithstanding, many English do still entrench upon the said Indians' land, which this assembly conceiving to be contrary to justice, and the true intent of the English plantation in this country, whereby the Indians might by all just and fair ways be reduced to civility and the true worship of God, have therefore thought fit to ordain and enact, and be it hereby ordained and enacted, that all the Indians of this colony shall and may hold and keep those seats of land which they now have, and that no person or persons whatsoever be suffered to entrench or plant upon such places as the said Indians claim or desire until full leave from the governor and council or commanders for the place. Yet this act not to be extended to prejudice those English which are now seated with the Indians' former consent unless, upon further examination before the Grand Assembly, cause shall be found for so doing. And the said commanders shall be accountable before the governor and council and the Grand Assembly if any wrong or injury be done to the Indians contrary to the intent of this act. And be it further enacted, that the Indians as either now or hereafter shall want seats to live on, or shall desire to remove to any places void or untaken up, they shall be assisted therein, and order granted them for confirmation thereof. And no Indians to sell their lands but at quarter courts. And that those English which are lately gone to seat near the Pamunkeys and the Chickahominies on the north side of Pamunkey River shall be recalled and such English to choose other seats elsewhere. And that the Indians, as by a former act was granted them, shall have free liberty of hunting in the woods without the English fenced plantations, these places excepted: between York River and James River and between the Blackwater and the Monacan town and James River. And no patent shall be adjudged valid which has lately passed or shall pass contrary to the sense of this act, not none to be of force which shall entrench upon the Indians' lands to their discontent without express order for the same. (Hening 1823, 1:467–68)

In 1659 Indians were even allowed to keep guns and to use them in their own territories (Hening 1823, 1:518). Whereas the Virginia colony prohibited trade for arms with the Indians, the neighboring colonies did not, and it was apparently not unusual for Indians to carry firearms at this time. The Virginia colony recognized both the impossibility of keeping guns out of the hands of the Indians and the profits to be gained from their trade, declaring in 1659 that free trade, including guns and ammunition, would begin the following spring, "it derogating nothing from our safety and adding much to our advantage" (Hening 1823, 1:525).

These acts provided greater protection to the Powhatans in their inter-actions with the colony, allowed any colonist to participate in the Indian trade, and recognized that the sovereignty of the Powhatan tribes was equal to that of the colony. Although this improved the legal position of the Powhatans, it also put pressure on individual colonial traders to be fair in their dealings by providing increasing government regulation of this trade. The colonial government at this time felt that the good will of the Pow-hatans was important. There are frequent references in the acts of the Gen-eral Assembly to fears of attack in response to unfair treatment, and in 1660 the protection of the Indians in trade relations went so far as to prohibit any Englishman from attempting to recover debts resulting from the ex-tension of credit to an Indian (Hening 1823, 1:541).

The separation of this ideal from the reality of colonial relations with the Powhatans began to be apparent by late 1660. Whereas payments were ordered at that time for Indian lands settled by colonists (Hening 1823, 2:13–14), the commissioners of Northumberland County, on the south bank of the Potomac River, were authorized to apprehend and sell overseas "so many of them as the court shall think fit" if necessary to compensate one colonist for "damages done to him by the Indians" (Hening 1823, 2:15–16). In 1661 the freedom to trade was again restricted to those who "first obtain a commission from the governor, who is desired to grant the same to none but persons of known integrity" (Hening 1823, 2:20). There are also increasing references through this period to runaway servants and slaves. They do not specify where the runaways went, but it can almost only have been to the Indians; even if their ultimate destination was an-other colony, where they might hope to be unknown and begin a new life, they would first have to pass through Indian territory. The 1661 General Assembly approved several sales of Indian lands to colonists (Hening 1823, 2:35, 36, 39), allowing the further restriction of their territory.

The assembly of 1662 completely rewrote the laws of the colony. The relative importance of the Indians may be indicated by the fact that they are not even mentioned until Act 114 (of 152), which allowed free trade to all colonists, "Provided always that no person or persons shall have any commerce or trade with any Indians for beaver, otter or any other furs except as commissioned by the governor" (Hening 1823, 2:124). Act 137 appointed Thomas Flood the colony's new interpreter, his father having recently died (Hening 1823, 2:138). Act 138 then presented all other laws "Concerning Indians." Most of these are related to earlier laws, but there are some important differences and clarifications. In response to common abuses, colonists were again forbidden from purchasing lands from the Indians, all such transactions were nullified, and colonists who had settled on Indian land without prior approval were to be evicted forcibly and their houses burned (Hening 1823, 2:139). Neighboring colonists were ordered to help build fences for the Indians' fields, but the maintenance of the fences was left to the Indians (Hening 1823, 2:139–40). Fishing and gathering in colonial territory were permitted to licensed, unarmed Indians only, and trade could only be conducted by licensed colonists (Hening 1823, 2:140). The boundaries between the colony and the Indians were to be reviewed annually, and new silver and copper badges were ordered for Indians to enter the colony (Hening 1823, 2:141–42). The penalties for offenses were to be similar whether the offender and the victim were Indian or English in most of these cases, providing the greatest legal equality to date, although they were still considered equivalent to runaway servants if found in the colony without their identifying badge from their chief (Hening 1823, 2:143). The role of the Powhatans as colonial buffer was also formally defined:

> And be it further enacted that all Indian kings tributary to the English when they have the least notice of any march by any strange Indians near our quarters shall repair themselves or at least send some one of their great men to the next of the militia, which shall be nominated and appointed by the governor for that purpose, and acquaint him with as much as they know concerning the nation, the numbers, and which way they conceive they will bend their course, and if they then shall desire any aid from us to secure them, that a party be presently sent out by the colonel of the militia to that purpose, which by this our assistance and reciprocal care will make them and us have an equal interest in each other's preservation, while on the other side, we being ignorant of the marches of foreigners impute all damages we receive, which is then commonly most, to our neighbors how innocent soever. (Hening 1823, 2:142–43)

As with all such acts of the assembly since the treaty of 1646, and most likely including that treaty, there does not seem to have been any consultation with the Powhatan leaders over these terms. The assembly was, in many ways, sincerely trying to protect the interests of the Powhatans, but only because they recognized that their own interests were inextricably tied to them.

Through the 1660s and early 1670s repeated troubles arose between the colony and various neighboring tribes and also between the tribes themselves (see Rountree 1990:94–96). Within the colony, which by this time had grown to about forty-one thousand, including about twenty-five hundred slaves of African descent (McCusker and Menard 1985:136), there were increasing differences, on the one hand, between the licensed Indian traders and those others who desired a share in the profits from that trade, and, on the other, between those who favored good relations with the Indians, primarily for trade, and those who wanted their lands for ever-larger plantations. The governor's control of such matters was also resented by some. The occasional violence kept all the factions uneasy.

In the summer of 1675 a dispute erupted over payment for goods between the Doeg Indians of Maryland and Thomas Mathew, a wealthy planter on the Potomac. Attempting to gain satisfaction, the Doegs first stole some of Mathew's hogs but were pursued, and some were killed by Mathew's men. A party of Doegs then attacked and killed one of Mathew's men. This prompted a militia party under the command of George Brent and George Mason to raid the Doeg village (Washburn 1957:20–21). They seem to have been anxious for a fight; not only were a Doeg chief and ten of his men killed by Brent and his horse troops, but fourteen Susquehannocks were killed by Mason's men before "an Indian came, who with both hands shook [Mason] (friendly) by one arm, saying 'Susquehanoughs netoughs,' i.e., 'Susquehannocks — friends,' and fled, whereupon [Mason] ran amongst his men, crying out 'For the Lord's sake shoot no more, these are our friends the Susquehannocks' " (Mathew 1963:8–9). This action initiated protests from Maryland over the incursion of Virginians into their colony and the killings of peaceful Indians (Washburn 1957:21). Governor Berkeley of Virginia tried to control his colonists — if for no other reason than to protect his profits from trade with the tributary Indians — but too many of them were ready to disregard his orders and attack Indians regardless of whether they were friendly or not. One such, who became their leader, was Nathaniel Bacon Jr., a gentleman-scoundrel — "impatient of labor" and "extravagant and improvident" — who had only arrived in the colony in 1674, "after he had become involved in a scheme to defraud a neighboring youth of a part of his inheritance" (Washburn 1957:18). Bacon began his actions against the Indians by seizing "some friendly Appomattox Indians allegedly

for stealing corn, although the corn was neither his nor his neighbors' "
(Washburn 1957:22). In 1676 Bacon led forces against two friendly settlements in Virginia, the Pamunkeys and the Occoneechees. Having gained
the support of many in the colony, Bacon returned to Jamestown in July
1676, and "the impotent Berkeley fled to the Eastern Shore" (Rountree
1990:99). Bacon's rule was short-lived; Berkeley and his loyalists began
their counterattack in September, and in October Bacon died of dysentery,
while plagued by lice (Washburn 1957:80–85, 211). Berkeley's men continued the attacks, and by January 1677 the courts-martial of the rebels had
begun (Washburn 1957:89–90). While the rebellion was dying down, however, Berkeley still had to defend his government before the king's commissioners, sent to investigate the uprising and its background. There were
many complaints of Berkeley's high-handedness, particularly in matters relating to the Indians, and Berkeley also came under fire from the commissioners for his seizures of the estates of reported rebels (Washburn
1957:120–31). Berkeley was returned to England, where he died soon after
(Washburn 1957:139).

Bacon's Rebellion has been variously interpreted by historians, some
viewing it as a democratic uprising, perhaps even a precursor to the War
for American Independence (Wertenbaker 1940; Webb 1984), and others
questioning the democratic motives of the rebels (Washburn 1957). Washburn noted what I believe to be the key issue, here and throughout the
colony's relations with the Powhatans — "the aggressiveness of the fron-
tiersmen"— and argued that historians have overlooked this cause because
of racial and political biases that encourage a view of Indians as primitive
and warlike and whites as civilized pursuers of democratic freedoms —
when "actually the American frontiersman of the seventeenth century paid
scant heed to such ideals" (1957:162–63).

Whatever its implications for the colony, the rebellion's relation to the
Powhatans was simple: "Out of the terribly confused situation existing in
Virginia in 1677, the commissioners found clear evidence on only one
point: the tributary Indians had been gratuitously attacked and despoiled"
(Rountree 1990:99). In May 1677 a new peace was signed between the
colony and the Powhatans, known as the "Treaty of Middle Plantation"
(i.e., Williamsburg). Three Powhatan chiefs — including Cockacoeske from
Pamunkey–signed, but the *werowance* of Appomattox was not allowed to
sign "because of some recent trouble with his people" (Rountree
1990:100). When the treaty was renewed in 1680 the leaders of several other
tribes also signed, including the *werowance* of Appomattox; it seems to have

been accepted as a fair agreement (McCartney 1989:193; Rountree 1990:100). The greatest difficulty with the treaty was the fact that Cocka-coeske, at her own and the colony's desire, was placed over several tribes in addition to the Pamunkeys, including the Chickahominies and the Rap-pahannocks, who "stubbornly refused to cooperate with her, claiming that they had not intended such subjection by subscribing to the peace treaty" (McCartney 1989:186; cf. Washburn 1957:135–36; Rountree 1990:101–3). Both seem to have maintained their independence, without abandoning the treaty (McCartney 1989:189).

The provisions of this treaty were similar to the laws in place prior to Bacon's Rebellion, with the Indians accepting the sovereignty of the king of England and the colony pledged to protecting the lands and rights of the tributary Indians (Washburn 1957:135). Similar abuses also appear to have continued; by the early eighteenth century, for example, the Pamunkey reservation was drastically reduced to a size insufficient to support the tribe; most tribes were to lose their lands entirely. Some of these land sales and leases were requested by the Indians, and after the 1680s the colony did not keep its treaty obligation to prevent such alienation (Rountree 1990:112–13, 115). It seems apparent that the Powhatans were reduced to selling and leasing their land when they were no longer able to maintain themselves on that land. John Clayton noted in 1687 that they were still making ceramic pots and pipes (Clayton 1965:38), which probably included those such locally made products found on colonial sites (Gleach 1990a), and John Banister noted that trade goods in the 1680s included, in addition to furs, "venison, deer-suit, feathers, baskets, etc." (1970:385), but their only commodifiable resource for which there was constant and strong demand was land.

The relatively friendly acquisition of Powhatan lands allowed the colony to expand without further conflict with either its colonial or Indian neigh-bors. The colonial population grew steadily from this time on, and wealthy landowners began to assemble the vast plantations that came to typify eighteenth-century Virginia, complete with greatly increased slave-hold-ings. The Powhatans were increasingly engaged in the struggle for their survival; Rountree (1990) has detailed the histories of the Powhatan tribes to the present. Although they continued to exist and to interact with each other, with other Indians, and with their neighboring colonists, their po-litical position — their ability to affect colonial policy — declined. From a position of power from which they could manipulate and exert some con-trol over colonial policy, they had become dependent on the colony. At times in this early period the colony tried — at least a token effort — to treat the Powhatans fairly, but by the eighteenth century the colonists' prejudices against Indians were all too apparent; the Reverend Burnaby, who visited the colony in 1759–60, wrote of the colonists: "Their ignorance of mankind and of learning exposes them to many errors and prejudices, especially in regard to Indians and negroes, whom they scarcely consider as of the human species; so that it is almost impossible, in cases of violence, or even murder, committed upon those unhappy people by any of the planters, to have the delinquents brought to justice: for either the grand jury refuse to find the bill, or the petit jury bring in their verdict, not guilty" (1904:54). Whereas the Powhatans had worked to accommodate the English colonists, had even come to accept and live with their political subordination to the English crown, the attitudes of the colonists were largely unchanged. By the later seventeenth century, however, the colony had grown in size and strength to the point where it could control many aspects of the Indians' lives.

✦ Conclusion

Of the pursuit of beauty and the husk that remains, perversions and mistakes, while the true form escapes in the wind, sing O Muse; of Raleigh, beloved by majesty, plunging his lust into the body of a new world — and the deaths, misfortunes, counter coups, which swelled back to certify that ardor with defeat. Sing! and let the rumor of these things make the timid more timid and the brave desperate, careless of monuments which celebrate the subtle conversions of sense and let truth go unrecognized. Sing! and this once let the song be an arrow through the brain.
— William Carlos Williams, "Sir Walter Raleigh"

THE PERIOD DISCUSSED here saw great changes in the inter-actions between the Powhatan tribes and the Virginia colony and great changes within each of these polities. The Powhatans allowed the Virginia colony to be planted in 1607, formally and ritually admitting it into their world in the winter of 1607–8, and for several decades they fought to enforce the control they believed they could exert over the colony. The Virginia colonists and their promoters in England never recognized Powhatan authority, and they also acted to control the situation. The period between the coups of 1622 and 1644 marked a turning point in the relations between the Powhatans and the English, from a situation where both sides felt that they not only could dictate, but were dictating, the terms of the relationship, to the period after 1646, where the colony was clearly in control of the situation. There is greater justification in defining the 1644 coup as an "uprising," but even in 1644 Opechancanough was expecting the political and military results to reflect the morally correct position (from the Powhatan perspective) that the colonists were violating their pledges to the Powhatans. After the death of Opechancanough, and following the repeated colonial attacks in 1644 and 1645, the remaining Powhatan tribes had little alternative but to accede to the demands of the colony. We know, from Beverley's notes of two *huskanaws* around 1690 and his entry into and description of a Powhatan temple (1947:196–98, 207–8), probably also in the 1690s (Rountree 1990:116), that the Powhatan religion continued in practice at least into the end of the seventeenth century, but the political union of tribes seems to have ended by around 1650.

The history of English-Powhatan relations demonstrates the importance of viewing the context, in this case a particular colonial situation, from the various perspectives of the participants. In many historical cases there is little detail recorded about such abstract cultural constructs, but the approach employed here uses comparative materials from related cultural contexts in order to reconstruct an approximation of systems of meaning that would otherwise be lost. This approach must be used carefully, grounded in the various cultural records — archaeological, historical, ethnographic, of native and Western traditions — to avoid the perils of sheer speculation, but it enables meaningful cultural interpretations in situations where otherwise such would not be possible. These reconstructed understandings can then be applied to the documented historical record.

My adoption of the term *coup* for these military actions that previously have been referred to as "massacres" or "uprisings" thus reflects the meanings of those actions within the particular contexts in which they took place, as closely as I can reconstruct them, and as accurately as I can find terminology to represent them. They were not uprisings or rebellions, they were not unnecessary and indiscriminate, nor were they attempts at genocide. They were military corrections, severe parallels to the slap on the wrist administered to a disobedient child — in this case administered to an unruly minority population who had been permitted to settle in Powhatan territory. But the colony's response to these actions, the interpretation of them as attempted genocide or uprising, is an equally essential part of an understanding of the events of seventeenth-century Virginia. Taken alone, the modern view of Indians as engaged in valiant but vain efforts to defend their cultures against European invaders is no more accurate than the earlier notion of Christian soldiers fighting against pagan savages to bring God to the New World.

It is not just the respective valorizations of the competing cultures, but the basic categories of meaning, that need revision. The Powhatans, and other American Indians, have suffered the results of such flawed Euro-American constructions for centuries, considered either as uncivilized warriors, capable of no response to the Europeans other than warfare; as romanticized natural beings, living in idealized close relation to nature; or as

rational, economic Everymen, calculating the costs and benefits in univer-
salized terms. It might never be possible to understand another world-view
fully, but with hard work, open-mindedness, and respect for cultural differences, we can always hope to improve.

I have explored here the repeated efforts of Powhatan and his successors
to establish parameters within which the English colony could exist, and
the various treaties and other formal relationships between the two peoples.
Only after repeated refusal of such offers and violations of these agreements
did the Powhatans attack the colony, and then only in a controlled action,
attacking the most offensive, invasive settlements. The situation bears a
striking parallel to later interactions in the west, here described by a former
Indian agent:

> We may as well make up our minds to the fact that the Indians are
> not disappearing, and will not disappear from natural causes, even in
> the face of our advancing civilization.
>
> We may exterminate them partially, as we did the heroic band who
> were led by Nez Perce Joseph; who lost fifty per cent of their number
> by sheer homesickness after their removal to the Indian Territory. Or
> we may inveigle them into a surrender by fraud as Crook did Geron-
> imo, and send them to die in the swamps of Florida. But they are a
> vital living fact with which we have to deal; and the most vital so far
> as our national honor is concerned. And we can only cause them to
> disappear by extermination or absorption.
>
> . . .
>
> I sometimes feel that if it could be arranged that this big, awkward
> and unjust machine that we call the Government, could be prevailed
> upon to take its hands off the Indians and let them alone, *that* would
> be one step in the right direction. In my twenty-two years of life in
> Indian country, I have seen a great many cases of controversy between
> Indians and white men; and I have never known of a single one in
> which the Indian was not right. Not a single one. (Riordan 1891:
> 234–35)

Although one may question certain points in Riordan's address, its essence — that the Indians would not disappear, and that it was primarily the
actions of the intruding Euro-Americans that have caused conflict between
the two peoples — is also supported by the events of the first seventy-five
years of English-Indian contact in Virginia.

But pointing a finger at the offending intruders is not sufficient in a modern context where the descendants of those intruders are the ultimate authorities over history and, in some ways, even over the Indian descendants themselves. By examining the history of these early interactions from both perspectives, I have illustrated some of the processes by which such authority was created. This is not intended to engender guilt; as Sioui notes, we need to set aside those feelings in order to come to terms with our historical past, so that we may improve our future (Sioui 1992, esp. 4–5). The historical fact is that the colonizing Europeans gained control of many aspects of the lives of American Indians. But there are also aspects of many American Indians' lives that have not come under the control of Euro-Americans. For some groups it has been a matter of withdrawal from contact or of keeping certain rituals secret from these outsiders. These have seen some success.

The Powhatans seem to have taken the path of withdrawal only in a limited sense through this period, and not entirely willingly. They actively sought trade with the English colonists and were willing to accept the English church alongside their own religious beliefs. The expectations in trade were grossly uneven, however; colonial Virginia was interested in its Indians only insofar as they were a resource. Despite the rhetoric about "civilizing" the Indians, the main effect of the program — when it had an effect at all — was to teach them English and turn them into servants. There was only limited acceptance of them as equals, as fully human. Few Powhatan ceremonies were recorded by the English writers, but the impression a reader receives repeatedly is that they were not recorded because they were thought to be of no significance, not because they were hidden from the colonists in order to preserve them.

The status of military power in England at this time, and its relations to other aspects of their culture, is also of critical importance to the study of their colony in Virginia and could well be applied in other colonial situations. The final shift in military tactics and technology from approaches based on the personal strength of the soldiers to a reliance on an impersonal external power that could be controlled by anyone may be related to the perspective that saw the entire universe as created for the use and benefit of humanity, as something to be manipulated. As discussed in chapter 2, the "great chain of being" was reflected in the English colonial hierarchy; the organization of armies can be seen as yet another form of this hierarchy. The perception of the importance of firearms in early colonial warfare with the Indians, despite their lack of any significant material advantage in the form of war fought in Virginia, demonstrates their symbolic importance in this English world-view; the acceptance of this perception by most scholars to the present reflects the extent to which this understanding of man's relationship to the universe, and to power, still pertains in contemporary Anglo-American culture. The difficulties the colonies — and later the United States — had in adjusting their ways of war to fight successfully against Indians in the eighteenth and nineteenth centuries further demonstrate the strength of this Anglo-American reliance on arms.

Despite the continued existence of a number of the Powhatan tribes, historians consistently noted their decline and predicted their demise. In the mid–eighteenth century Burnaby noted their "having dwindled away through intemperance and disease" (1904:62); Thomas Jefferson described their condition similarly:

> Very little can now be discovered of the subsequent history of these tribes severally. The *Chickahominies* removed, about the year 1661, to Mattaponi river. Their chief, with one from each of the tribes of the Pamunkies and Mattaponies, attended the treaty of Albany in 1685. This seems to have been the last chapter in their history. They retained however their separate name so late as 1705, and were at length blended with the Pamunkies and Mattaponies, and exist at present only under their names. There remain of the *Mattaponies* three or four men only, and they have more negro than Indian blood in them. They have lost their language, have reduced themselves, by voluntary sales, to about fifty acres of land, which lie on the river of their own name, and have, from time to time, been joining the Pamunkies, from whom they are distant but 10 miles. The *Pamunkies* are reduced to about 10 or 12 men, tolerably pure from mixture with other colours. The older ones among them preserve their language in a small degree, which are the last vestiges on earth, as far as we know, of the Powhatan language. They have about 300 acres of very fertile land, on Pamunkey river, so encompassed by water that a gate shuts in the whole. Of the *Nottoways*, not a male is left. A few women constitute the remains of that tribe. (Jefferson 1955:96–97)

Jefferson's description was not altogether accurate; as Mooney noted (1907:143), Jefferson omitted some groups known to have still existed, underestimated the Mattaponi and Pamunkey populations and the retention of the Powhatan language, and gave the wrong size for the Pamunkey reservation, which was 800 acres, not 300. The Powhatans were not very visible to the mainstream society in the later eighteenth and nineteenth centuries, however, and Jefferson's appraisal reflects the perceptions of most in Virginia at this time. Through the nineteenth century there were repeated statements and predictions of their end by historians, and laments by romantic poets; for example,

> Opechancanough lived to see the destruction of his people; and for any purpose of glory or security, might have justly considered himself as the last of his race. (Burk 1805:62)

> Modern industry may perchance still find in the counties of King William and Southampton the feeble remains of these tribes, sunk in indolence, and degraded by intermixture with a lower race; but a few years will sweep from eastern Virginia every vestige of the savage warriors who once held her soil. . . . Cold philosophy may explain their decay, and mark each step of their melancholy pilgrimage through years of diminution; but a sensitive heart will not refuse to let fall a tear upon the soil once trodden by the feet of these desolated sons of the forest. (Howison 1846:116)

> But the warrior race is fading away;
> The day of their prowess and glory is past;
> They are scathed like a grove where the lightnings play,
> They are scatter'd like leaves by the tempest blast.
> They must perish from earth with the deeds they have done;
> Already the pall of oblivion descends,
> Enshrouding the tribes from our view, one by one,
> And time o'er the straggling remnants bends,
> And sweeps them away with a hurried pace,
> Still sounding the knell of the warrior race.
> (S. Smith 1841:14)

Despite the decline in public recognition of the Powhatans, they continued — and do now continue — to exist. Rountree (1990) has documented their histories to the present-day, but any perceptive visitor to the Pamunkey and Mattaponi reservations in Virginia today can recognize a difference between their attitudes towards their history and towards their cultural and natural setting and the attitudes of their non-Indian neighbors.

The Powhatans today, like other American-Indian groups, survive and retain many distinctive qualities and ways of understanding and living in the world around them. But because they do not fit Euro-American stereotypes of Indians, they have become relatively invisible to the dominant culture. This is a particular problem for Indians east of the Mississippi, who have only recently gotten much recognition, and then only through such actions as the standoff at Oka and the revision of land leases at Salamanca, New York. The Lumbee Indians of North Carolina have been seeking federal recognition as Indians for over a hundred years, without success to date. Never having had a reservation or a treaty with the federal government — a common condition for eastern Indians — makes it difficult to gain recognition. Even now, none of the Powhatan tribes are federally recognized, and until relatively recently only the two reservation-based tribes, the Pamunkeys and the Mattaponis, were recognized by the Commonwealth of Virginia.

The Euro-American stereotypes of Indians are based in European colonists' misunderstandings of Indian culture and Indians' actions. The consequences of these misunderstandings continue to develop today, and it is only through an increased awareness of the processes by which they originate that there can be any possibility of resolving some of these differences. I have attempted to show here how some of these misunderstandings arose, what their bases were in both events and cultural understandings, and what were the more immediate consequences of the variant perceptions of events. The Powhatan construction of reality, the interrelationships they saw between aspects of culture and the natural world that were seen as separate by the English colonists, and the aesthetic sense in which they evaluated actions were all quite distinct from the colonial English understanding. It is precisely in these differences that this history is rooted.

✦ Notes

INTRODUCTION

1   The name was originally given as *Opitchapam*, also spelled *Opitchapan*. Smith (1986d:308) refers to "Opitchapam now called Toyatan" in a 1622 context, but Strachey used the spelling *Taughaiten* in 1612 (1953:69), and the new name Itoyatan took on in 1621 was *Sasawpen* (Virginia Council 1933c:584). To avoid unnecessary confusion, I have used the spelling *Itoyatan* throughout; since the first syllable in both forms (O- or I-) is an unstressed ǝ (easily missed by the untrained English-accustomed ear), it is possible that the other spelling variations simply represent speaking or hearing differences between individuals.

2   These are not necessarily mutually exclusive categories (see Sahlins 1981:67–72); "one may question whether the continuity of a system ever occurs without its alteration, or alteration without continuity" (1981:67).

3   There is a commonsense view of history that sees it as simply derived from authoritative statements of historical facts (Collingwood 1956:234–35), but this has long been recognized as fallacious.

4   There are also western Algonquian languages (e.g. Arapaho, Blackfoot, and Cheyenne), but these are divergent from both the Central and Eastern groups (see Bloomfield 1946; Goddard 1978b:586).

5   The latter usage may also be responsible for the mistaken attribution that one occasionally finds of *Powhatan* as a title of position, instead of a name. The contemporary sources are clear that this was used as a name (although rank was a component of his identity); he was a leader named Powhatan, *not* "the Powhatan" of the group. I discuss the likely meaning of this name in chapter 1.

I   THE NATIVE CONTEXT

1   Which they, in turn, had probably received in trade; the ultimate source was most likely near Lake Superior (see Tooker 1901, esp. p.28, Pendergast 1991).

2   Quinn (1955:854) cites linguistic notes supplied by James Geary, with "*ahkamikwi* being apparently 'land dwelt upon,' 'dwelling house,' 'house-site,' [Tsenacommacah] having *tsen = tcin* 'close together' as a prefix."

3   Smith (1986c:127) notes that this term could refer to any "commander," but English usage at the time, and historians' usage ever since, has applied the term to what Smith referred

to as Powhatan's "inferior kings," or district chiefs. Smith also notes the use of the word *caucorouse*, or "Captain" (1986c:127); elsewhere (1986c:103) he gives *caw-cawwassoughes* as the elders of the Chickahominies. This is apparently "the Algonkian word *caucawasu* meaning 'advisor,' from which the word caucus is derived" (Cooper 1992:2).

4 This idea was widely accepted among Virginia archaeologists in the early 1980s and is given in print by E. R. Turner (1993:239−40n.6).

5 The validity of the Walam Olum as a Delaware origin account may be questionable, and its recorded form appears to have been created by Constantine Rafinesque in the early nineteenth century (Oestreicher 1993), but Voegelin's knowledgeable and careful translations make it useful for this sort of general word identification.

6 See Galloway (1989:259−60) for a similar interpretation of Choctaw understandings of the French colonial structure.

7 The term possibly had a meaning approximating "he has a new body" (Gerard 1907:94).

8 Possibly a priestly village, since the name has the same root as *quioccosuk*.

2   THE ENGLISH COLONIAL CONTEXT

1 Note that the term *Virginia* as used at this time referred to all of North America claimed by England; that part described by Hariot was what is now coastal North Carolina.

2 Copland is an obscure figure, known chiefly from his few published sermons. He was admitted into the Virginia Company and given three shares in 1621 (Virginia Co. 1933:63). Like William Crashaw, he seems to have had puritan leanings.

3 A popular minister, Crashaw had strong puritan leanings, and his sermons were widely published; he was also a noted poet and father of the poet Richard Crashaw. An extensive entry can be found for him in the *Dictionary of National Biography*.

4 Another contemporary copy of this document, held at the Bodleian Library, has been published (Virginia Council 1933a). The published version, however, includes at least one miscopy from the document and differs from this copy in several particulars. My preference is for the contemporary copy in the British Library, which I have personally examined and which I cite here.

5 In a recent attempt to salvage the reputations of the Virginia colonists, Ransome has argued (1995) that they were more skilled and literate than previously described, basing his argument on passenger lists from 1619 to 1621 that list individuals by their skills (husbandman, gardener, bricklayer, etc.) and from book purchases by the company from 1620 to 1623. Unfortunately, the data do not warrant his conclusions; the fact that someone had a trained skill indicates neither his willingness to work nor his integrity, and the books purchased attest only that some in the colony could read — a fact that has never been in dispute. A printing order for 500 copies of pamphlets on growing mulberry trees and "500 more of the Rates of comoditie" (quoted in 1995:455) demonstrates only the press run demanded by the printer, not "a remarkable belief in the settlers' literacy, for the population of the colony at that time was less than 900" (1995:455). The other documented books purchased were barely sufficient for a few religious and political leaders. Some, perhaps even many, individuals undoubtedly carried books with them, but there is no real evidence for widespread literacy among the Virginia colonists.

Ransome's argument is also based entirely on information dating from 1619 and later;

Copland's comment cited above suggests that the situation then was very different from that of the early years of the colony. Lacking any reason to discard an extensive body of uniformly negative contemporary assessments of the Virginia colonists, including those of colonial and Company officials, Ransome's argument is questionable for the period after 1619, and entirely unpersuasive for the earlier period. His dismissal (1995:444) of the work of Morgan (1975) and Breen (1980) is thus also unwarranted.

6   This letter is mistakenly cited as 14 September 1613 in the catalog of the Stowe manuscripts in the British Library and in other publications. The correct date is 4 September 1613.

7   This work was originally attributed to Guillaume de Bellay, and is often cited thus (see Spaulding 1937:96). William de Bellay is the name given as author on the title page.

4 THE BIRTH OF VIRGINIA IN TSENACOMMACAH

1   The first river encountered on entering the Chesapeake Bay, the James River was named after the English king, as was the first settlement. Powhatan's original home territory lay upon this river, and it was similarly known to his people as Powhatan's river (Smith 1986b:145).

2   Smith frequently wrote his accounts in the third person.

3   In English usage, particularly in the early seventeenth century, "wheat" was the unmarked term for the grain of a cereal, and here refers to maize or Indian corn; "corns" was synonymous with kernels or grains.

4   Regna Darnell has observed that the shift to three as ritual number — four is much more common in Algonquian cultures, representing the principal cardinal directions — is a common indication of the influence of Christianity (personal communication). This may indicate that Don Luis and the Spanish Jesuit mission of 1570–71 had more effect on the Powhatans than is commonly assumed, and supports my interpretation of that episode in chapter 3.

5   The symbolic death and rebirth of young men in the *huskanaw* (Beverley 1947:207–9), discussed in chapter 1, provides a good parallel here.

5 VIRGINIA BEFORE THE 1622 COUP

1   This incident is not recorded in the *True Relation*, and the section of the *Proceedings* and the *Generall Historie* that includes it was probably actually written by Anas Todkill, one of the colonists with them (Smith 1986c:221n.8).

2   His contempt, in retrospect, is evident from the marginal note in the *Generall Historie*: "Captain Smith goes with four to Powhatan, when Newport feared with 120" (1986d:182).

3   This is the first recorded mention of Nemattanew, although the tone of the quotation suggests that he had been previously known to the English. His murder in 1622, seen as the proximate cause of the coup, is discussed in chapter 6.

4   Whitaker also described an attack by rain-conjuring attempted against another expedition (1611:ff 192ᵛ–93).

5   Hamor (1615:31) implies that this took place in the winter of 1612–13; Strachey (1953:64) dates it to the winter of 1610, but Dale had not arrived in the colony at that date.

6   Archaeological survey directed by L. Daniel Mouer in the mid-1980s identified what were
    most likely the remains of the Bermuda Hundred palisade, although no artifacts were
    found that clearly dated to this period (Gleach 1986). Most of the site of Henrico seems
    to have been destroyed during the Civil War by canal construction.

7   The taking of a new name did not eliminate the old for the Powhatans. Most later refer-
    ences to these chiefs use their earlier-known names, and I follow that usage here.

8   Rountree (1990:302 n.41) tentatively identifies the poison as the plant *Cicuta maculata*,
    noting that it is widespread on the Eastern Shore.

6   "THE GREAT MASSACRE OF 1622"

1   Browne's entry for the month of March in his 1622 almanac was oddly prophetic for the
    Virginia colony: the "phlebotomy" skillfully applied by the Powhatans that month, the
    coup of 22 March, proved to be truly dangerous medicine for the physician, since the
    English colony took this as stimulant to a war of revenge.

    Rountree (1990:71–72) has suggested that Nemattanew's killing occurred prior to No-
    vember 1621, but, as she notes, all contemporary accounts that mention the timing of these
    events "indicate a short lapse of time between his death and the attack" (1990:302 n.44).
    She bases her timing on an inferred sequence of events from a confusingly written passage
    in a letter from the Virginia Council (Rountree 1990:302 n.45). The critical statement
    reads, "neither was it to be imagined that upon the death of Nemattanew, a man so far
    out of the favor of Opechancanough that he sent word to Sir George Yeardley being then
    governor by his interpreter, that for his part he could be contented his throat were cut,
    there would fall out a general breach" (Virginia Council 1935a:10–11). The mention of
    Yeardley as governor places the cited message from Opechancanough prior to Wyatt's
    arrival in November 1621, but there is no reason that a character reference in a subordinate
    clause need refer to action precisely contemporary with the main text in which the clause
    is embedded. The primary text should be read thus: "Neither was it to be imagined that
    upon the death of Nemattanew there would fall out a general breach." The subordinate
    clause indicates why this should be so: prior to November 1621 some incident had
    prompted a message to the governor that Nemattanew was so out of favor that Ope-
    chancanough could be contented if Nemattanew's throat were cut. From this I assume
    that Nemattanew had raided other settlements. The statement is clearly not relevant to
    the immediate time of Nemattanew's death, since he died of gunshot wounds before he
    could be taken to the governor (Beverley 1947:53).

2   Like the Virginia "massacres," this attack may be misnamed, but it is the name by which
    it is generally known; I leave this matter to scholars of colonial Ireland.

3   Kingsbury's square brackets here denote portions of the text that are unclear in the manu-
    script, not editorial additions.

4   As I read it; Rountree disagrees, as already discussed.

7   VIRGINIA BETWEEN THE COUPS

1   Not 1634, as transcribed by Gethyn-Jones (1982:208, 214, 217–18). The manuscript (Smyth
    of Nibley papers, no. 43) plainly shows a "2" written over the "3" here, as done by the

same copyist on a 1623 court document (Smyth of Nibley papers, no. 38) in the same set of manuscripts.

2 Martin was a high-ranking gentleman colonist, a member of the original 1607 Council. He was granted the unique distinction of a land patent from the company that exempted him from all obligations to the colony, and several charges were made against him in the 1610s and 1620s stemming from his actions under this freedom (Virginia General Assembly 1933:155–58); he was apparently widely disliked, and in 1625 the Council in Virginia went so far as to remove him, against the expressed wishes of the Privy Council (Virginia Council 1935d:560, 1935e:565). His patent was known as Martin Brandon; Martin's Hundred was a different, later settlement not associated with John Martin.

3 The exception noted, allowing for licensed attack against Yeardley, seems intended to insure that he could be stopped if he were to overstep his bounds.

4 An "ancient planter," or settler who had been in the colony since 1615 or earlier. This William Pierce is not to be confused with Captain William Peirce, who sailed between England and Virginia on many occasions in the 1620s and 1630s. Variant spellings also include Perce and Perse, and the two must be identified by context (see Smith 1986c:468n and the *Dictionary of American Biography*).

5 An additional twenty-one colonists, including the interpreter Henry Spelman, were killed by the Potomacs in March 1623 in retaliation for the English killing of thirty or forty Potomacs the previous year (Smith 1986c:313–14, 320–21; cf. Mead 1963:410).

8 THE COUP OF 1644 AND ITS AFTERMATH

1 It is difficult to locate holidays and moon phases for 1644; there were no formal almanacs and no *Book of Common Prayer* published that year in England. A 1641 *Book of Common Prayer* (Church of England 1641:n.p.) provides the holiday calendar in "An Almanack for xxxviii. yeers," however; extrapolating from a 1643 almanac (Gallen 1643:B2v-B3) and considering the date of Easter, we can reckon 14 April, and no later than 20 April 1644, as the most likely date for the full moon.

2 This was a village almost due north of Jamestown on the north bank of the York River, east of where the Mattaponi and Pamunkey Rivers join to form the York River, and well within the coastal plain.

3 A woolen fabric.

4 This article drew the southern boundary between the colony and the Indians, permitting the colony all land from the south bank of the James River several miles into the interior throughout the coastal plain (see figure 8).

5 Capt. Flood was also appointed official interpreter of the colony (Hening 1823, 1:328).

✦ References

Archer, Armstrong. 1844. *A Compendium of Slavery, as it exists in the Present Day in the U S of A*. London: J. Haddon.

Archer, Gabriel [attribution from Barbour]. 1969. A relatyon of the Discovery of our River, from James Forte into the Maine: made by Captain Christopher Newport: and sincerely written and observed by a gent. of yᵉ Colony [May–June 1607]. In *The Jamestown Voyages under the First Charter, 1606–1609*, ed. Philip L. Barbour. Cambridge UK: Hakluyt Society.

Argall, Samuel. 1933a. A Letter, Probably to His Majesty's Council for Virginia [June 9, 1617]. In *The Records of the Virginia Company of London*, vol. 3. Ed. Susan M. Kingsbury. Washington DC: U.S. Government Printing Office.

——. 1933b. A Letter to the Virginia Company [March 10, 1618]. In *The Records of the Virginia Company of London*, vol. 3. Ed. Susan M. Kingsbury. Washington DC: U.S. Government Printing Office.

Ascham, Roger. 1571. *Toxophilus, The schole, or partitions of shooting contayned in ii. bookes, written by Roger Ascham, 1544, And now newlye perused*. London: Thomas Marshe.

Aubin, George F. 1975. *A Proto-Algonquian Dictionary*. Ottawa: National Museum of Man.

Axtell, James, and William C. Sturtevant. 1980. The Unkindest Cut, or Who Invented Scalping? *William and Mary Quarterly* (3d ser.) 37 (3): 451–72.

Banister, John. 1970. The General Natural History and Account "Of the Natives" [ca. 1691]. In *John Banister and His Natural History of Virginia, 1678–1692*, ed. Joseph and Nesta Ewan. Urbana: Univ. of Illinois Press.

Barbour, Philip L. 1964. *The Three Worlds of Captain John Smith*. Boston: Houghton Mifflin.

——. 1970. *Pocahontas and Her World*. Boston: Houghton Mifflin.

——. 1971. The Earliest Reconnaissance of the Chesapeake Bay Area: Captain John Smith's Map and Indian Vocabulary. *Virginia Magazine of History and Biography* 79:280–302.

——. 1972. The Earliest Reconnaissance of the Chesapeake Bay Area: Captain John Smith's Map and Indian Vocabulary. Part 2. *Virginia Magazine of History and Biography* 80: 21–51.

——. 1986a. Biographical Directory. In *The Complete Works of Captain John Smith (1580–1631)*, ed. Philip L. Barbour. Chapel Hill: Univ. of North Carolina Press.

——. 1986b. General Introduction to *The Complete Works of Captain John Smith (1580–1631)*, ed. Philip L. Barbour. Chapel Hill: Univ. of North Carolina Press.

Barker, Alex W. 1992. Powhatan's Pursestrings: On the Meaning of Surplus in a Seventeenth Century Algonkian Chiefdom. In *Lords of the Southeast: Social Inequality and the Native Elites of Southeastern North America*, ed. Alex W. Barker and Timothy R. Pauketat. Archeological Papers of the American Anthropological Association, no. 3. Washington DC: American Anthropological Association.

Barriff, William. 1635. *Military Discipline: Or the Yong Artillery Man*. London: Thomas Harper.

Barwick, Humfrey. 1973. A breefe Discourse, Concerning the force and effect of all manuall weapons of fire [1594]. Reprinted in *Bow versus Gun*, comp. E. G. Heath. Wakefield UK: EP Publishing Limited.

Bateson, Gregory. 1987. *Steps to an Ecology of Mind: Collected Essays in Anthropology, Psychiatry, Evolution, and Epistemology* [1972]. Northvale NJ: Jason Aronson.

Beaulieu, John. 1969. Letter to William Trumbell, 30 November 1609. In *The Jamestown Voyages under the First Charter, 1606–1609*, ed. Philip L. Barbour. Cambridge UK: Hakluyt Society.

Benedict, Ruth Fulton. 1923. *The Concept of the Guardian Spirit in North America*. Memoirs of the American Anthropological Association, no. 29.

Bennett, Robert. 1922. Letter to Edward Bennett [9 June 1623]. In Lord Sackville's Papers respecting Virginia, 1613–1631, 1. *American Historical Review* 27 (3): 493–538.

Beverley, Robert. 1947. *The History and Present State of Virginia* [1705]. Ed. Louis B. Wright. Chapel Hill: Univ. of North Carolina Press.

Biard, Pierre. 1896a. Missio Canadensis: Epistola ex Porturegali in Acadia, transmissa ad Praepositum Generalem Societatis Jesu [1612]. In *The Jesuit Relations and Allied Documents: Travels and Explorations of the Jesuit Missionaries in New France, 1610–1791*, vol. 2. Ed. Reuben Gold Thwaites. Cleveland: Burrows Brothers Co.

——. 1896b. Lettre au R. P. Chritophe Baltazar, Provincial de France, à Paris [10 June 1611]. In *The Jesuit Relations and Allied Documents: Travels and Explorations of the Jesuit Missionaries in New France, 1610–1791*, vol. 1. Ed. Reuben Gold Thwaites. Cleveland: Burrows Brothers Co.

——. 1897. Relation de la Novvelle France, de fes Terres, Natvrel du Pais, & de fes Habitans [1616]. In *The Jesuit Relations and Allied Documents: Travels and Explorations of the Jesuit Missionaries in New France, 1610–1791*, vol. 3. Ed. Reuben Gold Thwaites. Cleveland: Burrows Brothers Co.

Billings, Warren M. 1975. Some Acts Not in Hening's *Statutes*: The Acts of Assembly, April 1652, November 1652, and July 1653. *Virginia Magazine of History and Biography* 83 (1): 22–76.

Binford, Lewis R. 1964. Archaeological and Ethnohistorical Investigation of Cultural Diversity and Progressive Development among Aboriginal Cultures of Coastal Virginia and North Carolina. Ph.D. dissertation, University of Michigan.

Biswell, Harold H. 1967. The Use of Fire in Wildland Management in California. In *Natural Resources: Quality and Quantity: Papers Presented Before a Faculty Seminar at the University of California, Berkeley, 1961–1965*. Ed. S. V. Ciriacy-Wantrup and James J. Parsons. Berkeley: Univ. of California Press.

Blanchard, Kendall. 1981. *The Mississippi Choctaws at Play: The Serious Side of Leisure*. Urbana: Univ. of Illinois Press.

Bloomfield, Leonard. 1946. Algonquian. *Linguistic Structures of Native America*. Ed. Cornelius Osgood. Viking Fund Publications in Anthropology, no. 6. New York: Viking Fund.

Brady, Ciarán. 1986. Spenser's Irish Crisis: Humanism and Experience in the 1590s. *Past and Present* 111:17–49.

Breen, Timothy H. 1980. *Puritans and Adventurers: Change and Persistence in Early America*. New York: Oxford Univ. Press.

A Brief Account From the most Authentic Protestant Writers of the Irish Rebellion. 1747. London.

Brightman, Robert. 1993. *Grateful Prey: Rock Cree Human-Animal Relationships.* Berkeley: Univ. of California Press.

Brinton, Daniel G. 1885. The Chief God of the Algonkins, in his Character as a Cheat and Liar. *American Antiquarian* 7:137–39.

Brotherston, Gordon. 1979. *Image of the New World: The American Continent Portrayed in Native Texts.* London: Thames & Hudson.

Brown, M. L. 1980. *Firearms in Colonial America: The Impact on History and Technology, 1492–1792.* Washington DC: Smithsonian Institution Press.

Browne, Daniel. 1622. *A New Almanacke and Prognostication for the yeare of our Lord God, 1622.* London.

Bruce, Philip Alexander. 1895. *Economic History of Virginia in the Seventeenth Century.* 2 vols. Reprinted 1935. New York: Peter Smith.

———. 1910. *Institutional History of Virginia in the Seventeenth Century.* 2 vols. Reprinted 1964. Gloucester MA: Peter Smith.

Bucher, Bernadette. 1981. *Icon and Conquest: A Structural Analysis of the Illustrations of de Bry's Great Voyages.* Trans. Basia Miller Gulati. Chicago: Univ. of Chicago Press.

Burk, John. 1805. *The History of Virginia, from It's First Settlement to the Present Day,* vol. 2. Petersburg VA: Dickson & Pescud.

Burnaby, Andrew. 1904. *Burnaby's Travels through North America: Reprinted from the Third Edition of 1798.* New York: A. Wessels Company.

Byrd, William. 1967. History of the Dividing Line Run in the Year 1728. In *Histories of the Dividing Line betwixt Virginia and North Carolina,* ed. William K. Boyd. New York: Dover Publications.

Callender, Charles. 1978. Fox. In *Handbook of North American Indians,* vol. 15; *Northeast.* Ed. Bruce G. Trigger. Washington DC: Smithsonian Institution.

Campbell, Charles. 1860. *History of the Colony and Ancient Dominion of Virginia.* Facsimile reprint 1965. Spartanburg SC: The Reprint Company.

Canny, Nicholas P. 1973. The Ideology of English Colonization: From Ireland to America. *William and Mary Quarterly* (3d series) 30 (4): 575–98.

———. 1988. *Kingdom and Colony: Ireland in the Atlantic World, 1560–1800.* Baltimore: Johns Hopkins Univ. Press.

Carmack, Robert M. 1972. Ethnohistory: A Review of Its Development, Definitions, Methods, and Aims. *Annual Review of Anthropology* 1:227–46.

de la Carrera, Juan. 1953. Relation of Juan de la Carrera, Sent to Bartolomé Pérez, S.J., from Puebla de los Angeles, March 1, 1600. In *The Spanish Jesuit Mission in Virginia, 1570–1572,* trans. and ed. Clifford M. Lewis, S.J., and Albert J. Loomie, S.J. Chapel Hill: Univ. of North Carolina Press.

[Cass, Lewis]. 1826. [Unsigned book review; attribution from Kinietz and Voegelin 1939]. *North American Review* 22 (50): 94–107.

Castle, William. 1747. A Short Discovery of the Coast and Continent of America [ca. 1625]. In *A Collection of Voyages and Travels,* 3d ed., vol. 8. Ed. Awnsham Churchill. London.

Cataneo, Girolamo. 1574. *Most Briefe Tables to knowe redily howe manye ranckes of footemen armed with Corslettes, as unarmed, go to the making of a just battayle.* Trans. Henry Grantham. London: W. Williamson.

Chapman, George, Ben Jonson, and John Marston. 1926. *Eastward Hoe* [1605]. Ed. Julia Hamlet Harris. Yale Studies in English 73. New Haven: Yale Univ. Press.

Child, Josiah. [1733?] A Discourse concerning Plantations [1692]. In *Select Tracts Relating to Colonies*. London: Printed for J. Roberts.

Church of England. 1641. *The Book of Common Prayer and Administration of the Sacraments: and Other Rites and Ceremonies of the Church of England*. London: Robert Barker.

Clayton, John. 1965. The Aborigines of the Country: Letter to Dr. Nehemiah Grew [1687]. In *The Reverend John Clayton, a Parson with a Scientific Mind: His Scientific Writings and Other Related Papers*, ed. Edmund Berkeley and Dorothy Smith. Charlottesville: Univ. Press of Virginia.

Clifford, James. 1988. *The Predicament of Culture: Twentieth-Century Ethnography, Literature, and Art*. Cambridge: Harvard Univ. Press.

Cohn, Bernard S. 1987a. History and Anthropology: The State of Play [1980]. In *An Anthropologist among the Historians and Other Essays*, ed. Bernard S. Cohn. Delhi: Oxford Univ. Press.

———. 1987b. Anthropology and History in the 1980s: Towards a Rapprochement [1981]. In *An Anthropologist among the Historians and Other Essays*, ed. Bernard S. Cohn. Delhi: Oxford Univ. Press.

Collingwood, R. G. 1956. *The Idea of History* [1946]. New York: Oxford Univ. Press.

Cooper, John M. 1934. *The Northern Algonquian Supreme Being*. Anthropological Series no. 2. Washington DC: Catholic Univ. of America.

Cooper, Karen. 1990. When in Rome, or in the Woodlands. . . . *The Eagle: New England's American Indian Journal* 8 (4): 2.

———. 1992. Caucus: An Old American (Indian) Political Tradition. *The Eagle: New England's American Indian Journal* 10 (1): 2.

Copland, Patrick. 1622. *Virginia's God be Thanked, or A Sermon of Thanksgiving for the happie successe of the affayres in Virginia this last yeare*. London.

Cotter, John L. 1958. *Archeological Excavations at Jamestown, Virginia*. Washington DC: National Park Service.

Cotter, John L., and J. Paul Hudson. 1957. *New Discoveries at Jamestown*. Washington DC: National Park Service.

Crashaw, William. 1610. *A Sermon preached in London before the right honorable the Lord Lawarre, Lord Governour and Captaine Generall of Virginea*. Facsimile reprint 1937. Boston: Massachusetts Historical Society.

Craven, Wesley Frank. 1964. *Dissolution of the Virginia Company* [1932]. Gloucester MA: Peter Smith.

———. 1970. *The Southern Colonies in the Seventeenth Century, 1607–1689* [1949]. Baton Rouge: Louisiana State Univ. Press.

Cronon, William. 1983. *Changes in the Land: Indians, Colonists, and the Ecology of New England*. New York: Hill & Wang.

Crosby, Constance A. 1988. From Myth to History, or Why King Philip's Ghost Walks Abroad. In *The Recovery of Meaning: Historical Archaeology in the Eastern United States*, ed. Mark P. Leone and Parker B. Potter. Washington DC: Smithsonian Institution Press.

Dale, Sir Thomas. 1975. Letter to Lord Salisbury, August 1611. In *The Old Dominion in the Seventeenth Century: A Documentary History of Virginia, 1606–1689*, ed. Warren M. Billings. Chapel Hill: Univ. of North Carolina Press.

Davidson, Thomas E. 1993. Relations between the Powhatans and the Eastern Shore. In *Powhatan Foreign Relations, 1500–1722*, ed. Helen C. Rountree. Charlottesville: Univ. Press of Virginia.

Deetz, James. 1988. American Historical Archeology: Methods and Results. *Science* 239: 362–67.

DeMallie, Raymond J. 1993. "These Have No Ears": Narrative and the Ethnohistorical Method. *Ethnohistory* 40 (4): 515–38.

Dening, Greg. 1991. A Poetic for Histories: Transformations that Present the Past. In *Clio in Oceania: Toward a Historical Anthropology*, ed. Aletta Biersack. Washington DC: Smithsonian Institution Press.

Dickason, Olive Patricia. 1992. *Canada's First Nations: A History of Founding Peoples from Earliest Times*. Norman: Univ. of Oklahoma Press.

Digby, Sir John. 1612a. Letter to Sir Thomas Edmondes. Madrid, 20 June. British Library, Stowe MSS 172, ff 307–8^v.

———. 1612b. Letter to Sir Thomas Edmondes. Madrid, ? November. British Library, Stowe MSS 173, ff 222–23^v.

———. 1613. Letter to Sir Thomas Edmondes. Madrid, 4 September. British Library, Stowe MSS 174, ff 170–70^v.

Dobyns, Henry F. 1966. Estimating Aboriginal American Populations: An Appraisal of Techniques with a New Hemispheric Estimate. *Current Anthropology* 7:395–416.

Donne, John. 1622. *A Sermon upon the VIII. verse of the I. chapter of the acts of the Apostles. Preach'd To the Honourable Company of the Virginia Plantation. 13°. Novemb. 1622.* London.

du Praissac, ? 1639. *The Art of Warre, or Militarie Discourses.* Trans. John Cruso. Cambridge: Roger Daniel.

Earle, Carville V. 1979. Environment, Disease, and Mortality in Early Virginia. In *The Chesapeake in the Seventeenth Century: Essays on Anglo-American Society*, ed. Thad W. Tate and David L. Ammerman. New York: W. W. Norton.

Eburne, Richard. 1962. *A Plain Pathway to Plantations (1624).* Ed. Louis B. Wright. Ithaca: Cornell Univ. Press for The Folger Shakespeare Library.

Eggan, Fred. 1975. Social Anthropology and the Method of Controlled Comparison [1954]. In *Essays in Social Anthropology and Ethnology*. Chicago: Department of Anthropology, University of Chicago.

Eid, Leroy V. 1982. The Cardinal Principle of Northeast Woodland Indian War. In *Papers of the Thirteenth Algonquian Conference*, ed. William Cowan. Ottawa: Carleton University.

Elton, Richard. 1668. *The Compleat Body of the Art Military.* London.

Emerson, Matthew Charles. 1988. Decorated Clay Tobacco Pipes from the Chesapeake. Ph.D. dissertation, University of California, Berkeley.

Erickson, Vincent O. 1978. Maliseet-Passamaquoddy. In *Handbook of North American Indians*, volume 15, *Northeast*. Ed. Bruce G. Trigger. Washington DC: Smithsonian Institution.

Falls, Cyril. 1950. *Elizabeth's Irish Wars.* London: Methuen.

Fausz, J. Frederick. 1977. The Powhatan Uprising of 1622: A Historical Study of Ethnocentrism and Cultural Conflict. Ph.D. dissertation, College of William and Mary.

———. 1979a. George Thorpe, Nemattanew, and the Powhatan Uprising of 1622. *Virginia Cavalcade* 28 (3): 111–17.

———. 1979b. Fighting "Fire" with Firearms: The Anglo-Powhatan Arms Race in Early Virginia. *American Indian Culture and Research Journal* 3 (4): 33–50.

————. 1981. Opechancanough: Indian Resistance Leader. In *Struggle and Survival in Colonial America*, ed. David G. Sweet and Gary B. Nash. Berkeley: Univ. of California Press.

————. 1985. Patterns of Anglo-Indian Aggression and Accommodation along the Mid-Atlantic Coast, 1584–1634. In *Cultures in Contact: The Impact of European Contacts on Native American Cultural Institutions A.D. 1000–1800*, ed. William W. Fitzhugh. Washington DC: Smithsonian Institution Press.

————. 1988. Merging and Emerging Worlds: Anglo-Indian Interest Groups and the Development of the Seventeenth-Century Chesapeake. In *Colonial Chesapeake Society*, ed. Lois Green Carr, Philip D. Morgan, and Jean B. Russo. Chapel Hill: Univ. of North Carolina Press.

Feest, Christian F. 1966a. Powhatan: A Study in Political Organization. *Wiener Völkerkundliche Mitteilungen* 13:69–83.

————. 1966b. Virginia Indian Miscellany 1. *Archiv für Völkerkunde* 20:1–7.

————. 1967. Virginia Indian Miscellany 2. *Archiv für Völkerkunde* 21:5–25.

————. 1972. Virginia Indian Miscellany 3. *Archiv für Völkerkunde* 26:1–14.

————. 1973. Seventeenth Century Virginia Algonquian Populations Estimates. *Quarterly Bulletin of the Archeological Society of Virginia* 28 (2): 66–79.

————. 1978. Virginia Algonquians. In *Handbook of North American Indians*, vol. 15, *Northeast*. Ed. Bruce G. Trigger. Washington DC: Smithsonian Institution.

————. 1990. *The Powhatan Tribes*. New York: Chelsea House.

Fenton, William N. 1946. An Iroquois Condolence Council for Installing Cayuga Chiefs in 1945. *Journal of the Washington Academy of Sciences* 36 (4): 110–27.

Ferguson, Leland G. 1992. *Uncommon Ground: Archaeology and Early African America, 1650–1800*. Washington DC: Smithsonian Institution Press.

Fiske, John. 1897. *Old Virginia and Her Neighbours*. Boston: Houghton Mifflin.

Flaherty, David H. 1969. Introduction to *Lawes Divine, Morall and Martiall, Etc.* Charlottesville: Univ. Press of Virginia.

Flannery, Regina. 1939. *An Analysis of Coastal Algonquian Culture*. Anthropological series, no. 7. Washington DC: Catholic Univ. of America Press.

Fleet, Henry. 1876. A Brief Journal of a Voyage Made in the Bark Virginia, to Virginia and Other Parts of the Continent of America. In *The Founders of Maryland as Portrayed in Manuscripts, Provincial Records and Early Documents*, ed. Rev. Edward D. Neill. Albany: Joel Munsell.

Fogelson, Raymond D. 1962. The Cherokee Ball Game: A Study in Southeastern Ethnology. Ph.D. dissertation, University of Pennsylvania.

————. 1971. The Cherokee Ballgame Cycle: An Ethnographer's View. *Ethnomusicology* 15 (3): 327–38.

————. 1974. On the Varieties of Indian History: Sequoyah and Traveller Bird. *Journal of Ethnic Studies* 2 (1): 105–12.

————. 1989. The Ethnohistory of Events and Nonevents. *Ethnohistory* 36 (2): 133–47.

————. 1990. On the "Petticoat Government" of the Eighteenth-Century Cherokee. In *Personality and the Cultural Construction of Society*, ed. David Jordan and Marc Swartz. Birmingham: Univ. of Alabama Press.

Foreman, Carolyn Thomas. 1943. *Indians Abroad, 1493–1938*. Norman: Univ. of Oklahoma Press.

Fourquevaux, Raimond de Beccarie de Pavie, Baron de. 1589. *Instructions for the Warres*. Trans. Paule Ive. London.

Friederici, Georg. 1985. Scalping in America [1906]. Reprinted in *Scalping and Torture: Warfare Practices among North American Indians*, comp. W. G. Spittal. Oshweken ON: Iroqrafts.

Furet, François. 1984. *In the Workshop of History*. Trans. Jonathan Mandelbaum. Chicago: Univ. of Chicago Press.

Gallen, T. 1643. *An Almanack and Prognostication For the yeare of God 1643*. London: James Young.

Galloway, Patricia. 1989. "The Chief Who Is Your Father": Choctaw and French Views of the Diplomatic Relation. In *Powhatan's Mantle: Indians in the Colonial Southeast*, ed. Peter H. Wood, Gregory A. Waselkov, and M. Thomas Hatley. Lincoln: Univ. of Nebraska Press.

Gatschet, Albert S. 1899. The Deities of the Early New England Indians. *Journal of American Folklore* 12 (46): 211–12.

——. n.d. Pamunkey Notebook [ca. 1890]. National Anthropological Archives, MS 2197.

Gerard, William R. 1904. The Tapahanek Dialect of Virginia. *American Anthropologist*, n.s., 6 (2): 313–30.

——. 1907. Virginia's Indian Contributions to English. *American Anthropologist*, n.s., 9 (1): 87–112.

Gethyn-Jones, Eric. 1982. *George Thorpe and the Berkeley Company: A Gloucestershire Enterprise in Virginia*. Gloucester UK: Alan Sutton.

Gewertz, Deborah B., and Edward E. Schieffelin, eds. 1985. *History and Ethnohistory in Papua New Guinea*. Sydney: Univ. of Sydney Press.

Gleach, Frederic W. 1986. ". . . Where the Pale ran": Sir Thomas Dale's Palisades in Seventeenth-Century Virginia. *Archaeological Society of Virginia Quarterly Bulletin* 41 (3): 160–68.

——. 1987. The Reynolds-Alvis Site (44He470): A Summary Report. *Quarterly Bulletin of the Archeological Society of Virginia* 42 (4): 205–32.

——. 1988. A Rose by Any Other Name: Questions on Mockley Chronology. *Journal of Middle Atlantic Archaeology* 4:85–98.

——. 1990a. Ceramics under Fire: Chesapeake Pipes and Colono-Indian Pots in the Context of Seventeenth-Century Virginia. Paper, Society for Historical Archaeology Annual Meeting, Tucson.

——. 1990b. "Hatchets and Copper wee should make him": Powhatan's Constructions of the English in Early Virginia. Paper, American Society for Ethnohistory Annual Meeting, Toronto.

——. 1992a. English and Powhatan Approaches to Civilizing Each Other: A History of Indian-White Relations in Early Colonial Virginia. Ph.D. dissertation, University of Chicago.

——. 1992b. A Traditional Story of the Powhatan Indians Recorded in the Early Nineteenth Century. In *Papers of the Twenty-third Algonquian Conference*, ed. William Cowan. Ottawa: Carleton University.

——. 1993. The Powhatan Indians and an Algonquian Aesthetic of War: A Work in Progress. In *Papers of the Twenty-fourth Algonquian Conference*, ed. William Cowan. Ottawa: Carleton University.

———. 1994. Pocahontas and Captain John Smith Revisited. In *Actes du vingt-cinquième congrès des algonquinistes*, ed. William Cowan. Ottawa: Carleton University.

———. 1996a. Controlled Speculation: Interpreting the Saga of Pocahontas and Captain John Smith. In *Reading beyond Words: Contexts for Native History*, ed. Jennifer S. H. Brown and Elizabeth Vibert. Peterborough ON: Broadview Press.

———. 1996b. Mimesis, Play, and Transformation in Powhatan Ritual. In *Papers of the Twenty-Sixth Algonquian Conference*, ed. David Pentland. Winnipeg: University of Manitoba.

Goddard, Ives. 1978a. Eastern Algonquian Languages. In *Handbook of North American Indians*, vol. 15, *Northeast*. Ed. Bruce G. Trigger. Washington DC: Smithsonian Institution.

———. 1978b. Central Algonquian Languages. In *Handbook of North American Indians*, vol. 15, *Northeast*. Ed. Bruce G. Trigger. Washington DC: Smithsonian Institution.

Gradie, Charlotte M. 1988. Spanish Jesuits in Virginia: The Mission that Failed. *Virginia Magazine of History and Biography* 96 (2): 131–56.

———. 1993. The Powhatans in the Context of the Spanish Empire. In *Powhatan Foreign Relations, 1500–1722*, ed. Helen C. Rountree. Charlottesville: Univ. Press of Virginia.

Gutierrez de la Vega, Luis. 1582. *A Compendious Treatise entituled, De re militari, containing principall orders to be observed in Martiall affaires*. Trans. Nicholas Lichefild. London: Thomas East.

Hakluyt, Richard. 1935. Divers Voyages Touching the Discoverie of America [1582]. In *The Original Writings and Correspondence of the Two Richard Hakluyts*, vol. 1. Ed. E. G. R. Taylor. Cambridge UK: Hakluyt Society.

Hallowell, A. Irving. 1946. Some Psychological Characteristics of the Northeastern Indians. In *Man in Northeastern North America*, ed. Frederick Johnson. Papers of the Robert S. Peabody Foundation for Archaeology, vol. 3. Andover MA: Phillips Academy.

———. 1976a. Ojibwa Ontology, Behavior, and World View [1960]. In *Contributions to Anthropology: Selected Papers of A. Irving Hallowell*, comp. Raymond D. Fogelson. Chicago: Univ. of Chicago Press.

———. 1976b. Ojibwa World View and Disease [1963]. In *Contributions to Anthropology: Selected Papers of A. Irving Hallowell*, comp. Raymond D. Fogelson. Chicago: Univ. of Chicago Press.

Hamor, Raphe [Ralph]. 1615. *A true discourse of the present estate of Virginia, and the successe of the affaires there till the 18 of June. 1614*. Facsimile reprint 1860. Albany: J. Munsell.

Hanson, Victor David. 1989. *The Western Way of War: Infantry Battle in Classical Greece*. New York: Alfred A. Knopf.

Hantman, Jeffrey L. 1990. Between Powhatan and Quirank: Reconstructing Monacan Culture and History in the Context of Jamestown. *American Anthropologist* 92:676–90.

———. 1993. Powhatan's Relations with the Piedmont Monacans. In *Powhatan Foreign Relations, 1500–1722*, ed. Helen C. Rountree. Charlottesville: Univ. Press of Virginia.

Hariot, Thomas. 1588. *A Briefe and True Report of the New Found Land of Virginia*. Facsimile reprint 1903. New York: Dodd, Mead & Company.

Harrington, John P. 1955. The Original Strachey Vocabulary of the Virginia Indian Language. *Bureau of American Ethnology Bulletin* 157, Anthropological Paper no. 46. Washington DC: U.S. Government Printing Office.

Harris, Julia Hamlet. 1926. Introduction to *Eastward Hoe*, ed. Juliet Hamlet Harris. New Haven: Yale Univ. Press.

Harvey, Captain. 1629? Captaine Harvey, his Propositions touching Virginia. Great Britain, Public Record Office CO 1/5/1, ff 65–66v.

Heath, E. G. 1973. Introduction to *Bow versus Gun*, comp. E. G. Heath. Wakefield UK: EP Publishing Limited.

Heckewelder, Rev. John. 1876. *History, Manners, and Customs of the Indian Nations Who Once Inhabited Pennsylvania and the Neighboring States*. Philadelphia: Historical Society of Pennsylvania.

Helms, Mary W. 1988. *Ulysses' Sail: An Ethnographic Odyssey of Power, Knowledge, and Geographical Distance*. Princeton: Princeton Univ. Press.

Hening, William Waller, ed. 1823. *The Statutes at Large; being a Collection of all the Laws of Virginia, from the First Session of the Legislature, in the year 1619*. New York: R. & W. & G. Bartow.

Hexham, Henry. 1642. *The First Part of the Principles of the Art Military, Practiced in the Warres of the United Netherlands*. Delft.

———. 1643. *The Third Part of the Principles of the Art Military, Practiced in the Warres of the United Netherlands*. Delft.

Hildreth, Richard. 1849. *The History of the United States of America from the Discovery of the Continent to the Organization of Government under the Federal Constitution*. New York: Harper & Brothers.

Hill, Jonathan D., ed. 1988. *Rethinking History and Myth: Indigenous South American Perspectives on the Past*. Urbana: Univ. of Illinois Press.

Holland, C. G. 1979. The Ramifications of the Fire Hunt. *Quarterly Bulletin of the Archeological Society of Virginia* 33 (4): 134–40.

Horse Capture, George. 1991. An American Indian Perspective. In *Seeds of Change: A Quincentennial Celebration*, ed. Herman Viola and Carolyn Margolis. Washington DC: Smithsonian Institution Press.

Horsman, Reginald. 1982. Well-Trodden Paths and Fresh Byways: Recent Writing on Native American History. *Reviews in American History* 10 (4): 234–44.

Howison, Robert R. 1846. *A History of Virginia, from its Discovery and Settlement by Europeans to the Present Time*, vol. 1. Philadelphia: Carey & Hart.

Hudson, Charles. 1966. Folk History and Ethnohistory. *Ethnohistory* 13 (1–2): 52–70.

Hulme, Peter. 1992. *Colonial Encounters: Europe and the Native Caribbean, 1492–1797* [1986]. London: Routledge.

Hulton, Paul. 1984. *America 1585: The Complete Drawings of John White*. Chapel Hill: Univ. of North Carolina Press.

Hunter, Robert R., Jr., Patricia Samford, and Marley R. Brown III. 1984. Phase II Archaeological Testing of the Proposed Second Street Extension, York County and Williamsburg, Virginia. Report submitted by Colonial Williamsburg Foundation, Office of Excavation and Conservation, to Virginia Department of Highways and Transportation.

The Indians of Southern Virginia, 1650–1711: Depositions in the Virginia and North Carolina Boundary Case. 1900. *Virginia Magazine of History and Biography* 7 (4): 337–58.

The Indians of Southern Virginia, 1650–1711: Depositions in the Virginia and North Carolina Boundary Case [Concluded]. 1900. *Virginia Magazine of History and Biography* 8 (1): 1–11.

Issac, Rhys. 1982. *The Transformation of Virginia 1740–1790*. Chapel Hill: Univ. of North Carolina Press.

James I [King of England]. 1969a. Letters patent to Sir Thomas Gates and others [10 April 1606]. In *The Jamestown Voyages Under the First Charter, 1606–1609*, ed. Philip L. Barbour. Cambridge UK: Hakluyt Society.

———. 1969b. Instructions for Government [20 November 1606]. In *The Jamestown Voyages under the First Charter, 1606–1609*, ed. Philip L. Barbour. Cambridge UK: Hakluyt Society.

Jefferson, Thomas. 1955. *Notes on the State of Virginia*, ed. William Peden. Chapel Hill: Univ. of North Carolina Press.

Jenness, Diamond. 1935. *The Ojibwa Indians of Parry Island: Their Social and Religious Life*. Bulletins of the Canadian Department of Mines, no. 78. Ottawa: National Museum of Canada.

Jennings, Francis. 1975. *The Invasion of America: Indians, Colonialism and the Cant of Conquest*. Chapel Hill: Univ. of North Carolina Press.

Johnson, Thomas Cary. 1946. Introduction to *A Proclamation for Settling the Plantation of Virginia*. Charlottesville: Univ. of Virginia.

Johnston, Basil. 1990. *Ojibway Heritage* [1976]. Lincoln: Univ. of Nebraska Press.

Jones, William. 1905. The Algonkin Manitou. *Journal of American Folk-lore* 18:183–90.

Jouvency, Joseph. 1896a. De Regione et Moribus Canadensium seu Barbarorum Novæ Franciæ [1710]. In *The Jesuit Relations and Allied Documents: Travels and Explorations of the Jesuit Missionaries in New France, 1610–1791*, vol. 1. Ed. Reuben Gold Thwaites. Cleveland: Burrows Brothers Co.

———. 1896b. Canadicæ Missionis Relatio [1710]. In *The Jesuit Relations and Allied Documents: Travels and Explorations of the Jesuit Missionaries in New France, 1610–1791*, vol. 1. Ed. Reuben Gold Thwaites. Cleveland: Burrows Brothers Co.

Kelso, William M. 1984. *Kingsmill Plantations, 1619–1800: Archaeology of Country Life in Colonial Virginia*. New York: Academic Press.

———. 1989. Comments on the 1987 Society for Historical Archaeology Landscape Symposium. *Historical Archaeology* 23 (1): 48–49.

Kidwell, Clara Sue. 1992. Indian Women as Cultural Mediators. *Ethnohistory* 39 (2): 97–107.

Kimball, Jeffrey. 1967. The Battle of Chippawa: Infantry Tactics in the War of 1812. *Military Affairs* 31 (4): 169–71.

Kinietz, Vernon, and Erminie W. Voegelin. 1939. *Shawnese Traditions: C. C. Trowbridge's Account*. Occasional Contributions from the Museum of Anthropology of the University of Michigan, no. 9. Ann Arbor: Univ. of Michigan Press.

Knowles, Nathaniel. 1985. The Torture of Captives by the Indians of Eastern North America [1940]. Reprinted in *Scalping and Torture: Warfare Practices Among North American Indians*, comp. W. G. Spittal. Oshweken ON: Iroqrafts.

Krech, Shepard, III. 1991. The State of Ethnohistory. *Annual Review of Anthropology* 20: 345–75.

Kugel, Rebecca. 1990. Religion Mixed with Politics: The 1836 Conversion of Mang'osid of Fond du Lac. *Ethnohistory* 37 (2): 126–57.

———. 1994. Of Missionaries and Their Cattle: Ojibwa Perceptions of a Missionary as Evil Shaman. *Ethnohistory* 41 (2): 227–44.

Kulikoff, Allan. 1986. *Tobacco and Slaves: The Development of Southern Cultures in the Chesapeake, 1680–1800*. Chapel Hill: Univ. of North Carolina Press.

Kupfer, Joseph H. 1983. *Experience as Art: Aesthetics in Everyday Life*. Albany: State Univ. of New York Press.

Kupperman, Karen Ordahl. 1980. *Settling with the Indians: The Meeting of English and Indian Cultures in America, 1580–1640*. Totowa NJ: Rowman & Littlefield.

Land, Robert Hunt. 1938. Henrico and Its College. *William and Mary Quarterly* (2d ser.) 18 (4): 453–98.

Lederer, John. 1672. *The Discoveries of John Lederer, In three several Marches from Virginia, To the West of Carolina, And other parts of the Continent*. Facsimile reprint 1966. Readex Microprint.

Lemay, J. A. Leo. 1992. *Did Pocahontas Save Captain John Smith?* Athens: Univ. of Georgia Press.

Lescarbot, Marc. 1896. La Conversion des Savvages qui ont esté baptizés en la Novvelle France, cette annee 1610. In *The Jesuit Relations and Allied Documents: Travels and Explorations of the Jesuit Missionaries in New France, 1610–1791*, vol. 1. Ed. Reuben Gold Thwaites. Cleveland: Burrows Brothers Co.

Lévi-Strauss, Claude. 1963. *Structural Anthropology*. New York: Doubleday.

Lewis, Clifford M., and Albert J. Loomie. 1953. *The Spanish Jesuit Mission in Virginia 1570–1572*. Chapel Hill: Univ. of North Carolina Press.

Lindeström, Peter. 1925. *Geographia Americae, with an Account of the Delaware Indians, Based on Surveys and Notes Made in 1654–1656*. Trans. Amandus Johnson. Philadelphia: Swedish Colonial Society.

Livingston, Luther S. 1903. Introductory Note to *A Briefe and True Report of the New Found Land of Virginia*. New York: Dodd, Mead.

Loskiel, George Henry. 1794. *History of the Mission of the United Brethren among the Indians in North America*. Trans. Christian Ignatius LaTrobe. London: Printed for the Brethren's Society for the Furtherance of the Gospel.

Lovejoy, Arthur O. 1936. *The Great Chain of Being: A Study in the History of an Idea*. Cambridge: Harvard Univ. Press.

Lowie, Robert H. 1908. The Test Theme in North American Mythology. *Journal of American Folk-Lore* 21 (81–82): 97–148.

Lurie, Nancy Oestreich. 1959. Indian Cultural Adjustment to European Civilization. In *Seventeenth-Century America: Essays in Colonial History*, ed. James Morton Smith. Chapel Hill: Univ. of North Carolina Press.

Malone, Patrick M. 1991. *The Skulking Way of War: Technology and Tactics among the New England Indians*. Lanham MD: Madison Books.

Markham, Gervase. 1643. *The Souldiers Exercise*. London: John Dawson.

Martin, John. 1933. The Manner Howe to Bringe the Indians into Subiection. In *The Records of the Virginia Company of London*, vol. 3. Ed. Susan M. Kingsbury. Washington DC: U.S. Government Printing Office.

Martínez, Bartolomé. 1953. Relation of Bartolomé Martínez [24 October 1610]. In *The Spanish Jesuit Mission in Virginia, 1570–1572*. Trans. and ed. Clifford M. Lewis, S.J., and Albert J. Loomie, S.J. Chapel Hill: Univ. of North Carolina Press.

Mathew, Thomas. 1963. The Beginning, Progress, and Conclusion of Bacon's Rebellion in Virginia, in the Years 1675 and 1676 [1705]. In *Tracts and Other Papers, Relating Principally to the Origin, Settlement, and Progress of the Colonies in North America, from the Discovery of the Country to the Year 1776*, vol. 1. Comp. Peter Force. Gloucester MA: Peter Smith.

McCartney, Martha W. 1989. Cockacoeske, Queen of Pamunkey: Diplomat and Suzerain. In

Powhatan's Mantle: Indians in the Colonial Southeast, ed. Peter H. Wood, Gregory A. Waselkov, and M. Thomas Hatley. Lincoln: Univ. of Nebraska Press.

McCusker, John J., and Russell R. Menard. 1985. *The Economy of British America, 1607–1789*. Chapel Hill: Univ. of North Carolina Press.

McIlwaine, H. R., ed. 1915. *Journals of the House of Burgesses of Virginia, 1619–1658/59*. Richmond: Virginia State Library.

——. 1979. *Minutes of the Council and General Court of Colonial Virginia*. Richmond: Virginia State Library.

Mead, Rev. Joseph. 1963. The Indian Massacre of 1622: Some Correspondence of the Reverend Joseph Mead. Ed. Robert C. Johnson. *Virginia Magazine of History and Biography* 71 (4): 408–10.

Mechling, W. H. 1958. The Malecite Indians, with Notes on the Micmacs [1916]. *Anthropologica* 7:1–160.

Merrell, James H. 1989a. Some Thoughts on Colonial Historians and American Indians. *William and Mary Quarterly*, 3d ser., 46:94–119.

——. 1989b. *The Indians' New World: Catawbas and Their Neighbors from European Contact through the Era of Removal*. Chapel Hill: Univ. of North Carolina Press.

Michelson, Truman. 1933. The Linguistic Classification of Powhatan. *American Anthropologist* 35 (3): 549.

Miller, Christopher L., and George R. Hamell. 1986. A New Perspective on Indian-White Contact: Cultural Symbols and Colonial Trade. *The Journal of American History* 73 (2): 311–28.

Miller, Jay. 1991. Delaware Personhood. *Man in the Northeast* 42:17–27.

Miller, Walter B. 1955. Two Concepts of Authority. *American Anthropologist* 57:271–89.

Mook, Maurice A. 1943a. The Anthropological Position of the Indian Tribes of Tidewater Virginia. *William and Mary Quarterly*, 2d ser., 23 (1): 27–40.

——. 1943b. Virginia Ethnology from an Early Relation. *William and Mary Quarterly*, 2d ser., 23 (2): 101–29.

Mooney, James. 1907. The Powhatan Confederacy, Past and Present. *American Anthropologist*, n.s., 9 (1): 129–52.

Morgan, Edmund S. 1975. *American Slavery, American Freedom: The Ordeal of Colonial Virginia*. New York: W. W. Norton.

Mossiker, Frances. 1976. *Pocahontas: The Life and Legend*. New York: Alfred A. Knopf.

Mouer, L. Daniel. 1981. Powhatan and Monacan Settlement Hierarchies: A Model of Relationship between Social and Environmental Structure. *Quarterly Bulletin of the Archeological Society of Virginia* 36 (1–2): 1–21.

——. 1987. Everything in Its Place: Locational Models and Notions of the Elite in Colonial Virginia. Paper, Society for Historical Archaeology Annual Meeting, Savannah.

——. 1991. Rebecca's Children: A Critical Look at Old and New Myths Concerning Indians in Virginia's History and Archaeology. Paper, Society for Historical Archaeology Annual Meeting, Richmond.

Mouer, L. Daniel, and Frederic W. Gleach. 1984. Bermuda Hundred: From Frontier Fort to Planters' Port. Paper, Middle Atlantic Archeology Conference, Rehobeth Beach, Delaware.

Mouer, L. Daniel, Jill C. Woolley, and Frederic W. Gleach. 1986. Town and Country in the Curles of the James (1660–1830): Social and Geographic Place and the Material Culture of James River Plantations. Paper, Middle Atlantic Archeological Conference, Rehobeth Beach, Delaware.

Nash, Rev. Treadway Russel. 1835. [Notes to Samuel Butler's] *Hudibras* [1793]. London: John Murray.

Neill, Edward D. 1876. *The Founders of Maryland as Portrayed in Manuscripts, Provincial Records and Early Documents*. Albany: Joel Munsell.

———. 1878. *Early Settlement of Virginia and Virginiola, as Noticed by Poets and Players*. Minneapolis: Johnson, Smith & Harrison.

———. 1885. *Virginia Vetusta, during the reign of James the First*. Albany: Joel Munsell's Sons.

———. 1886. *Virginia Carolorum: The Colony Under the Rule of Charles the First and Second, A.D. 1625–A.D. 1685*. Albany: Joel Munsell's Sons.

Newcomb, William W., Jr. 1956. *The Culture and Acculturation of the Delaware Indians*. Anthropological Papers, no. 10. Ann Arbor: Museum of Anthropology, University of Michigan.

Nicolar, Joseph. 1893. *The Life and Traditions of the Red Man*. Bangor ME: C. H. Glass & Co.

Noël Hume, Ivor. 1962. An Indian Ware of the Colonial Period. *Quarterly Bulletin of the Archeological Society of Virginia* 17:1–16.

———. 1982. *Martin's Hundred*. New York: Alfred A. Knopf.

Notestein, Wallace. 1954. *The English People on the Eve of Colonization, 1603–1630*. New York: Harper & Row.

Nugent, Nell Marion. 1934. *Cavaliers and Pioneers: Abstracts of Virginia Land Patents and Grants, 1623–1800*, vol. 1. Richmond: Dietz Printing Co.

O'Farrell, Patrick. 1971. *Ireland's English Question: Anglo-Irish Relations 1534–1970*. New York: Schocken Books.

O'Mack, Scott. 1990. The Sun, the King, and *El Paso de Cortes*. Paper, American Society for Ethnohistory Annual Meeting, Toronto.

Obeyesekere, Gananath. 1992. *The Apotheosis of Captain Cook: European Mythmaking in the Pacific*. Princeton: Princeton Univ. Press.

Oestreicher, David M. 1993. The Deconstruction of the Walam Olum: A Nineteenth-Century Hoax. Paper, 25th Algonquian Conference, Montreal.

Oré, Luis Gerónimo de. 1953. Relation of Luis Gerónimo de Oré [ca. 1617–1620]. In *The Spanish Jesuit Mission in Virginia, 1570–1572*, trans. and ed. Clifford M. Lewis, S.J., and Albert J. Loomie, S.J. Chapel Hill: Univ. of North Carolina Press.

Parry, J. H. 1982. The Spaniards in Eastern North America. In *Early Maryland in a Wider World*, ed. David B. Quinn. Detroit: Wayne State Univ. Press.

Pendergast, James F. 1991. *The Massawomeck: Raiders and Traders into the Chesapeake Bay in the Seventeenth Century*. Transactions of the American Philosophical Society 81(2). Philadelphia: American Philosophical Society.

Penn, William. 1855. Character, Manners, and Customs of the Indians [ca. 1701]. In *History of the Shawnee Indians, from the year 1681 to 1854, Inclusive*, ed. Henry Harvey. Cincinatti: Ephraim Morgan & Sons.

Percy, George. 1922. A Trewe Relacyon of the Procedinges and Ocurrentes of Momente wch have hapned in Virginia from the Tyme Sr Thomas Gates was shippwrackte uppon the Bermudes an^o 1609 untill my departure outt of the Country wch was in an^o Dñi 1612. *Tyler's Quarterly Historical and Geneaological Magazine* 3 (4): 259–82.

———. 1969. Observations gathered out of a Discourse of the Plantation of the Southerne

Colonie in Virginia by the English, 1606. In *The Jamestown Voyages under the First Charter, 1606–1609*, ed. Philip L. Barbour. Cambridge UK: Hakluyt Society.

A Perfect Description of Virginia [1649]. 1963. In *Tracts and Other Papers, Relating Principally to the Origin, Settlement, and Progress of the Colonies in North America, from the Discovery of the Country to the Year 1776*, vol. 2. Comp. Peter Force. Gloucester MA: Peter Smith.

Peterson, Harold L. 1956. *Arms and Armor in Colonial America, 1526–1783*. Harrisburg PA: Stackpole Co.

Philip II [King of Spain]. 1953. Cedula of Philip II, From Madrid, February 19, 1571. In *The Spanish Jesuit Mission in Virginia, 1570–1572*, trans. and ed. Clifford M. Lewis, S.J., and Albert J. Loomie, S.J. Chapel Hill: Univ. of North Carolina Press.

Pierce, William. 1629? A relation in generall of the present state of his Matie's Colony in Virginia, by Capt. William Perse, an antient planter of twenty yeares standing there. Great Britain, Public Record Office CO 1/5/1, ff 69–70v.

Plantagenet, Beauchamp. 1963. A Description of the Province of New Albion. In *Tracts and Other Papers, Relating Principally to the Origin, Settlement, and Progress of the Colonies in North America, from the Discovery of the Country to the Year 1776*, vol. 2. Comp. Peter Force. Gloucester MA: Peter Smith.

Porter, H. C. 1979. *The Inconstant Savage: England and the North American Indian 1500–1660*. London: Gerald Duckworth & Co.

Potter, Stephen R. 1982. An Analysis of Chicacoan Settlement Patterns. Ph.D. dissertation, University of North Carolina.

———. 1993. *Commoners, Tribute, and Chiefs: The Development of Algonquian Culture in the Potomac Valley*. Charlottesville: Univ. Press of Virginia.

Purchas, Samuel. 1617. *Purchas His Pilgrimage*, 3d ed. London.

Quinn, David Beers. 1955. The Map of Raleigh's Virginia. In *The Roanoke Voyages, 1584–1590: Documents to Illustrate the English Voyages to North America under the Patent Granted to Walter Raleigh in 1584*, vol. 2. Ed. David Beers Quinn. London: Hakluyt Society.

———. 1961. The Argument for the English Discovery of America Between 1480 and 1494. *Geographical Journal* 127:277–85.

———. 1974. *England and the Discovery of America, 1481–1620*. New York: Alfred A Knopf.

———. 1985. *Set Fair for Roanoke: Voyages and Colonies, 1584–1606*. Chapel Hill: Univ. of North Carolina Press.

Quirós, Luis de, and Juan Baptista de Segura. 1953. Letter of Luis de Quirós and Juan Baptista de Segura to Juan de Hinistrosa [12 September 1570]. In *The Spanish Jesuit Mission in Virginia, 1570–1572*, trans. and ed. Clifford M. Lewis, S.J., and Albert J. Loomie, S.J. Chapel Hill: Univ. of North Carolina Press.

Ragueneau, Paul. 1898. Relation of What Occurred in the Mission of the Fathers of the Society of Jesus among the Hurons, a country of New France, in the years 1648 and 1649 [1650]. In *The Jesuit Relations and Allied Documents: Travels and Explorations of the Jesuit Missionaries in New France, 1610–1791*, vol. 34. Ed. Reuben Gold Thwaites. Cleveland: Burrows Brothers Co.

Ransome, David R. 1995. "Shipt for Virginia": The Beginnings in 1619–1622 of the Great Migration to the Chesapeake. *Virginia Magazine of History and Biography* 103 (4): 443–58.

Rhodes, Richard A., and Evelyn M. Todd. 1981. Subarctic Algonquian Languages. In *Hand-*

book of North American Indians, vol. 6, *Subarctic*. Ed. June Helm. Washington DC: Smithsonian Institution.

Ricouer, Paul. 1981. *Hermeneutics and the Human Sciences*. Trans. and ed. John B. Thompson. Cambridge: Cambridge Univ. Press.

Riordan, D. M. 1891. What Shall We Do With Our Indians? In *Echoes of the Sunset Club, Comprising a Number of the Papers Read, and Addresses Delivered, Before the Sunset Club of Chicago During the Past Two Years*, comp. W. W. Catlin. Chicago: Howard, Bartels & Co.

Rogel, Juan. 1953a. Letter of Juan Rogel to Francis Borgia, From the Bay of the Mother of God, August 28, 1572. In *The Spanish Jesuit Mission in Virginia, 1570–1572*, trans. and ed. Clifford M. Lewis, S.J., and Albert J. Loomie, S.J. Chapel Hill: Univ. of North Carolina Press.

———. 1953b. Relation of Juan Rogel, Between 1607 and 1611, as edited by Juan Sánchez Vaquero, S.J. In *The Spanish Jesuit Mission in Virginia, 1570–1572*, trans. and ed. Clifford M. Lewis, S.J., and Albert J. Loomie, S.J. Chapel Hill: University of North Carolina Press.

Rogers, Colonel Hugh Cuthbert Basset. 1960. *Weapons of the British Soldier*. Imperial Services Library, vol. 5. London: Seeley Service.

Rohan, Henri, Duc de. 1640. *A Treatise of Modern War*. Trans. John Cruso. Cambridge UK: Roger Daniel.

Rolfe, John. 1933. A Letter to Sir Edwin Sandys [June 8, 1617]. In *The Records of the Virginia Company of London*, vol. 3. Ed. Susan M. Kingsbury. Washington DC: U.S. Government Printing Office.

Rountree, Helen C. 1972a. Being an Indian in Virginia: Four Centuries in Limbo. *The Chesopiean* 10 (1): 2–7.

———. 1972b. Powhatan's Descendants in the Modern World: Community Studies of the Two Virginia Indian Reservations, with Notes on Five Non-reservation Enclaves. *The Chesopiean* 10 (3): 62–96.

———. 1975. Change Came Slowly: The Case of the Powhatan Indians of Virginia. *The Journal of Ethnic Studies* 3 (3): 1–19.

———. 1989. *The Powhatan Indians of Virginia: Their Traditional Culture*. Norman: Univ. of Oklahoma Press.

———. 1990. *Pocahontas's People: The Powhatan Indians of Virginia through Four Centuries*. Norman: Univ. of Oklahoma Press.

———, ed. 1993a. *Powhatan Foreign Relations, 1500–1722*. Charlottesville: Univ. Press of Virginia.

———. 1993b. Who Were the Powhatans and Did They Have a Unified "Foreign Policy"? In *Powhatan Foreign Relations, 1500–1722*. Ed. Helen C. Rountree. Charlottesville: Univ. Press of Virginia.

Rubertone, Patricia E. 1989. Landscape as Artifact: Comments on "The Archaeological Use of Landscape Treatment in Social, Economic and Ideological Analysis." *Historical Archaeology* 23 (1): 50–54.

Rutman, Anita H. 1987. Still Planting the Seeds of Hope: The Recent Literature of the Early Chesapeake Region. *Virginia Magazine of History and Biography* 95:3–24.

Sacchini, Francisco. 1953. Borgia, the Third Part of the History of the Society of Jesus [1622]. In *The Spanish Jesuit Mission in Virginia, 1570–1572*, trans. and ed. Clifford M. Lewis, S.J., and Albert J. Loomie, S.J. Chapel Hill: Univ. of North Carolina Press.

Sahlins, Marshall. 1976. *Culture and Practical Reason*. Chicago: Univ. of Chicago Press.

———. 1981. *Historical Metaphors and Mythical Realities: Structure in the Early History of the Sandwich Islands Kingdom*. Ann Arbor: Univ. of Michigan Press.

———. 1985. *Islands of History*. Chicago: Univ. of Chicago Press.

———. 1988. Cosmologies of Capitalism: The Trans-Pacific Sector of "The World System." *Proceedings of the British Academy* 74:1–51.

———. 1991. The Return of the Event, Again; With Reflections on the Beginnings of the Great Fijian War of 1843 to 1855 between the Kingdoms of Bau and Rewa. In *Clio in Oceania: Toward a Historical Anthropology*, ed. Aletta Biersack. Washington DC: Smithsonian Institution Press.

———. 1995. *How "Natives" Think: About Captain Cook, for Example*. Chicago: Univ. of Chicago Press.

Said, Edward W. 1978. *Orientalism*. New York: Pantheon Books.

Sale, Kirkpatrick. 1990. *The Conquest of Paradise: Christopher Columbus and the Columbian Legacy*. New York: Alfred A. Knopf.

Sandys, Sir Edwin, Henry Timberlake, and John Ferrar. 1933. Meeting of a Committee for Smythes Hundred. In *The Records of the Virginia Company of London*, vol. 3. Ed. Susan M. Kingsbury. Washington DC: U.S. Government Printing Office.

Saussure, Ferdinand de, 1966. *Course in General Linguistics*. Trans. Wade Baskin. New York: McGraw-Hill.

Shea, William L. 1983. *The Virginia Militia in the Seventeenth Century*. Baton Rouge: Louisiana State Univ. Press.

Sheehan, Bernard W. 1980. *Savagism and Civility: Indians and Englishmen in Colonial Virginia*. Cambridge: Cambridge Univ. Press.

Shineberg, Dorothy. 1971. Guns and Men in Melanesia. *Journal of Pacific History* 6:61–82.

Shkilnyk, Anastasia M. 1985. *A Poison Stronger than Love: The Destruction of an Ojibwa Community*. New Haven: Yale Univ. Press.

Siebert, Frank T., Jr. 1975. Resurrecting Virginia Algonquian from the Dead: The Reconstituted and Historical Phonology of Powhatan. In *Studies in Southeastern Indian Languages*, ed. James M. Crawford. Athens: Univ. of Georgia Press.

Simmons, William S. 1986. *Spirit of the New England Tribes: Indian History and Folklore, 1620–1984*. Hanover NH: Univ. Press of New England.

Sioui, Georges E. 1992. *For an Amerindian Autohistory*. Trans. Sheila Fischman. Montreal: McGill-Queen's Univ. Press.

Smith, Captain John. 1986a. A True Relation of Such Occurrences and Accidents of Noate as Hath Hapned in Virginia [1608]. In *The Complete Works of Captain John Smith (1580–1631)*. Ed. Philip L. Barbour. Chapel Hill: Univ. of North Carolina Press.

———. 1986b. A Map of Virginia, With a Description of the Countrey, the Commodities, People, Government and Religion [1612]. In *The Complete Works of Captain John Smith (1580–1631)*, ed. Philip L. Barbour. Chapel Hill: Univ. of North Carolina Press.

———. 1986c. The Proceedings of the English Colonie in Virginia [1612]. In *The Complete Works of Captain John Smith (1580–1631)*, ed. Philip L. Barbour. Chapel Hill: Univ. of North Carolina Press.

———. 1986d. The Generall Historie of Virginia, New-England, and the Summer Isles [1624]. In *The Complete Works of Captain John Smith (1580–1631)*, ed. Philip L. Barbour. Chapel Hill: Univ. of North Carolina Press.

———. 1986e. Advertisements For the Unexperienced Planters of New-England, or Any Where [1631]. In *The Complete Works of Captain John Smith (1580–1631)*, ed. Philip L. Barbour. Chapel Hill: Univ. of North Carolina Press.

Smith, Seba. 1841. *Powhatan; a Metrical Romance, in Seven Cantos*. New York: Harper & Brothers.

Smyth, John, of Nibley. n.d. Virginia Papers, 1613–1634. New York: New York Public Library.

Smythe, Sir John. 1973. Certain Discourses, written by Sir John Smythe, Knight: Concerning the formes and effects of divers sorts of weapons [1590]. Reprinted in *Bow versus Gun*, comp. E. G. Heath. Wakefield UK: EP Publishing Limited.

Spaulding, Thomas M. 1937. Early Military Books in the Folger Library. *Journal of the American Military History Foundation* 1 (3): 91–100.

Speck, Frank G. 1919. The Functions of Wampum among the Eastern Algonkian. *Memoirs of the American Anthropological Association* 6:3–71.

———. 1924. The Ethnic Position of the Southeastern Algonkian. *American Anthropologist* 26 (2): 184–200.

———. 1925. *The Rappahannock Indians of Virginia. Indian Notes and Monographs* 5(3). New York: Museum of the American Indian, Heye Foundation.

———. 1926. Culture Problems in Northeastern North America. *Proceedings of the American Philosophical Society* 65 (4): 272–311.

———. 1928. *Chapters on the Ethnology of the Powhatan Tribes of Virginia. Indian Notes and Monographs* 1(5). New York: Museum of the American Indian, Heye Foundation.

———. 1931. *A Study of the Delaware Indian Big House Ceremony*. Harrisburg: Pennsylvania Historical Commission.

———. 1977. *Naskapi: The Savage Hunters of the Labrador Peninsula* [1935]. Norman: Univ. of Oklahoma Press.

———. 1995. *Midwinter Rites of the Cayuga Long House* [1949]. Lincoln: Univ. of Nebraska Press.

———. n.d. Papers. Library of the American Philosophical Society, Philadelphia.

Spelman, Henry. 1910. Relation of Virginia [1613?]. In *Travels and Works of Captain John Smith*, ed. Edward Arber and Arthur G. Bradley. Edinburgh: John Grant.

Spencer, Oliver M. 1907. *The Indian Captivity of O. M. Spencer*, ed. Milo Lilton Quaife. Chicago: R. R. Donnelley & Sons.

Stern, Theodore. 1951. *Pamunkey Pottery Making. Southern Indian Studies* 3. Chapel Hill: Archaeological Society of North Carolina.

———. 1952. Chickahominy: The Changing Culture of a Virginia Indian Community. *Proceedings of the American Philosophical Society* 96 (2): 157–225.

Stith, William. 1865. *The History of the First Discovery and Settlement of Virginia* [1747]. New York: Reprinted for Joseph Sabin.

Strachey, William. 1906. A true repertory of the wracke, and redemption of Sir Thomas Gates Knight; upon, and from the Ilands of the Bermudas: his comming to Virginia, and the estate of that Colonie then, and after, under the government of the Lord La Warre, July 15, 1610. In *Hakluytus Posthumus or Purchas His Pilgrimes*, vol. 19. Ed. Samuel Purchas. Glasgow: James MacLehose & Sons.

———. 1953. *The Historie of Travell into Virginia Britania* [1612]. Ed. Louis B. Wright and Virginia Freund. London: Hakluyt Society.

———. 1969. *Lawes Divine, Morall and Martiall, Etc.* [1612]. Ed. David H. Flaherty. Charlottesville: Univ. Press of Virginia.

Sturtevant, William C. 1964. Studies in Ethnoscience. *American Anthropologist* 66 (3 pt. 2): 79–131.

———. 1966. Anthropology, History, and Ethnohistory. *Ethnohistory* 13 (1–2): 1–51.

Styward, Thomas. 1581. *The Pathwaie to Martiall Discipline*. London.

Swanton, John R. 1979. *The Indians of the Southeastern United States* [1946]. Washington DC: Smithsonian Institution Press.

Tate, Thad W. 1979. The Seventeenth-Century Chesapeake and Its Modern Historians. In *The Chesapeake in the Seventeenth Century: Essays on Anglo-American Society*, ed. Thad W. Tate and David L. Ammerman. New York: W. W. Norton.

Thomas, David Hurst, Grant D. Jones, Roger S. Durham, and Clark Spencer Larsen. 1978. *The Anthropology of St. Catherines Island I: Natural and Cultural History*. Anthropological Papers of the American Museum of Natural History, no. 55, pt. 2. New York: American Museum of Natural History.

Thompson, Raymond H. 1970. The Subjective Element in Archaeological Inference [1956]. In *Introductory Readings in Archaeology*, ed. Brian M. Fagan. Boston: Little, Brown.

Todorov, Tzevetan. 1984. *The Conquest of America: The Question of the Other*. Trans. Richard Howard. New York: Harper & Row.

Tooker, Elizabeth. 1970. *The Iroquois Ceremonial of Midwinter*. Syracuse: Syracuse Univ. Press.

Tooker, William Wallace. 1895. The Algonquian Appellatives of the Siouan Tribes of Virginia. *American Anthropologist* 8:376–92.

———. 1901. *The Bocootawanaukes or the Fire Nation*. The Algonquian Series, 4. New York: Francis P. Harper.

Trigger, Bruce G., ed. 1978. *Handbook of North American Indians*, Volume 15: *Northeast*. Washington: Smithsonian Institution.

Trumbull, J. Hammond. 1870a. On the Composition of Algonkin Geographical Names. In *Collections of the Connecticut Historical Society*, vol. 2. Hartford: Connecticut Historical Society.

———. 1870b. On the Algonkin Name "Manit" (or "Manitou"), Sometimes Translated "Great Spirit," and "God." *Old and New* 1 (3): 337–42.

Turner, E. Randolph, III. 1976. An Archaeological and Ethnohistorical Study on the Evolution of Rank Societies in the Virginia Coastal Plain. Ph.D. dissertation, Pennsylvania State University.

———. 1978. An Intertribal Deer Exploitation Buffer Zone for the Virginia Coastal Plain-Piedmont Regions. *Quarterly Bulletin of the Archeological Society of Virginia* 32 (3): 42–48.

———. 1982. A Re-examination of Powhatan Territorial Boundaries and Population, ca. A.D. 1607. *Quarterly Bulletin of the Archeological Society of Virginia* 37:45–64.

———. 1985. Socio-Political Organization within the Powhatan Chiefdom and the Effects of European Contact, A.D. 1607–1646. In *Cultures in Contact: The Impact of European Contacts on Native American Cultural Institutions A.D. 1000–1800*, ed. William W. Fitzhugh. Washington DC: Smithsonian Institution Press.

———. 1993. Native American Protohistoric Interactions in the Powhatan Core Area. In *Powhatan Foreign Relations, 1500–1722*, ed. Helen C. Rountree. Charlottesville: Univ. Press of Virginia.

Turner, Terence S. 1977. Transformation, Hierarchy and Transcendence: A Reformulation of van Gennep's Model of the Structure of *Rites de Passage*. In *Secular Ritual*, ed. Sally F. Moore and Barbara G. Myerhoff. Amsterdam: Van Gorcum.

———. 1988. Ethno-Ethnohistory: Myth and History in Native South American Representations of Contact with Western Society. In *Rethinking History and Myth: Indigenous South American Perspectives on the Past*, ed. Jonathan D. Hill. Urbana: Univ. of Illinois Press.

———. n.d. The Poetics of Play: Ritual Clowning, Masking and Performative Mimesis Among the Kayapo. In *The Ludic: Forces of Generation and Fracture*, ed. Bruce Kapferer and Peter Koepping. Oxford: Berg Press. In press.

Turner, Victor. 1967. Betwixt and Between: The Liminal Period in *Rites de Passage*. In *The Forest of Symbols: Aspects of Ndembu Ritual*. Ithaca: Cornell Univ. Press.

———. 1969. *The Ritual Process: Structure and Anti-Structure*. Ithaca: Cornell Univ. Press.

———. 1977. Variations on a Theme of Liminality. In *Secular Ritual*, ed. Sally F. Moore and Barbara G. Myerhoff. Amsterdam: Van Gorcum.

Tyler, Lyon Gardiner. 1904. *England in America, 1580–1652*. Facsimile reprint 1968. New York: Cooper Square Publishers.

Upton, Dell. 1988. New Views of the Virginia Landscape. *The Virginia Magazine of History and Biography* 96 (4): 403–70.

Vance, James E., Jr. 1970. *The Merchant's World: The Geography of Wholesaling*. Englewood Cliffs NJ: Prentice-Hall.

van Gennep, Arnold. 1960. *The Rites of Passage* [1908]. Trans. Monika B. Vizedom and Gabrielle L. Caffee. Chicago: Univ. of Chicago Press.

Virginia Company of London. 1878. Letter to the Mayor of Northborne, *via* Edwin Sandys, 28 February 1610/11. In *Early Settlement of Virginia and Virginiola, as Noticed by Poets and Players*, ed. Edward D. Neill. Minneapolis: Johnson, Smith & Harrison.

———. 1906a. At a Court held for Virginia the 14th of August 1622. In *The Records of the Virginia Company of London*, vol. 2. Ed. Susan M. Kingsbury. Washington DC: U.S. Government Printing Office.

———. 1906b. A Præparative Court held on Monday in the Afternoone the 17th of November 1623. In *The Records of the Virginia Company of London*, vol. 2. Ed. Susan M. Kingsbury. Washington DC: U.S. Government Printing Office.

———. 1933. Shareholders in the Virginia Company from 1615 to 1623. In *The Records of the Virginia Company of London*, vol. 3. Ed. Susan M. Kingsbury. Washington DC: U.S. Government Printing Office.

———. 1935. Discourse of the Old Company [April 1625]. In *The Records of the Virginia Company of London*, vol. 4. Ed. Susan M. Kingsbury. Washington DC: U.S. Government Printing Office.

Virginia Council. 1609. Instructions orders and constitutions by way of advice set doune declared and propounded to Sir Thomas Gates Knight governour of Virginia and of the Colony there planted, and to bee planted, and of all the Inhabitants thereof, by his Ma[tis] Councell for direction of the affaires of that Countrey, for his better disposeing and proceeding in the government theireof, attending to the authority and power given unto us by vertue of his Ma[ts] twoe pattents. Copy in the British Library, Additional MSS 21993, f 178[v]-183.

———. 1906. Letter to Virginia Company of London [14 June 1623]. Quoted in A Quarter Court held for Virginia on Wednesday in the Afternoone the 19th of November 1623. In

The Records of the Virginia Company of London, vol. 2. Ed. Susan M. Kingsbury. Washington DC: U.S. Government Printing Office.

———. 1933a. Instruccions orders and constitucions . . . to Sr Thomas Gates knight Governor of Virginia [May 1609]. In *The Records of the Virginia Company of London*, vol. 3. Ed. Susan M. Kingsbury. Washington DC: U.S. Government Printing Office.

———. 1933b. The putting out of the Tenants that came over in the B. N. wth other orders of the Councell [11 November 1619]. In *The Records of the Virginia Company of London*, vol. 3. Ed. Susan M. Kingsbury. Washington DC: U.S. Government Printing Office.

———. 1933c. Letter to Virginia Company of London [January 1622]. In *The Records of the Virginia Company of London*, vol. 3. Ed. Susan M. Kingsbury. Washington DC: U.S. Government Printing Office.

———. 1933d. A Letter to the Virginia Company of London [(after 20) April 1622]. In *The Records of the Virginia Company of London*, vol. 3. Ed. Susan M. Kingsbury. Washington DC: U.S. Government Printing Office.

———. 1935a. Letter to Virginia Company of London [20 January 1623]. In *The Records of the Virginia Company of London*, vol. 4. Ed. Susan M. Kingsbury. Washington DC: U.S. Government Printing Office.

———. 1935b. Letter to Virginia Company of London [4 April 1623]. In *The Records of the Virginia Company of London*, vol. 4. Ed. Susan M. Kingsbury. Washington DC: U.S. Government Printing Office.

———. 1935c. Letter to the Earl of Southampton and the Council and Company of Virginia [2 December 1624]. In *The Records of the Virginia Company of London*, vol. 4. Ed. Susan M. Kingsbury. Washington DC: U.S. Government Printing Office.

———. 1935d. Letter to the Privy Council [15 June 1625]. In *The Records of the Virginia Company of London*, vol. 4. Ed. Susan M. Kingsbury. Washington DC: U.S. Government Printing Office.

———. 1935e. Letter to the Commissioners for the Affairs of Virginia [15 June 1625]. In *The Records of the Virginia Company of London*, vol. 4. Ed. Susan M. Kingsbury. Washington: U.S. Government Printing Office.

Virginia General Assembly. 1901. The Virginia Assembly of 1641 [i.e., 1642]: A List of Members and Some of the Acts. *Virginia Magazine of History and Biography* 9 (1): 50–59.

———. 1915. Acts, Orders and Resolutions of the General Assembly of Virginia, at Sessions of March 1643–1646. *Virginia Magazine of History and Biography* 23 (3): 225–55.

———. 1933. A Reporte of the Manner of Proceeding in the General Assembly Convented at James City [July/August 1619]. In *The Records of the Virginia Company of London*, vol. 3. Ed. Susan M. Kingsbury. Washington DC: U.S. Government Printing Office.

Voegelin, C. F. 1954. Translation of the Walum Olum text. In *Walum Olum, or Red Score: The Migration Legend of the Lenni Lenape or Delaware Indians*. Indianapolis: Indiana Historical Society.

Ward, Robert. 1639. *Anima'dversions of Warre; or, A Military Magazine of the Truest Rules, and Ablest Instructions, for the Managing of Warre*. London: John Dawson.

Warren, William W. 1984. *History of the Ojibway People* [1885]. Saint Paul: Minnesota Historical Society Press.

Washburn, Wilcomb E. 1957. *The Governor and the Rebel: A History of Bacon's Rebellion in Virginia*. Chapel Hill: Univ. of North Carolina Press.

Waterhouse, Edward. 1933. A Declaration of the State of the Colony and Affaires in Virginia

[1622]. In *The Records of the Virginia Company of London*, vol. 3. Ed. Susan M. Kingsbury. Washington DC: U.S. Government Printing Office.

Watteville, Colonel H. de. 1954. *The British Soldier: His Daily Life from Tudor to Modern Times*. London: J. M. Dent & Sons.

Webb, Stephen Saunders. 1984. *1676: The End of American Independence*. Cambridge: Harvard Univ. Press.

Wertenbaker, Thomas Jefferson. 1927. *The First Americans, 1607–1690*. New York: Macmillan.

———. 1940. *Torchbearer of the Revolution: The Story of Bacon's Rebellion and Its Leader*. Princeton: Princeton Univ. Press.

Whitaker, Alexander. 1611. Letter to Wm. Crashaw. Jamestown, 9 August. British Library, Additional MS 21993, ff 192ᵛ-193.

White, Richard. 1991. *The Middle Ground: Indians, Empires, and Republics in the Great Lakes Region, 1650–1815*. Cambridge: Cambridge Univ. Press.

Whitehorne, Peter. 1573. *Certayne wayes for the ordering of Souldiers in battelrey, and setting of battayles*. London: W. Williamson.

Williams, Sir Roger [1540?–1595]. 1964. *The Actions of the Low Countries* [1618]. Ed. D. W. Davies. Ithaca: Cornell Univ. Press.

Williams, Roger [1604?–1683]. 1973. *A Key into the Language of America* [1643]. Ed. John J. Teunissen and Evelyn J. Hinz. Detroit: Wayne State Univ. Press.

Williams, William Carlos. 1924. Sir Walter Raleigh. *Broom: An International Magazine of the Arts* 6 (1): 23–25.

Williamson, Margaret Holmes. 1979. Powhatan Hair. *Man*, n.s., 14:392–413.

Wingfield, Edward. 1910. A Discourse of Virginia [1608]. In *Travels and Works of Captain John Smith*, ed. Edward Arber and Arthur G. Bradley. Edinburgh: John Grant.

Witherspoon, Gary. 1977. *Language and Art in the Navajo Universe*. Ann Arbor: Univ. of Michigan Press.

Wolf, Eric. 1982. *Europe and the People without History*. Berkeley: Univ. of California Press.

Wright, Louis B. 1943. *Religion and Empire: The Alliance between Piety and Commerce in English Expansion 1558–1625*. Chapel Hill: Univ. of North Carolina Press.

Wyatt, Francis. 1933. A Commission to Sir George Yeardley [20 June 1622]. In *The Records of the Virginia Company of London*, vol. 3. Ed. Susan M. Kingsbury. Washington DC: U.S. Government Printing Office.

Yeardley, George. 1933. A Letter to Sir Henry Peyton [November 18, 1610]. In *The Records of the Virginia Company of London*, vol. 3. Ed. Susan M. Kingsbury. Washington DC: U.S. Government Printing Office.

Zeisberger, Rev. David. 1910. David Zeisberger's History of the Northern American Indians. Ed. Archer Butler Hulbert and William Nathaniel Schwarze. *Ohio Archaeological and Historical Quarterly* 19 (1&2): 1–189.

✦ Index

In *Studies in the Anthropology of North American Indians*